GREGG

**applied
typing**

Second edition

GREGG

applied typing

Second edition

A. M. Drummond
Matthew Boulton Technical College, Birmingham

I. E. Scattergood
British School of Commerce, Birmingham

07 094271 4

McGRAW-HILL · LONDON

New York · St. Louis · San Francisco · Dusseldorf · Johannesburg
Kuala Lumpur · London · Mexico · Montreal · New Delhi · Panama
Rio de Janeiro · Singapore · Sydney · Toronto

Printed in Great Britain by
William Clowes and Sons, Limited, London, Beccles and Colchester

Preface

Applied Typing presents a systematic and comprehensive programme for perfecting and applying typing skill up to the standard of the intermediate and advanced stages of any typing examination.

This new edition is a complete and thorough revision, and teachers will welcome its special features:

- *International size paper* is required for all exercises.
- *Metric Units* are used for most measurements.
- *Decimal Currency* is used in all monetary examples.
- *Manuscript exercises* have been doubled in number.
- *Many more letters* are in manuscript.
- *Production jobs* have increased in number.
- *Five Consolidation Units* have been included in addition to the ten pages of examination preview at the end of the book.
- *Accuracy/Speed Practice* is now an integral part of the Skill Building Section of each unit.

Applied Typing, Second Edition, thus combines a much greater emphasis on realistic production work with the carefully planned unit structure of the first edition. Each of the 28 units is divided into three sections:

Skill Building

This section provides a constant review of the typing and machine techniques that are essential for accurate and quick production work. It contains:

(a) Review of Alphabet keys.
(b) Intensive drills on
  (i) Figures
  (ii) Letter combinations
  (iii) Suffixes and Prefixes
  (iv) Common Phrases
  (v) Fluency
  (vi) Shift Key.
(c) Accuracy/Speed practice graded according to syllabic intensity (S.I.), Speed, and Timing.

Technique Development

This section provides a thorough review of all machine and typing techniques and develops them to the higher levels required for fast and accurate production typing. It contains abundant instructions and practice in, for example, centring, word division, tabulation, manuscript correction (both amended typescript and manuscript), letter styles, agendas, minutes, plays, etc.

Production Typing

The purpose of *Applied Typing* is to develop quick and accurate production typing, and this new edition contains 103 realistic production jobs. Each job has a target time based on average timings of a variety of students. Most production jobs are in manuscript form, and the total number of manuscript exercises in the book has been doubled.

Accuracy/Speed Practice

All accuracy/speed practice passages are graded for syllabic intensity, speed, and timing. Syllabic intensity, which is the average number of syllables per word contained in a passage, gives the teacher an indication of the relative difficulty of copy. In *Applied Typing*, students are presented with graded and controlled copy so that they build speed with accuracy and sustain their speed for gradually lengthening periods of time.

The following table shows the controlled development of speed and accuracy:

Page	Timings — Number in Minutes	Number of Words	Syllabic Intensity	Error Tolerance
1	1	70	1.10–1.30	1
7	2	140	1.13	2
11	3	210	1.27	3
16	4	280	1.25	3
21	5	350	1.27	3
29	1	80	1.19–1.24	1
35	2	160	1.20	2
40	3	240	1.28	3
47	4	320	1.34	3
55	5	400	1.28	3
65	1	80	1.25–1.27	1
72	2	160	1.24	2
77	3	240	1.33	3
83	4	320	1.37	3
90	5	400	1.30	3
100	1	80	1.26–1.29	1
107	2	160	1.30	2
112	3	240	1.32	3
119	4	320	1.37	3
129	5	400	1.38	3
138	1	80	1.30–1.32	1
145	2	160	1.33	2
150	3	240	1.40	3
157	4	320	1.37	3
165	5	400	1.38	3
176	5	400	1.50	3
182	6	480	1.33	3

Since students starting to use this book may have different typing speeds, they should begin by typing as much as possible of the first accuracy/speed passage on page 1 to establish their speed. Then if:

(a) in the first timing, they have not more than 1 error, they should aim at a speed of 5 words a minute above the speed reached in the first typing. For example, if a student's present speed with not more than 1 error is 35 words a minute, her starting point for building speed will be 40 words a minute;

(b) a student has more than 1 error in the first timing, she should continue to practise the passage at the speed reached in the first timing until she can type it with not more than 1 error.

As the length of timing increases by one minute in each of the next four units, the student should continue to practise at the selected starting speed up to the end of Unit 5.

At the beginning of Units 6, 11, 16, and 21, the student is asked to increase speed by 5 words a minute. Each time the speed is increased, the student should practise the one-minute timing until she reaches her goal within the error tolerance, and then continue with the next four units at the same speed.

The student's ultimate aim should be a minimum of 80 words a minute with not more than 3 errors.

Review Quizzes

The five review quizzes give a thorough and rapid review of punctuation, styling, and display. Self-checking answers are included at the end of the text.

Secretarial Aids

The five secretarial aids give the typist useful information about:

- Proof-reading
- Stationery
- Personality
- Responsibility
- Care of the typewriter.

Teacher's Handbook and Solutions

A teacher's handbook and solutions is planned to accompany the text.

Acknowledgments

The authors wish to express their gratitude to Mrs. Hilary Dorman and Mr. P. C. Pratt for their kind permission to use extracts from their plays 'Bloggs' Big Day' and 'Imprint for Murder'. They also wish to thank their colleagues for the valuable help given in testing the exercises under practical conditions and with students of varying ages and ability, as well as for assisting with the copying of the manuscript work.

Index

Abbreviations, 3, 163, M1, M2, M8
  Spacing, M9
Accuracy + Speed Passages
  1 min., 1, 29, 66, 100, 138
  2 mins., 7, 35, 72, 107, 145
  3 mins., 11, 40, 77, 112, 150
  4 mins., 16, 47, 83, 129, 157
  5 mins., 21, 55, 90, 129, 165, 176
  6 mins., 182
Addressing envelopes:
  Exercises, 79, 80
  Forms of address, 79, 80
  Postcode, 78
  Punctuation, 78
Addressing machines, 114
Agenda, 41, 42, 46
  Chairman, 43, 44, 46
  Staff meeting, 43, 46
Agreement, 168, 171
Alphabetical reviews, 1, 7, 11, 16, 21, 29, 35, 40, 47, 55, 66, 72, 77, 83, 90, 100, 107, 112, 119, 129, 138, 145, 150, 157, 165, 176
Annual General Meeting, 45
Answers to Review Quizzes, 199
Answers to Exercise 8 page 103, 199
Application Form, 144
Apostrophe, 10
Arabic Numbers, 12
Asterisk, 17
Attention Line, 68
Back-feeding, 76
Balance Sheets, 140, 141, 142, 143
Bibliography, 186
Bills of Quantities, 122, 123, 124, 125, M2
Blind Carbon Copies, 85
Block Paragraphs, 3
Borders, Ornamental, M9
Brace, M3
Business Letters, 67
  Attention Line, 68
  Enclosure, 68
  Folding, M8
  Fully Blocked, 67
  Indented Letter, 67
  Inset Matter:
    Fully-blocked, 69
    Semi-blocked, 73
  Layout, 67, 73
  Manuscript, 70, 71, 75, 84, 85, 88, 94, 99, 106, 136, 149, 164, 174, 175, 189, 192
  Open Punctuation, 74
  Postscript, 74
  Semi-blocked, 67, 73
  Steps in Typing a Letter, M3
  Subject Heading:
    Fully-blocked, 69
    Semi-blocked, 73
Carbon Copies, 84
  Additional Copies, 84
  Blind Copies (cc), 85
  Carbon Packs, Insertion of, 113
Caret Sign, M3
Centring:
  Horizontal, 2
  Vertical, 30
Chairman's Agenda, 43, 44, 46
Civil Service Letters, 101, 102, 104
Column Headings, 131, 147
Columnar Statements, 130, 131, 132, 133
  Vertical, 158, 159, 161
  Diagonal, 160, 163
Combination Characters, 17, M3
Common Word Drill, 150, 165
Composing at Machine, 26, 62, 96, 135, 172

Concentration Drills, 16, 72, 83, 145
Consolidation, 27, 28, 63, 64, 97, 98, 99, 136, 137, 173, 174, 175
Consular Invoice, 113
Continuation Sheets:
  Business Letters, 86
  Manuscript, 24, 50
Copy of Letter, M8
Correction Signs, 8, 10, 95, M3, M4
Dagger, 17
Dash, 17, 36
Dead Keys, M8
Decimals, 66
Degree Sign, 17
Diagonal Headings, 160
Display:
  Effective Display, 31
  Exercises, 19, 28, 54, 64, 82, 128, 133, 137, 181, 191, 193
  Lay-out, 30
Division of Words, 2, M5
Division Sign, 17
Dollar Sign, 17
Double Dagger, 17
Double Underscore (Totals), 9
Drills:
  Alphabetic—see Alphabetic Reviews
  Common Words, 150, 165
  Concentration, 16, 72, 83, 145
  Fluency, 1, 21, 65, 107, 119, 150
  Figures, 7, 40, 72, 100, 157
  Letter Combinations, 7, 35, 65, 100, 119, 138
  Phrases, 7, 11, 35, 77, 107, 138
  Prefixes, 7, 11, 47, 77, 112
  Shift Key, 1, 29, 35, 72, 145
  Shift Lock, 16, 40, 83, 112, 145
  Special Characters, 29
  Suffixes, 47, 107
Duplicating:
  Offset-Litho Process, 185
  Photo-copying, 185
  Proto-copying, 185
  Spirit, 185
  Stencilling, 177
    Cutting Stencil, 177, 178
  Interleaving, 184
  Manifolding, 177
    Joining, 179
    Running off, 183
Effective Display, 31
Ellipsis, 14
Enclosure, 68
Endorsement:
  Bill of Quantities, M2
  Legal Documents, M4
  Specification, M6
Enumerations, 13
Envelopes:
  Exercises, 79, 80
  Forms of Address, 79, 80
  Sizes, 78
  Postcode, 78
  Punctuation, 78
  Window, M9
Equation Sign, 17
Erasing, 25
Examination Hints, 187
Exclamation Mark, 17
Export Invoices, 113
Figure Drills, 7, 40, 72, 100, 157
Figures and Words, Use of, 18, M7
Fluency Drills, 1, 21, 65, 107, 119, 150
Folding
  Letters, M8
  Legal Documents, M4
  Programmes, 32
  76, 79, 80, 81, 97, 105, 127, 173, 174, 180

Footnotes:
  Exercises, 22, 23, 24, 25, 53, 97, 177, 187
Formal Notes, 92
Forms of Address, 79, 80
Fractions, 48
Fully-blocked Letters, 67
  Attention Line, 68
  Enclosures, 68
  Inset Matter, 69
  Subject Heading, 69
Grafting, 183
Hanging Paragraphs, 3
Headings:
  Columns, 131, 147
  Diagonal, 160, 163
  Letters, 4
  Main, 4
  Manuscript, 4
  Paragraph, 4, 5, 6
  Shoulder, 4, 5, 6
Horizontal Centring, 2
Horizontal Ruling, 146
Hyphen, 17
Income and Expenditure Account, 140, 143
Indented Letter, 67
Indented Paragraphs, 3
Inferior Characters, 9
Inset Matter, 12
Interliner, 9
Interleaving, 184
Internal Telephone-Index, 18, 19
Inter-Office Memoranda, 93, 94, 137, 189
Invoicing, 113, 114, 115, 118
Itinerary, 37, 38, 39, 189
Jobs—see Production Typing
Justifying, M8
Keyboard Reviews—see Drills
Lay-out, Display, 30, 31
Leader Dots, 152
Legal Work, 166, 168, 171, M4
Letter Combination Drills, 7, 35, 65, 100, 119, 138
Line-end Division of Words, 2, M5
Literary Matter, 50
Longhand Abbreviations, 3

Main Headings, 4
Manifolding, 177
Manuscript, Miscellaneous Exercises, 6, 10, 15, 20, 27, 28, 50, 51, 53, 63, 76, 79, 80, 81, 97, 105, 127, 173, 174, 180
Margins, 4
Meetings, Notice of, 41, 42, 46
  Annual General Meetings, 45
  Staff Meetings, 43, 46
Memoranda, Inter-Office, 93, 94, 137, 189
Menu, 36, 39, 53, 136
Message Forms, 37, 39
Minutes, 48, 49, 53, 134
Minutes Sign, 17
Money, Sums of, 66
Notice, Lay-out, 30, 31
Notice of Meetings, 41, 42, 46
Numbers:
  Arabic, 12
  Cardinal, 12
  Omission of comma, 132
  Ordinal, 12
  Roman Numerals, 12, M6
Official Letters, 101, 102, 104
Offset-Litho, 185
Omission of Words, 14
Open Punctuation:
  Business Letters, 86
  Envelopes, 78
Order, 109
Ordinal Numbers, 12
Ornamental Border, M9
Pamphlet, 196
Paper Sizes, M5
Paragraphs, Types of, 3
Paragraph Headings, 4
Personal Letters, 91, 111
Photo-copying, 186
Phrase Drills, 11, 35, 77, 107, 138
Play, 57, 60
Plus Sign, 17
Poetry, 56, 61, 63
Postcards, 95
Postcode, 78
Postscripts, 74
Prefix Drills, 7, 11, 47, 77, 112
Printers' Correction Signs, 8, 10, 95, M3, M4
Production Typing
  Annual Reports, Jobs Nos. 8:20, 90:180
  Abbreviations, Job No. 80:163
  Advertisement, Job No. 91:181
  Agenda:
    Chairman's, Job No. 21:46
    Committee Meeting, Job No. 20:46
    Staff Meeting, Job No. 22:46
  Agreement, Job No. 84:171
  Application Form, Job No. 71:144
  Balance Sheet, Job No. 70:143
  Bill of Quantities, Job. No. 59:126
  Business Letters, Job No. 32:70, 33:71, 34:75, 38:88, 39:94, 45:99, 46:99, 49:106, 65:136, 74:149, 81:164, 83:170, 87:174, 88:175, 93:189, 98:192
  Correction Signs, Jobs Nos. 4:10, 41:95
  Display, Jobs Nos. 6:19, 13:28, 31:64, 37:82, 61:128, 97:191, 102:196
  Examination Hints, Job No. 92:187
  Footnotes, Jobs Nos. 9:24, 10:25, 11:27, 23:53, 44:97, 92:187
  Form Letters, Jobs Nos. 50:110, 89:175; 51:110, 52:110,
  Income and Expenditure Account, Job No. 69:143
  Internal Telephone-Index, Jobs Nos. 7:19, 69:143
  Invitation, Job No. 42:95

Index

Production Typing—*contd.*
Invoice, Job No. 55:118
Itinerary, Jobs Nos. 19:39, 95:189
Legal Documents, Will, Job No. 82:170
Manuscript, Miscellaneous, Jobs Nos. 1:6, 3:10, 5:15, 11:27, 12:28, 30:63, 35:76, 36:81, 44:97, 48:105, 60:127, 85:173, 86:174, 90:180, 99:193
Meetings, Notice of, Jobs Nos. 20:46, 21:46, 22:46, 68:137
Memoranda, Jobs Nos. 40:94, 67:137, 94:189
Menu, Jobs Nos. 17:39, 24:53, 66:136
Message, Job No. 18:39
Minutes, Jobs Nos. 25:53, 64:134
Official Letter, Job No. 47:104
Personal Letter, Job No. 54:111
Play, Jobs Nos. 27:60, 43:95
Programmes, Jobs Nos. 15:34, 16:34, 53:111
Punctuation, Jobs Nos. 2:10, 14:34
Specification, Job No. 58:125
Statements, Jobs Nos. 56:118, 57:118
Tabulation, Jobs Nos. 62:133, 63:133, 72:148, 73:148, 75:155, 76:156, 77:161, 78:162, 79:163, 96:190, 100:194, 101:195, 103:198
Ticket, Job No. 26:54
Programmes, 31, 32, 33, 34, 111
Proof-correction Signs, 8, 10, M3, M4
Proof-reading, 26, 103
Punctuation (Open), 78

Punctuation Reviews:
Apostrophe, 10
Dash, 17, 36
Hyphen, 17
Quotation Marks, 10

Quizzes, 1:26, 2:62, 3:96, 4:135, 5:172
Answers, 199
Quotation Marks, 10

Ratchet Release (Interliner), 9
Receipts and Payments Account, 139
Reference Signs and Footnotes, 22, 154
Reviews—see Drills
Ribbons:
Fitting, M8
Types of, M9
Roman Numerals, 12, M6
Ruled Lines, Typing on, 108
Ruling, Tabulation, 146, 147, 153

Seconds Sign, 17
Secretarial Aids, 1:26, 2:62, 3:96, 4:135, 5:172
Section Sign, M3
Semi-blocked Letter, 67, 73
Shift-key Reviews, 1, 29, 35, 72, 145
Shift-lock Reviews, 16, 40, 83, 112, 145
Shoulder Headings, 4, 5
Single Actor's Part, 59, 61

Sizes of Paper, M5
Spacing—Measurements and Weights, M9
Special Characters, 29
Special Signs, 17
Specifications, 120, 125, M6
Endorsement, 121, M7
Speed + Accuracy—see under Accuracy
Spirit Duplicating, 185
Square Brackets, M3
Staff Meetings, 43, 46
Standard Abbreviations, 3, M1
Standard Sizes of Paper, M5
Statements, 116, 117, 118
Stencilling:
Cutting Stencil, 177, 178
Grafting, 183
Interleaving, 184
Joining, 179
Running off, 183
Steps in Typing a Letter, M3
Subdivided Headings (Tabulation), 151
Subject Heading (Business Letters):
Fully-blocked, 69
Semi-blocked, 73
Suffix Drills, 47, 107
Sums of Money, 66
Superior Characters, 9

Tabular Statements, 130, 146, 148, 151, 152, 153, 155, 156, 158, 159, 160, 161, 162, 163, 190, 194, 195
Tabulation:
Headings:
Column, 147

Tabulation—*contd.*
Headings—*contd.*
Diagonal, 160, 163
Subdivided, 151
Vertical, 158, 159, 161
Hints, 153
Leader Dots, 152
Re-arrangement of, 159, 190, 194, 195, 198
Reference Signs and Footnotes, 154
Ruling, 146
Ink, 147
Typewriter, 153
Tailpiece, M9
Telephone-Index, Internal, 18
Tips for Typists, 24

Underscore (Double), 9
Underscoring, M9

Variable line spacer, 92
Vertical Centring, 30
Vertical Column Headings, 158, 159, 161
Vertical Ruling, 146

Will, 169, 170
Window Envelopes, M9
Word-division, 2, M5
Words and Figures, 18, M7

Introductory Notes

Reminders before starting to type

1. Insert paper by means of interliner and remove by means of paper release.
2. Set margins according to instructions given in each Unit. Bear in mind that right-hand margin must never be wider than left-hand.

Example: Writing line   60 spaces
Set Margins: Pica   12—72
Elite   20—80

In Production Typing, if margins are not stated, select what you consider to be the most suitable for the particular job.

3. Set line-spacing.
4. Clear previous tab. stops and re-set where required.
5. Date all your work.

Keyboard techniques

At the beginning of each Unit there are keyboard reviews. Type each of these as instructed. Whenever you have time, repeat any which cause you difficulty.

Folders

We suggest you should keep the following folders:

1. Production Jobs.
2. Reference Notes.
3. Miscellaneous completed exercises which you are required to keep.

Unit 1

Skill building

Type each line or sentence (A, B, and C) *three* times, and, if time permits, complete your practice by typing each group once as it appears.

A. Review alphabet keys

1.   On the journey they visited an extremely quaint cottage where a wizened old woman kept an aviary of many fine birds.

B. Review shift key

2. June York Aden Ward Mary Fife Kate Peter Roger Nancy Tom Pat

3. June, Mary, Kate, Peter, Roger, Nancy, and Tom left for Ayr.

4. Telephone Mr. L. H. Ward about the Annual General Meeting of The National Union of Teachers which will be held on Friday.

C. Improve fluency

5. Why not let her try the new hat and fur she has got for you?

6. Now the boy has cut his leg and his arm on that old tin can.

7. She did not say why she had put her big red bag in the road.

8. The lad can now pay you for the new pen nib you got for him.

Accuracy/Speed Practice

Read page iv in Preface under heading 'Accuracy and Speed Practice'. Then, having selected your starting point for building speed, practise the following passage as far as you can in one minute at that speed until you can do so within the Accuracy Standard indicated.

One-minute timing   *Not more than 1 error*

		words
AS.1	As he came close to the town, he met a crowd of folk he	11
	did not recognize. This was strange, for he thought he knew	23
	all of the people on that side of the town. When he came to	35
	the main street, he found all of his old haunts had gone and	47
	rows of shops stood in their place. Then it struck him that	59
	all that was thirty years ago — a fact he had forgotten.	70

(S.I. 1.10)

		words
AS.2	You should be prompt to time not only at work, but also	11
	when you arrange to meet anyone. To keep someone waiting is	23
	very bad manners. Some people are always late, but are wild	35
	if they themselves are kept waiting. If you know you cannot	47
	be in time to keep your appointment, you should endeavour to	59
	let the person know, and explain why you cannot do so.	70

(S.I. 1.30)

MANUSCRIPT 'FIT'

1. It is sometimes necessary to divide a long manuscript among several typists. If the manuscript is in chapter form, the division should be made at the end of a chapter. If, however, the matter is continuous, the division must be made in such a way that the last line of each typist's section comes to the bottom of a page, so that it may run on without a break to the start of the next typist's section. This is known as 'fit'. To do this, it may be necessary to make some adjustment to the line-spacing on the last page.

2. When a manuscript is divided in this way, care must be taken to see that each typist adopts the same margins, style for headings, etc., and that the ribbons and type-faces on all machines match.

ORNAMENTAL BORDERS

Display work, such as programmes, menus, etc., can be made more artistic by the use of a suitable ornamental border or corners, such as the following. You should be able to make up other artistic borders, but in doing so take care not to make the border too heavy, as this will detract from the general appearance.

```
*  *  *  *  *  *        0 : 0 : 0 : 0 : 0
                             :            :
*                 *          :            :
                        0 : 0 : 0 : 0 : 0
* *  *  *  *  *


        ***                 ***
        *                     *
        *                     *

        *                     *
        *                     *
        ***                 ***
```

RIBBONS

Typewriter ribbons can be obtained in three main kinds:

Record ribbons are inked with a fast dye, and are used for letters and ordinary work. They may be in various colours, such as black, purple, blue, red, etc.

Bichrome ribbons are two-coloured, usually black and red, although other combinations are obtainable.

Copying ribbons: These are specially inked ribbons used for press-copying work.

SPACING

Where abbreviations are used for measurements or weights, such as in., ft., lb., mm, kg, there must always be a space left between the figures and the abbreviations. Examples: 2 mm, 3 kg. On no account must the figure and abbreviation be typed without a space between.

TAILPIECE

This is an ornamental arrangement frequently used at the end of a chapter or section of a book, and is made up by combining characters, such as hyphen, colon, etc.

UNDERSCORING

1. Never underscore final punctuation marks.

2. In manuscript or typescript copy, words double-underlined are intended to be typed in UNSPACED CAPITALS. Words treble-underscored are to be typed in S P A C E D C A P I T A L S. Double or treble underscoring, however, must not be used for underlining such typewritten headings. A <u>single</u> underscore line is permissible.

3. In matter to be submitted to printers, if words are underlined this is an indication to the printers that these words are to be printed in italics.

4. Column headings in tabulations should never be underscored.

WINDOW ENVELOPES

Some firms use envelopes from which a panel has been cut out at the front. This is known as a 'window' envelope. The object of window envelopes is two-fold:

1. It saves time in typing the name and address on both letter and envelope.

2. It avoids the possibility of error in copying the address on the envelope.

When a window envelope is used, the name and address of the addressee must be typed in full on the letter itself, and in such a position that, when the letter is folded the position of the address will coincide with the cut-out portion on the envelope. To help the typist, the position of the cut-out is sometimes marked on the letter heading either by marks in the corner or by a ruled box. Window envelopes may also be provided with a transparent cover over the cut-out part.

This type of envelope is not normally used for personal letters. It is used without the transparent cover mainly for statements, invoices, form letters, etc.

M9

Technique development

To centre any line, set the carriage at the centre, then back-space once for each two letters and spaces that the typed lines will occupy (ignore any odd letter) and begin typing at the point to which you have back-spaced. Example: To centre *Amount* as a heading, back-space AM OU NT. To centre *The Amount*, back-space TH E-space AM OU NT. To centre *The Total*, back-space TH E-space TO TA (ignore odd L). Say the letters to yourself as you back-space.

Special Notes: When the paper is inserted so that its left edge is at 0, note the scale-point at which the right edge appears; half that number is the centre. For example: A4 paper extends from 0 to 82 (pica) or 0 to 100 (elite); the centre would be 41 (pica) or 50 (elite). If margins have already been set, to find the centre add the margins and divide their total by 2. For example, with margins at 20 and 85 the centre is 105 ÷ 2 = 52. (Ignore any fraction left over.) If you have a machine with 0 in the centre of the scale, the centre point of the paper must be brought to 0. To do this, instead of inserting the paper with the left-hand edge at 0, see that the left-hand edge is at the scale-point indicated on page M5 of the Reference Manual for the centre point of the various sizes of paper. This will ensure that the centre of the paper corresponds with 0 on the scale. By bringing the paper guide against the left-hand edge of paper, you will be able to insert any subsequent sheet of paper of the same size in the correct position.

9. Practise horizontal centring. Read the above explanation, then
    (*a*) display the headings below on A5 (210 × 148 mm) paper;
    (*b*) display another copy on A5 (148 × 210 mm) paper with margins set at 10 and 55 pica, 10 and 65 elite.

NEW ERA SUPPLIES
Phoenix Place, Brighton, Sussex, BN1 5NA
Stationery
Envelopes
Duplicating Paper
Carbon Paper
Typewriter Ribbons
QUICK DELIVERY GUARANTEED

10. Practise word-division. Type one copy of the following words, inserting a hyphen at the most suitable point if the word can be divided. If necessary, review rules, Reference Manual, p. M5.

incompetent condemnation Bristol inspection doorway UNICEF niece occurrence disastrous non-existent gauges mortgage infatuation although shouldn't children brilliant 5,000,000 can't problem university transcription appropriate coated

11. Practise line-endings. Type a copy of the following in double-line spacing, using a 60-space line.

The object of the Department of Research was to facilitate and co-ordinate, wherever possible, all aspects of educational research. Its aim is, moreover, to avoid duplication of effort by developing a rapid means of collecting and disseminating research results, and of decreasing the great time lag between research and application of the results in practice. Documents of significance are sent to the clearing centre.

ABBREVIATIONS

1. Do not abbreviate Street, Road, Avenue, etc., in the address of a letter.

2. When preceding a name, titles of honour are usually contracted by the omission of all but the first syllable, or of all but the first and last letter. Examples: Lieut.-Col., Rear Adm., Right Hon.

As a rule, words of four or five letters only and forming parts of titles are not abbreviated.

COPY

To distinguish a copy of a document from an original, type the word 'COPY' at the top, and the word 'SIGNED' before the signature (if any).

DEAD KEYS

Some machines are provided with keys which, when depressed, do not cause the carriage to move forward the usual single character space. These are known as 'dead keys'. They are usually fitted for foreign accents, so that the accent can be struck first and, without the necessity of back-spacing, the letter key is then struck.

Building firms also sometimes have dead keys fitted on the machine for the denominator of certain fractions which they use frequently, and the typist merely inserts the numerator, e.g., $\overline{16}$ or /16.

FITTING A NEW RIBBON

Instructions for fitting a new ribbon are given in the Instruction Manual furnished by the typewriter companies. If, however, you have not one of these available, before changing your ribbon, note how the old one is wound. The following steps will be a guide to you.

1. Lift the ribbon cover (if any) up or off.

2. Depress shift lock.

3. Wind the old ribbon on to one spool, preferably the right, as on some machines the left- and right-hand spools are different, and new ribbons for such machines are usually supplied on right-hand spools. However, on most machines the spools can now be fitted on either side.

4. To make the ribbon carrier more accessible, depress G and H keys simultaneously, and lock them in the V-shaped guide. Then remove ribbon from the carrier, having first noted how it is fitted (i.e., behind the carrier, and then looped forward).

5. Remove spools and ribbon from the cups of the typewriter.

6. Loosen end of ribbon from empty spool (first taking careful note to see how it is fastened to the spool).

7. Take full spool with new ribbon and fasten loose end of ribbon in the empty spool.

8. Wind a little of the ribbon onto the empty spool, seeing that you wind it in the correct direction. On some machines the ribbon approaches the spool from the back and on others from the front.

9. Take both spools and place them in the cups (the spool with the new ribbon on the same side as that from which you took the full spool).

10. Thread the ribbon through the guides (if any) and slip the centre of the ribbon behind the ribbon carrier, then pull the ribbon forward from each side and thread it through the carrier-guide arms.

11. Release the shift lock, and replace ribbon cover (if any).

12. Check to see that the ribbon is operating correctly.

FOLDING LETTERS

Letters and papers should be neatly folded to fit the particular size of envelope used.

JUSTIFYING

The right-hand margin in typewriting cannot be completely regular as in printing, but for purposes of display it may be made regular by adopting the printer's method. This is known as 'justifying'—i.e., the space between the words is adjusted, so that each line is brought out to the same margin point. (The printer can adjust the space between letters, as he has different sizes of spaces.)

For this purpose a draft must be typed, and the additional spaces indicated at suitable points. The first line should be the required length, and the other lines should have spaces suitably adjusted to bring them to the length of the first line.

A typewriter which has a special device for this justifying can be obtained. It equalises the spaces between every word when the draft has been made, and the required number of spaces to be added to each line is known. This device is known as the Automatic Right Margin Justifying Device, and it is mainly used for the preparation of matter such as bulletins, booklets, etc.

M8

Longhand abbreviations

Abbreviations are often made in letters or matter written by hand for the typist to copy. In such cases the writer may make his own abbreviations, such as the following: / or . (full stop) for *the*, g for *ing*, w for *with*, wh for *which*, wd for *would*, shd for *should*, sh for *shall*, amt for *amount*, abt for *about*, tog for *together*, mfr for *manufacturer*, ōr for *other*, th for *that*, and so on. The typist must, of course, type these words in full, and common-sense will decide what the word is.

12. Practise longhand abbreviations. Read the above explanation, then type a copy of the handwritten draft below, spelling in full all words that are abbreviated.

Standard abbreviations

Apart from longhand abbreviations which anyone writing a rough copy may adopt, there are certain standard abbreviations which are always used, and others which may be used in certain circumstances. Study the list of these abbreviations and their uses which is given in the Reference Manual, page M1.

13. Practise standard abbreviations. Read the above explanation, then type a copy of the following in double spacing, using abbreviations or writing these in full where necessary.

Paragraphing

There are three different styles of paragraphing.

1. *Indented:* The first line is usually typed five spaces to the right of the left margin or of the following lines. The tab. stop is set for this type of paragraph.

2. *Block or flush:* All lines start at the same point on the scale.

3. *Hanging:* The second and subsequent lines are typed two spaces to the right of the first line.

UNIT 1

3

7. *Marginal headings.* These start 25 mm from left-hand edge of paper (to allow room for binding if necessary). They are typed in closed capitals and underscored (each line, if more than one).

Single-line spacing is used, and no full stop is typed at end of marginal headings.

Note: The margin release is used for marginal headings. It is a good plan to return the carriage to 0 on scale by means of the margin release and to set a tab. stop 25 mm from edge of paper for start of headings.

8. *Continuation sheets.* On continuation sheets, the heading is repeated above the marginal headings and underscored, as follows: Specification (Contd.), and unless the section on the previous page was completed, the sub-heading is also repeated underneath the word Specification, e.g. Bricklayer (Contd.).

9. *Numbering of pages.* At bottom, in centre. In a long specification the marginal headings are also numbered.

10. *Endorsement.* This contains brief details of work to be done, date, name of person for whom it is to be carried out, and name and address of Architect.

In the case of a short specification the endorsement is typed on the back of the last sheet in such a way as to be read easily when the sheets are folded (lengthways down middle). The folded edge should be to the left and the open edges to the right.

It is usual for long specifications to be bound, and in this case the endorsement is typed on the front cover.

Use of words and figures

USE WORDS

In General and Literary Matter

1. For all numbers below 100 and all round numbers over 100, also for indefinite numbers. Examples: There were three hundred people present. About a hundred and six packages are lost.

2. At the beginning of a sentence. Example: Twenty-one people attended the Show.

3. For indefinite ages: Examples: The ages ranged between eleven and twelve years.

4. For ordinal numbers in expressing ages, centuries, etc. Examples: He was in his seventy-sixth year. It happened in the nineteenth century.

5. For time when 'o'clock' is used. Example: Ten o'clock.

6. To express population. Example: The population of the town is five thousand.

7. For names of streets. Example: Second Avenue.

In Commercial Matter

8. Numbers from 1 to 9 inclusive in text are typed in words, unless they refer to measurements, weights or distances.

USE FIGURES

In General and Literary Matter

9. To express definite ages. Example: 12 years 1 month.

10. For street numbers and postcodes. Example: 4 Frederick Road, Birmingham B29 6PB.

11. For percentages, prices, and discounts. Example: Terms: 5% discount. *Note:* The words 'per cent' are written in full, except in commercial matter such as invoices, quotations, price-lists, etc.

12. Sums of money. Example: £10.30. *Note:* Sometimes written in both figures and words to ensure accuracy.

13. Before a.m. and p.m. Examples: 6.30 a.m. 2.30 p.m. *Note:* The full stop is used to separate hours and minutes.

In Commercial Matter

14. From 10 upwards.

15. When reference is made to quantities, measurements, weights, money items, or dates. Example: We require 20 reams of A4 Paper 210 × 297 mm.

16. For numbers in series: Example: 8 bags, 4 boxes, 2 crates.

Note: Avoid mixing figures and words. Example: Type £10m. as: Ten million pounds, or £10,000,000.

Note: The tendency is to type in words numbers which occur at the beginning of a sentence, and also the number ONE, while all other numbers are typed in figures.

Except in tabulation and display work, when using A4 paper the left margin must never be less than 10 pica, 12 elite, and when using A5 (148 × 210 mm) paper, the left margin must never be less than 5 pica, 6 elite. Whichever paper is used, the right margin must *never* be wider than the left.

14. Practise typing heading and indented paragraphs. Type a copy of the following on A4 (210 × 297 mm) paper in double spacing, using a 65-space typing line. Leave 6 clear line-spaces at top. Keep your typed copy for future reference in Folder No. 2.

HEADINGS IN MANUSCRIPT

Of the many kinds of headings, the three most commonly used are: main, shoulder, and paragraph.

MAIN HEADINGS

These are centred on the typing line and are usually in all-capitals, followed by two blank lines. Any heading typed in lower case with initial capitals MUST be underscored. It should be noted that only after main headings at the beginning of an exercise should two blank lines be left. The title of this exercise is a main heading. No full stop is used at the end of headings unless the last word is abbreviated. If there is a full stop, it is NOT underscored.

SHOULDER HEADINGS

These are generally typed in all-capitals at the left margin, preceded and followed by one blank line. The heading written above this paragraph is a shoulder heading. There is never a full stop after a shoulder heading unless the last word is abbreviated. Main headings and shoulder headings may be single-underscored but double or treble underlining must NEVER be used.

PARAGRAPH HEADINGS

Paragraph headings are typed with initial capitals and lower-case letters and are underscored. The first two words of this paragraph are a paragraph heading.

Second Style. Paragraph headings may be run into the first sentence of the paragraph, as in the paragraph above, or the heading may be displayed as in this paragraph.

Roman numerals

1. *Units:* I (1); X (10); C (100); M (1000)
   Fives: V (5); L (50); D (500).

2. The four *unit* symbols can be repeated to express 2 or 3 units of the *same* symbol.
   Examples: 1 = I; 2 = II; 3 = III;
   10 = X; 20 = XX; 30 = XXX;
   100 = C; 200 = CC; 300 = CCC;
   1000 = M; 2000 = MM; 3000 = MMM.

3. The symbol I may be used or repeated (up to III) *after* any of the above units or fives, in which case it *adds* to the symbol in front. Examples:

   I = 1; VI = 6; XI = 11; LI = 51;
   II = 2; VII = 7; XII = 12; LII = 52;
   III = 3; VIII = 8; XIII = 13; LIII = 53;
   CI = 101; DI = 501; MI = 1001;
   CII = 102; DII = 502; MII = 1002;
   CIII = 103; DIII = 503; MIII = 1003.

4. To express 4, 9, 40, 400 and 900, take the symbol immediately *above* and put the appropriate unit symbol *in front*, which means that it is *subtracted* from the higher symbol. Examples:

   4 = 5 − 1 = IV; 9 = 10 − 1 = IX;
   40 = 50 − 10 = XL; 90 = 100 − 10 = XC;
   400 = 500 − 100 = CD; 900 = 1000 − 100 = CM.

NOTE: I can be placed *only* before V or X;
   X „ „ „ „ „ L or C;
   C „ „ „ „ „ D or M.

5. To express numbers other than those in Rule 4, take the unit or five symbol immediately *below* and *add* to it the remaining symbols by putting these *after* the unit or five symbol. Examples:

   6 = 5 + 1 = VI; 14 = 10 + 4 = XIV;
   7 = 5 + 2 = VII; 15 = 10 + 5 = XV;
   8 = 5 + 3 = VIII; 16 = 10 + 6 = XVI;
   17 = 10 + 7 = XVII;
   18 = 10 + 8 = XVIII;
   60 = 50 + 10 = LX; 600 = 500 + 100 = DC;
   70 = 50 + 20 = LXX; 700 = 500 + 200 = DCC;
   80 = 50 + 30 = LXXX; 800 = 500 + 300 = DCCC.

6. A horizontal line drawn over the unit symbol means that the unit is multiplied by 1000. Example:

   $\overline{M}$ = 1000 × 1000 = 1,000,000.

7. To convert Arabic figures into Roman numerals, take each figure in turn. Example: To convert 467, proceed as follows:

   400 = 500 − 100 = CD; 60 = 50 + 10 = LX;
   7 = 5 + 2 = VII;
   467 = CDLXVII.

Note: When typing roman numerals for numbering paragraphs, always leave sufficient space so that units are typed under units, tens under tens, etc.

Guide to typing of specifications

Size of paper
   A4 (210 × 297 mm)

Ribbon
   Normally a black ribbon is used.

Parts of Specification
   Three, viz. Main heading; Body; Marginal headings.

Spacing
   Main heading in double-line spacing. Body typed in double-line spacing if the Specification is a short one, or in single-line spacing, with double spacing between paragraphs, if it is long.

LAY-OUT
1. *Main heading.* The word 'SPECIFICATION' in heading at top is typed in spaced capitals, starting at 30 Pica, 35 Elite.

2. Subsequent lines of heading are indented 5 spaces, i.e. 35 Pica, 40 Elite.

3. The name and address of architect are typed two single-line spaces underneath the heading, in single-line spacing, either in indented form, when each line of the address is indented five spaces, or it may be blocked.

4. Date, usually at left margin, two single-line spaces below last line of Architect's address. It is sometimes typed on right-hand side underneath Architect's address.

5. *Body.* Left-hand margin set at 63 mm from edge of paper, i.e. 25 Pica, 30 Elite. Right-hand margin 13 mm.

Paragraph indentation 5, unless blocked style used.

6. *Sub-headings in body.* The word PRELIMINARIES (when used) is usually typed in spaced capitals, centred on typing line, and underscored.
   When a section or trade is started, the name of the trade is centred in typing line, typed in closed capitals, and underscored.

15. Type the following on A4 (210 × 297 mm) paper in double spacing. Use shoulder headings and block paragraphs.

MOTOR VEHICLE LICENCE

When you have need to re-license a motor vehicle you should have the following information available:

DOCUMENTS

Registration book and a valid certificate of insurance (not the policy) in respect of Third Party risks. You will also require a Test Certificate, where appropriate, and your expiring licence if application for new licence is being made at a Post Office.

LICENSING PARTICULARS

Date from which licence has to run, and date of expiry of previous licence. The vehicle's registration number and taxation class.

ADDITIONAL PARTICULARS

Information as to the uses to which the vehicle will be put.

16. Type the following on A5 (210 × 148 mm) paper in double spacing, centring the main heading and using indented paragraphs.

POST OFFICE GUIDE

The Post Office Guide is the official book of reference regarding postal information and post offices throughout the United Kingdom. It is a wise plan always to keep a copy in the office for use when needed. Two of the services provided by the Post Office are given below:

Express Letters. If a letter is marked 'Express' and an extra fee is paid, it receives priority and is delivered by special messenger.

Business Reply Service. For this service a licence must be obtained from the Post Office. By this means a person may receive replies from his customers without their having paid the postage, this being collected from the receiver.

Line-end division

General rules

1. If possible, avoid dividing a word at the end of a line.

2. If it is necessary to do so to avoid an irregular right-hand margin, you should not divide on more than two consecutive lines.

3. Divide according to syllables *provided that the pronunciation of the word is not thereby changed.*

4. Wherever possible, let the portion of the word left at the end of the line indicate what the word is.

Specific rules

DIVIDE:

5. After a prefix and before a suffix. Examples: inter-sect, absorp-tion.

6. *Before* the repeated consonant if the final consonant is doubled (to apply spelling rule). Example: shop-ping.

7. *After* the repeated consonant if the root word ends in a double consonant. Example: miss-ing.

8. Between the two consonants (usually) when a consonant is doubled medially. Example: bag-gage.

9. After a single-letter syllable in the *middle* of a word. Example: manu-script.

10. Between two *different* consecutive consonants in the *middle* of a word. Example: desig-nation.

11. After the first of three consecutive consonants in the middle. Example: magis-trate.

12. At the original point of junction in compound words and words already hyphenated. Example: fisher-man, pre-eminent.

13. Between two separately sounded vowels. Example: radi-ator.

DO NOT DIVIDE:

14. Words of one syllable or their plurals. Examples: course, courses.

15. After or before one or two letters only. Examples: again, aided.

16. Proper names. Example: Wilson.

17. Sums of money, sets of figures, or contracted words. Examples: £14.32, isn't, 123,456,789.

18. At a point which alters the pronunciation. Examples: prod-uct (*not* pro-duct), kin-dred (*not* kind-red).

19. The last word of a paragraph or a page.

20. Foreign words—unless you know the language and where to divide.

Reference table for standard sizes of paper

Paper	Size		Horizontal spacing				Vertical spacing	
			Number of horizontal spaces		Centre point of paper		Total number of single-line spaces	Number of single-line spaces from top edge to centre of paper
	inches	millimetres	Pica	Elite	Pica	Elite		
International								
A4	$8\frac{1}{4} \times 11\frac{3}{4}$	210 × 297	82	100	41	50	70	35
A5	$8\frac{1}{4} \times 5\frac{7}{8}$	210 × 148	82	100	41	50	35	17
		or						
	$5\frac{7}{8} \times 8\frac{1}{4}$	148 × 210	59	70	29	35	50	25
A6	$5\frac{7}{8} \times 4\frac{1}{8}$	148 × 105	59	70	29	35	25	12
Octavo (8vo)	5 × 8	127 × 203	50	60	25	30	48	24
Sixmo (6mo)	$6\frac{1}{2} \times 8$	165 × 203	65	78	32	39	48	24
	$8 \times 6\frac{1}{2}$	203 × 165	80	96	40	48	39	19
Memorandum (memo.)	8 × 5	203 × 127	80	96	40	48	30	15
Quarto (4to)	8 × 10	203 × 254	80	96	40	48	60	30
Foolscap (fcp)	8 × 13	203 × 330	80	96	40	48	78	39

M5

Type the following manuscript in double spacing on A4 paper with suitable margins, bearing in mind that the right margin should never be wider than the left. Centre the main heading and use paragraph headings for the others. Insert necessary apostrophes and spell out abbreviations where needed.

FORMATION OF LIMITED COMPANIES

→ indent

Formation. When a ~~tnt~~ Ltd. Co. is formed it is necessary to submit to/Registrar of Cos. in h/n certain docs, in wh. connection fees & stamp duties are payable.

Registration of a co. Some of the documents required by/Registrar are given below.

Memorandum of Assoc. This controls the powers of/co. & states the cos. objects. It also tells/shareholders & other persons dealing w./co. in what activities/co. may engage, & also its capital, etc.

Articles of Assoc. These concern/regulations apply to/internal management of/co, but they cannot grant powers to/management wh. are not laid down in the Memorandum.

Registered Office. There must be kept a register of directors, secretaries, & directors/holdings of shares, as well as a/Minute Book of general meetings.

Prospectus. A prospectus is defined by the Companies Act as any prospectus, notice, circular, advert. or other invitation offering to/public for subscription or purchase any shares or debentures of a Co.

Issuing Shares. Shares may be issued by a new co. to raise/capital needed to commence business, or they may be issued by a co. already established in order to raise more capital for expansion.

Sign in margin	Meaning		Mark in text	
N.P. or / /	new paragraph		[	placed before first word of new paragraph.
Run on /	no new paragraph—carry straight on		⌢⌣	between paragraphs.
Stet/	let it stand—as it was originally		. . .	under word(s) struck out. These words to be put in as originally.
‖	straighten margin			
ital.	italics		———	(underscored)
⊙	insert full stop			
;/	„	semi-colon		
⊙:	„	colon		
,/	„	comma		
⌄	„	apostrophe		
/–/	„	hyphen		
|—|	„	dash		
⌄⌄ ⌄⌄	„	quotation marks	⋋	
#	„	space		
⋏	„	words		
(/)/	„	brackets		

Double underscore underneath words usually means that such words are to be typed in unspaced capitals.

Treble underscore underneath words usually means that such words are to be typed in spaced capitals (one space between each letter, and three spaces between words).

Legal documents

Folding

A4 documents are folded into two lengthwise or into four horizontally. Documents which are larger than A4 are folded into four.

To fold into two lengthwise:

Place the sheet or sheets face upwards on the table, and turn left-hand side over to meet right.

To fold into four:

Place the sheet or sheets face upwards on the table, turn bottom edges to meet top, crease flat, then take folded edge, turn upwards, and crease again.

Endorsement

When the document is folded, the endorsement is typed on the uppermost side, with the open edges to the right and the fold to the left.

It is advisable to make a pencil mark to show the top of the endorsement before the document is inserted into the machine for the typing of the endorsement.

Details for Endorsement

1. Centre date across top on approximately the seventh single-line space from top edge, starting with the word 'Dated'.

2. Where two parties are concerned the name of the first party (in capitals) is centred about 9–12 single-line spaces below the date.

3. The word 'and' (centred) on the third single-line space below the name of the first party.

4. Name of second party (in capitals) centred on the third single-line space below 'and'.

5. Nature of document in spaced capitals and underscored, centred in middle of page, followed by description of subject-matter in double-line spacing below the title of document (each line centred if more than one).

6. Name and address of solicitors at foot, first line to start about 51 mm from bottom edge.

Unit 2

Skill building

Type each exercise (A, B, C, and D) *once* for practice, *once* for speed, and finally *once* for accuracy.

A. Review alphabet keys

1.   Hire Purchase is a vexed question which dozens of young married couples have solved by just visiting a bank manager.

B. Review figures

2. w2e3 we23 e3r4 er34 t5y6 ty56 y6u7 yu67 u7i8 ui78 i8o9 io89.

3. The 240 men, 137 women, 58 girls, and 69 boys were on board.

4. The estimated expenditure for 1963/64 was: Primary £745,000; Secondary Schools £8,360,000; Further Education £10,275,000.

C. Build accuracy on common prefixes

5. dispose, display, discount, district, discussed, disappoint.

6. I am disappointed that the discount is so low. I hope to be in your district on Tuesday, when we can discuss it further.

7. We have just discovered that there is a display next Monday.

D. Practise common letter combinations

8. the they that this thank their month thought through nothing

9. We think that their order was not sent through as usual. At least there is nothing we can do about it now as this is the last day of the month. Thank them for settling the account.

Accuracy/Speed Practice

Two-minute timing   *Not more than 2 errors*

	words
AS.3 . Some time ago you asked us about some chairs and stools	11
of a style which you could use in your branch shops. At the	23
time we had none in stock to suit you. Now we have just had	35
in a supply of the type of chair and stool which we think is	47
just what you want. Not only is the style suitable for your	59
purpose, but the price is right. As you have always come to	71
us for all your needs, we are giving you the first option on	83
these goods. We do not, of course, wish to keep them in our	95
store too long, so we would ask you to call and inspect them	107
as soon as you can, and decide if they are what you require.	119
In the meantime, we are not putting the goods on show in our	131
shop until you have decided if you want them. (S.I. 1.13)	140

Steps in typing a letter

1. Ascertain number of copies required.
2. Assemble paper and carbon. (a) Insert paper with left edge at 0 on carriage-position scale; (b) Adjust if necessary.
3. Turn down three spaces after last line of heading or allow 9 spaces (38 mm) for heading.
4. Decide margins and set margin stops.
5. If necessary, set tab. stop for 5 indents.
6. If necessary, set tab. stop for centre of writing line.
7. Set line-spacing.
8. Back-space from right-hand margin for each character or space in date. Type date. This does not apply to fully-blocked letters, in which the date starts at left margin.
9. Insert reference(s) at left-hand margin.
10. Turn up 3 single-line spaces.
11. Type name and address of addressee in single-line spacing.
12. Turn up 3 single-line spaces.
13. Type salutation.
14. Turn up 2 single-line spaces.
15. (a) If there is a heading—from tab. stop in centre of writing line, back-space once for every two letters or spaces in heading. Type and under-score heading. Note: In fully-blocked letters the heading starts at left margin. (b) If there is no heading—indent if necessary and type first paragraph.
16. *Always leave double spacing between paragraphs,* irrespective of whether the letter is in single or double spacing.
Note: If 1½ spaces are used, leave only 1½ spaces between paragraphs.
17. Continue to type body of letter.
18. After last line of last paragraph, *turn up two single-line spaces only* and type complimentary close, commencing approximately at middle or slightly to the right of typing line. In fully-blocked letters, type at left margin.
19. If applicable, type name of firm *immediately below* complimentary close.
20. Turn up 5 single-line-spaces and type name and/or official status of person signing letter.
21. Check to see if there is an enclosure. If so, type 'Enc.' near bottom left-hand corner. If more than one enclosure, type 'Encs.'
22. Read letter through very carefully *before* removing from machine, making any necessary corrections neatly on top and carbon copies.
23. Remove papers from machine by means of paper release.
24. Type envelope(s).
25. Attach enclosure (if any) and envelope to letter.

Combination characters

Brace	Brackets typed one beneath the other	( ) ( ) ( )	
Caret	Underscore and solidus	∠	
Cedilla	Small c and comma	ç	
Cent	Small or capital c and solidus	¢ ¢	
Diaeresis	Quotation mark	ü	

Divide into	Right bracket and under-score on line above	⟍)
Paragraph	Capital I and small c	¶
Section	Two capital S's or small s's	§ §
Square brackets	Solidus and underscore	⌐ ¬
Square root	Small v and solidus, followed by underscore on line above	√

Correction signs

Sign in margin	Meaning		Mark in text
l/c or l.c.	lower case = small letters	—	under letter to be altered, or / struck through letter or word
u.c. or caps	upper case = capital letter	—	under letter to be altered or / struck through letter or word
♂	delete (take out)	—	through letter or word
⌒	close up (less space)	⌒	between letter or words
trs.	transpose	～	between letters or words

M3

Technique development

Proof-correction signs

Alterations in printers' proofs are indicated in the original copy by standard correction signs recognized by all who are concerned with this type of work. The letter or word to be altered is struck through, and the appropriate sign is written in the margin against the line in which the correction is to be made, followed by the solidus (/), which marks the end of the marginal note. Refer to Reference Manual pages M3—4 for the most common of these correction signs.

10. Practise correction signs. Read the above explanation and then type a copy of the following on A5 paper (210 × 148 mm) making the required corrections. Use double spacing and typing line of 60 spaces.

stet   We regret to ~~inform~~ *advise* you that we are extremely dissatis-

de/   fied with delay which has occured in conection with the

l.c.   delivery of our Autumn Catalogue, which should have been in

A/   the hands of our customers in the third week of August and

trs. ,/   which atcually reached them in the course of last week long

   after the ~~publication~~ *receipt* s of the ~~receipt~~ of *other* wholesale houses.

Run on   You will find that you gave a definite delivery promise

of one month, and had we known you would have exceeded this

stet N.P.   period, we ~~would~~ *should* have placed the printing elsewhere. [As a

,/   result of the delay we have already lost a great deal of

⊙   business

11. Type a copy of the following on A5 paper (210 × 148 mm), making the required corrections. Use double spacing and block paragraphs.

stet.
4 Kate ~~that~~ *in the* afternoon, John's father persuaded Norah +
N.P. John to drive out w. him to see the child. [Norah
)/ gave one look at / child/ + whatever doubts she/ *still* had
N.P. vanished. [It wasn't just her curly hair + brown *4 4*
   eyes + the ears which were just like mine, Norah *4*
4 recalled./ It was everything abt her.
Run on I wanted to run + take her up in my arms, but
4 John wouldn't let me." "If y. go to her," he said,
4 "we'll both break down. It won't be any good for
   the girl, + it won't be any good for us." *4*

c/o	= care of. Used only in addresses.		Junr., Jnr.	= Junior. Used in addresses—preferably typed in full.
c/f	= carried forward. Used in accounts, statements, etc.		Ltd.	= Limited. Used in name of company.
Co.	= company. Used in names of firms.		M.A.	= Master of Arts. Degree after person's name.
c.i.f.	= cost, insurance, freight. Used in commercial matter.		O.H.M.S.	= On Her Majesty's Service. Usually abbreviated.
c.o.d.	= cash on delivery. Used in commercial matter.		PS.	= Postscript. Used at foot of letter— never in body.
Dr.	= debit, debtor. Used in accounts.		Senr., Snr.	= Senior. Used in addresses— preferably typed in full.
Cr.	= credit, creditor. Used in accounts.		S/S, SS.	= Steamship. Used before name of ship.
D.Sc.	= Doctor of Science. Degree after person's name.		v.	= versus. Abbreviated or typed in full.
E. & O.E.	= Errors and omissions excepted.			
f.o.b.	= free on board. Used in commercial matter.			

Bills of quantities

The following notes will be a guide to the typing of Bills of Quantities:

1. The name of each trade is centred, and in the case of a lengthy Bill of Quantities each trade begins on a new sheet. In shorter Bills of Quantities the document is continuous, i.e., a fresh sheet is not used for each trade. At the end of the document the total of each separate trade is carried to a final summary sheet.

2. The main heading giving details of the Bill of Quantities is set out as in the specimen copy, each line being centred and the important lines underscored.

3. The name of the architect is typed in the same way as on a Specification.

4. The date is also typed in the same way as on a Specification.

5. The preliminary details headed PRELIMINARIES —usually in spaced capitals—are generally typed right across the page (irrespective of the columns ruled), with indented paragraphs, while the details of measurements, etc., are kept to the corresponding columns.

6. The separate items are typed in single-line spacing with double between the items, and are usually numbered as in the case of a Specification, the space at the left of the ruled columns on the left-hand side of the sheet being used for this purpose.

7. The pages are numbered at the foot in the centre.

8. Short Bills of Quantities are folded lengthwise from left to right in two folds and endorsed on the uppermost side, i.e., with folded edge to the left. The endorsement is worded in a similar manner to that of a Specification. Long Bills of Quantities are bound and endorsed on the front page.

Parts of a business letter

The main parts of a business letter are as follows:

1. *Date.* Correct order is: day, month, year. Typed on third single-line space below printed heading.
2. *Reference.* Usually typed on same line as date. Sometimes space is provided for this.
3. *Name and address of addressee.* In single-line spacing. First line typed on third single-line space below reference.

4. *Salutation.* On third single-line space below last line of address.
5. *Body of letter.* Starts on second single-line space below salutation.
6. *Complimentary close.* On second single-line space below last line of body.
7. *Name of sender.* On line immediately below complimentary close. If person signing has official position, turn up six single-line spaces for his signature and type his official status.

M2

Interliner

The interliner lever (sometimes called ratchet release) releases the platen temporarily from the line-spacing mechanism. It is usually on the left side of the carriage. Locate it on your machine. When the interliner is returned to its normal position, the platen goes back to the original writing line.

The interliner is used for typing:
(a) Inferior and superior characters.
(b) Double lines underneath totals.
(c) Certain combination characters.

Superior (raised) characters

Some characters have to be typed above the normal typing line, such as degrees (small o), mathematical formulae, and raised reference marks. These are called 'superior' characters. To type them you should proceed as follows:
(a) Turn platen back half a space.
(b) Type superior character(s).
(c) Return platen to original typing line.

Note: If no half-line spacing is provided on your machine, use interliner as follows:

(a) Release platen from line-spacing mechanism by means of the interliner lever.
(b) Turn platen back about half a space.
(c) Type superior character(s).
(d) Return interliner to normal position.
(e) See that platen returns to original typing line.

12. Practise superior characters. Read the above explanation, then type one copy of the following in double-line spacing.

$9y^2$ x $5y^2$; a^2b^2 x a^5b^4; a^2 x a^2b x $5ab^4$; $5a^2 - 3b^2$ x $3ab^2c^4$.

They said that 160 °C. equals 367 °F. and they were correct.

b.h.p. = 0.85 x $CR^{0.34}$ x $d^{1.75}$ x $S^{0.4}$ x number of cylinders.

Inferior (lowered) characters

Inferior characters are those which have to be typed below the normal typing line as in chemical formulae. To type these, follow the same steps as for superior characters, but turn platen *forward* half a space instead of backward.

13. Practise inferior characters. Read the above explanation, then type one copy of the following in double-line spacing.

O_2; H_2; $T_1°T_2°$ $(T_1 - T_2)$ T_1; $C_{12}H_{22}O_{11}$; W_a x R; $t_1 - T$; C_nH_m
Symbols: Water H_2O; Hydrogen H_2; Oxygen O_2; Sugar $C_{12}H_{22}O_{11}$.

14. Type a copy of the following, using the interliner for the double lines. Set margin at 20 and tab. stops for second and third columns at 35 and 50.

1,643	4,585	3,120
2,456	3,219	286
1,021	3,222	5,012
5,120	11,026	8,418

Abbreviations

Many abbreviations used in English are made up of separate letters, each of which stands for a single word. Some of these have a full stop between each letter, while others may be written without a full stop, although there is a growing tendency for the full stop to be omitted in all cases. A few of these abbreviations are listed below. In your work from time to time you will probably come across others, in which case you should look up their meaning in a dictionary, and then add them to the list we have given.

Common abbreviations

Cantab.	= of Cambridge.	
C.B.E.	= Commander of the British Empire.	
D.S.O.	= Distinguished Service Order.	
EFTA	= European Free Trade Association.	
G.L.C.	= Greater London Council.	
G.M.T.	= Greenwich Mean Time.	
L.R.C.P.	= Licentiate of the Royal College of Physicians.	
M.B.E.	= Member of the Order of the British Empire.	
M.P.	= Member of Parliament.	
M.P.S.	= Member of the Pharmaceutical Society.	
m.p.h.	= miles per hour.	

O.B.E. = Officer of the Order of the British Empire.
P.C. = Privy Councillor.
R.S.V.P. = Please reply (Répondez s'il vous plaît).
T.U.C. = Trades Union Congress.
U.D.C. = Urban District Council.
UNO or U.N.O. = United Nations Organization.
U.N.E.S.C.O. or UNESCO = United Nations Educational Scientific and Cultural Organization.
U.N.R.R.A. or UNRRA = United Nations Relief and Rehabilitation Administration.

Standard abbreviations

A list of the most common standard abbreviations with their uses is given below.

I. *Always Used*

ad lib	= ad libitum	= at pleasure
e.g.	= exempli gratia	= for example
Esq.	= Esquire	= courtesy title
etc.	= et cetera	= and others
et seq.	= et sequentes	= and those that follow
i.e.	= id est	= that is
Messrs.	= Messieurs	= courtesy title
Mr.	= Mister	= courtesy title
Mrs.		= courtesy title
N.B.	= nota bene	= note well

II. *Used with Figures only*
(and usually in commercial matter)

a.m.	= ante meridiem	= before noon
h.p., H.P.	= horse power	
No., Nos.	= number, numbers	
p.m.	= post meridiem	= after noon
%	= per centum (used only in invoices and similar forms)	
Vol.	= volume	
*in.	= inch or inches	
ft.	= foot or feet.	

*yd.	= yard or yards
*oz.	= ounce or ounces
*lb.	= pound or pounds (weight)
*qr.	= quarter or quarters (weight)
*cwt.	= hundredweight or hundredweights
*m	= metre, metres
*mm	= millimetre, millimetres
*cm	= centimetre, centimetres
*g	= gramme, grammes
*kg	= kilogramme, kilogrammes

* These do not require 's' in plural.

III. *Used in Cases Indicated*

*&	= ampersand = and
@	= at, at the price of
B.A.	= Bachelor of Arts. Degree after person's name
Bros.	= Brothers. In names of firms or companies only.
b/f	= brought forward. In accounts or statements.

* Used in names of firms and numbers (such as Nos. 25 & 26—Never in ordinary matter).

Production typing

Type the following on A5 (148 × 210 mm) paper in double spacing, inserting any necessary apostrophes and quotation marks, and dividing at line-ends as required. Abbreviations should be typed in full where necessary.

[handwritten passage]

We hv. recvd. a ltr. from a customer who complains abt an electric iron, which, he states, is unsatisfactory after only 2 whs use. He says: I am returning the iron to y., & in view of the 6 mnths guarantee y. gave me, I must ask y. to send this iron back to / manfrs w. / request th. they give it a thorough exam. & test. We are sending the iron to y. by. tomorrows post & hope y. will give this complaint yr. immediate attention.

Type the following on A5 (148 × 210 mm) paper in double spacing, making any necessary corrections as indicated.

[handwritten passage with corrections]

Every month, for over 3 years, I hv. purchased first yr. radio magazine & this is my complaint. This is the situation. Excellent as yr. mag. is, I do not care personally for combination of light & heavy reading matter, & I am confident th. all of readers feel as I do, few really splendid mags. are directed particularly to those of us who are interested in building our own radios. On the other hand, there are several good publications for those of us who want the popular point of view.

Type the following as it appears on A5 (148 × 210 mm) paper in double spacing. Make your own line-endings. Remove from machine and mark in ink any necessary corrections with the recognized signs. Then type the passage again, making the corrections indicated by you.

I often passed a house where two little boys of about eight and ten lived, they invariably came dashing out to pet my dog & they seemed to have such fun with him that I asked, havent you ever had a dog of your own. They shook there heads, Dad wont let us have one. So I was surprised, a few days later, to find the two children romping about on there lawn with a puppy. Well, I said, so Dad bought you a dog after all. The children grinned. No, hes Dads dog. We gave him to Dad for his birthday — but he lets us play with him.

Answers to review quizzes

No. 1 (page 26)
1. Ten, Twelve
2. 210 mm × 297 mm
3. 148 mm × 210 mm
4. Twelve, Ten
5. Six, Five
6. Prefix, Suffix
7. Capital I
8. Below
9. Interliner
10. ‡
11. 2nd
12. Let it stand (as it was)
13. Check, Before
14. Left, Capitals
15. Bottom
16. Below
17. Horizontal Line
18. Three, One

No. 2 (page 62)
1. Six
2. Seventy
3. Fifty
4. Spaced, Unspaced
5. Agenda
6. Minutes, Minute Book
7. Double, A4
8. Not, Top
9. Dropped Head
10. Small Roman
11. Red
12. A5, Double
13. Left Margins, Capitals, Underscored
14. Cues
15. Capital
16. Third, Past
17. Indent
18. Middle

No. 3 (page 96)
1. Five
2. Two, Left
3. Left
4. Two
5. Enc., Left, Signature, Label
6. £, p, Never
7. Centred, Above, Below
8. Addressee's, Page, Date, One
9. Separate
10. Last, Punctuation, One
11. Right
12. Second, Left
13. Third
14. Units, Units

No. 4 (page 138)
1. Above
2. Underscored
3. Underscored
4. Paper Release
5. Dead
6. Tailpiece
7. Specification
8. Equal
9. Longer
10. Opposite
11. Assets, Liabilities
12. Single, Double
13. Foot
14. Divided

No. 5 (page 172)
1. Top, Bottom
2. Deepest
3. Two, Three
4. Underneath
5. One
6. Beyond
7. Once, Twice
8. Five Hyphens
9. No, One
10. Raised
11. Headings, Descriptive
12. Following
13. Continuous

Answers to exercise 8 (Page 103)
(*Corrected errors are underscored*)

1. Messrs. Barrett & Patterson,
2. Newport, Monmouthshire. (County must be stated—there are other towns 'Newport'.)
3. Dear Sir,
4.   It has been kindly suggested to us by the Oldham Manufacturing
5. Co. of Oldham, Lancashire, that we invite your advice on the following
6. problem.
7.   We are re-modelling our two-storey factory in Cardiff and wish to
8. instal the most up-to-date automatic sprinkler equipment procur-
9. able. We should appreciate your answer to the following ques-
10. tions:—1. What would be the approximate cost of installing a satis-
11. factory sprinkler system on both floors? 2. How soon after you
12. receive our order could installation be completed? 3. Judg-
13. ing by your experience, what is the average percentage of saving in
14. insurance costs resulting from such installations?
15.   We are enclosing the floor plans of the factory. If you require
16. further information in order to answer the foregoing,
17. please let us know.
18.   Your early reply will be appreciated.
19.   Yours faithfully,
20.   J. M. STEEL & CO.

Questions should be displayed one underneath the other and indented.

        (5 spaces)
        J. Haywood
        Secretary.

Enc.

Unit 3

Skill building

Typing line:
60 spaces

Type each line or sentence (A, B, and C) *three* times, and, if time permits, complete your practice by typing each group once as it appears.

A. Review alphabet keys

1.   Through the haze four ships could be seen slinking very slowly from the quay towards the ocean, just as we expected.

B. Practise common prefixes

2. prefer, prepaid, prepare, present, prevail, prevent, predict
3. They prefer not to predict the outcome of their predicament.
4. Be prepared to prevail upon your President to act forthwith.
5. All present must try to prevent the predicted rise in price.

C. Practise common phrases

6. we are, we may, we did, we will, we hope, we have, we should
7. We should like to know if we may visit you on Saturday next.
8. We are not sure when he will have the suite you asked about.
9. We hope that we have sent you the correct shade of material.

Accuracy/Speed Practice

Three-minute timing

Not more than 3 errors

words

AS.4   Did you know that more than 80 per cent of all business 11
is carried on, at least in part, by mail? It is not surpris- 23
ing, therefore, that most firms deal with thousands of letters 35
every year. Add to these figures the many internal memoranda 48
written in each firm, and you can see why every worker needs 60
to know how to write letters. 66

A business letter is not a descriptive essay: it is a 76
polite statement of facts, easy to understand. In most cases 88
you do not know the person to whom you are writing; so you 100
should use simple words, short sentences and short paragraphs. 112
Do not say, "We are in receipt of your note of the 12th instant, 125
the contents of which have been noted." Say, "Thank you for 137
your note (or whatever was sent to you) of the 12th May." If 149
you have had the letter, one assumes that you have read it and 162
you know what the writer had to say. Do not use words which 174
are not needed. It is a waste of the dictator's time and that 186
of the typist. It also takes up the receiver's time. No one 198
in business can afford the time to read superfluous words. 210

(S.I. 1.27)

UNIT 3

11

Typist – The following list is a bit jumbled. Please prepare 3 lists for me. On the first sheet type all items marked 'A' (in alph. order) Use heading – <u>SECRETARIES – SHORTHAND-TYPISTS – TYPISTS</u>
All items marked 'B' on another sheet of paper in alpha. order. Heading : CLERKS. All items marked 'C' on a third sheet of paper in alpha. order – heading : OTHERS.

JOB	DESCRIPTION
Ⓒ JUNIOR CASHIERS	Record cash receipts & disbursements. Prepare daily cash reports. In charge of <u>Petty Cash</u> /lc.
Ⓑ POSTAL CLERKS	Open mail, date stamp, sort & distribute. Prepare outgoing mail.
Ⓑ SHIPPING CLERKS	Prepare shipping docs; compute transportation costs, & trace lost shipments.
(or delayed)	
Ⓐ SHORTHAND-TYPISTS	Take dictation in s'hand & transcribe notes to produce finished correspondence. May do some filing. *(Use telephone)*
Ⓒ SWITCHBOARD OPERATORS	Operate co. switchboard & equipment. Keep /© records of h calls. Take messages.
telephone h	
Ⓐ TYPISTS	Type forms, reports, & or business papers Prepare stencils, lists, etc.
Ⓐ SECRETARIES	As for s'hand-typists, plus: Receiving & entertaining visitors. Making travel arrangements. Keeping employers diary.
(Attending meetings + recording minutes) ²/h	
PAY ROLL CLERKS Ⓑ	Compute pay roll from time & piecework records. Issue pay cheques & envelopes.
PUNCHED CARD OPERATORS Ⓒ	Prepare & verify punched cards from business papers & or data.
Ⓒ RECEPTIONISTS	Greet & direct callers. Use tel. Keep reception area neat & tidy. Keep records
Ⓑ FILING CLERKS	Check papers for release for filing.
DUPLICATING M/C OPERATORS Ⓒ	Operate stencil & spirit duplicators. Use photo-copying equipment.
Ⓑ INVOICE CLERKS	Price Orders. Prepare invoices. Check computations.
Ⓑ PURCHASING CLERKS	Locate sources of supply. Issue letters of enquiry. Maintain records & verify estimates.
	(File & find papers. Help in transfer & storage)

Technique development

Numbers

Cardinal numbers are Arabic numbers—1, 2, 3, etc.

NOTE: The figure 1 is expressed either by the lower-case letter L or by the figure 1 if this is provided on the typewriter, but these must not be mixed, i.e., the same key must be used for figure 1 throughout an exercise. *Never* use capital I for the cardinal number 1. Ordinal numbers denote order or sequence, e.g., 1st, 2nd, etc.

NOTE: These are not abbreviations and must not, therefore, be followed by a full stop. Roman numerals are formed from seven symbols known as Units and Fives, viz.,

Units: I (1)   X (10)   C (100)   M (1,000)
Fives: V (5)   L (50)   D (500)

10. Practise formation of Roman numerals. Read the above explanation and study rules in Reference Manual, page M6; then type the following in double spacing: (a) In words and Roman numerals; (b) in words and Arabic numbers.

(a)   1865   1964   386   1999   444

(b)   MCDXXXIV   CIX   LVII   DXCIV   XLIX

Uses of Roman numerals

1. For Monarchs, Form and Class numbers. George VI, Form IV, Class II.

2. For chapters, tables or paragraphs instead of Arabic figures. Chapter III, Table II.

3. Sometimes to express the year. 1961—MCMLXI

4. In enumerations to distinguish between sets of figures. Article I, Clause 1, Paragraph (i).

5. Small roman numerals used for preface, sub-sections, Biblical references. 1 John iii. 23. See page xi of preface.

11. Practise using Roman numerals. Study the above rules and then type the following, using Roman numerals for Arabic where rule applies.

Forms 3 and 4 have been told to read Chapters 6, 9, and 12, and to study Tables 19 and 20 (Chapters 16 and 17).

The year of its erection, 1125, was cut into the stonework.

And a certain man drew a bow at a venture. 1 Kings 22 34.

Inset Matter

If matter is to be inset from the left margin, the longest line of the inset portion should end the same number of spaces from the right margin, so that the space from the left margin to the start of the inset portion equals the space from the end of the longest line to the right margin.

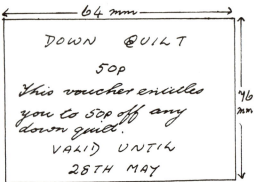

DOWN QUILT

50p

This voucher entitles you to 50p off any down quilt.

VALID UNTIL 28TH MAY

64 mm — 76 mm

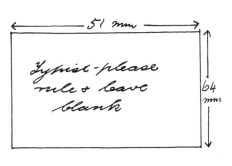

Typist - please rule & leave blank

51 mm — 64 mm

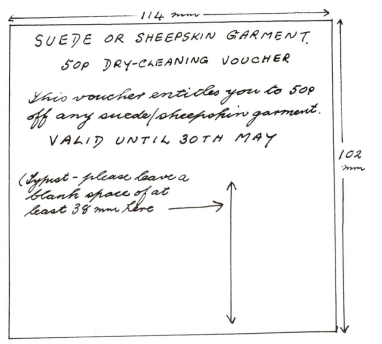

15p DRY-CLEANING VOUCHER

This voucher entitles you to 15p off any garment brought for cleaning & retexturing which would normally cost 30p or over.

VALID UNTIL 30TH MAY

57 mm

108 mm

Page 3

114 mm

SUEDE OR SHEEPSKIN GARMENT.

50p DRY-CLEANING VOUCHER

This voucher entitles you to 50p off any suede/sheepskin garment.

VALID UNTIL 30TH MAY

(Typist - please leave a blank space of at least 38 mm here ——→

102 mm

Typist. Please also type a memo. to the M. D. and say: I attach a draft of the pamphlet we will be sending to the printers next Tuesday. Please let me know if you wish me to make any alterations. R. S. Parkinson.

Enumerations

An enumeration is a set of paragraphs or lines, which are usually displayed as follows:

1. The numbers usually project to the left of the first line of the paragraph, and the second and subsequent lines are blocked underneath the first line (as in this paragraph). Leave two spaces after full stop following numeral.

2. In some cases the numbers are put in brackets (2), in which case one space is left after bracket.

3. Letters may be used in place of numbers.

4. Where there are subdivisions of enumerated items, these can be distinguished in order of importance as follows:

Capital roman numerals for main division. I
Upper case letters for first subdivision. A
Arabic numbers, small letters or small roman numerals.

5. When roman numerals are used in enumerations the unit figures must be typed underneath the unit of the previous roman numeral, as follows:

I.
II.
III.
IV.

12. Practise typing inset enumerations. Type the following on A4 paper (210 × 297 mm) in double spacing, using a 65-space typing line. Leave 6 clear line-spaces at top of paper, and follow layout. Keep your typed copy for future reference in Folder No. 2.

HIRE PURCHASE

Hire Purchase is a system of buying goods over a period of time. You hire the goods and payment is made by instalments over a fixed period. The goods are not your property until the last instalment has been paid. Let us look at the advantages and disadvantages of this system.

    I.   ADVANTAGES

        (a) You can afford to buy more expensive goods.

        (b) You can have the goods straight away.

        (c) Payments by instalments are simple and may be made:

            i. weekly;

          ii. monthly; or

        iii. at other agreed intervals.

   II.   DISADVANTAGES

        (a) You pay more than you would if you paid cash.

        (b) You may acquire the goods when money is plentiful — husband and wife both working. But what will happen if either or both are not working?

        (c) Goods may be out of date before the final payment is made.

NOTE:
The roman numeral I is here inset one space to right of paragraph indent to allow for the roman numeral II.

Typist - This is a rough lay-out of the pamphlet which we must send to the printers on Tuesday. It shd. fit on to a folded sheet of A4 paper. I have numbered the pages so that you can see what I would like on ea. page. Right & left margins on ea. page must not be less than 13 mm. Draw the rectangles to size, but do not type in measurements.

Page 1

D R Y - C L E A N I N G ← (spaced caps)

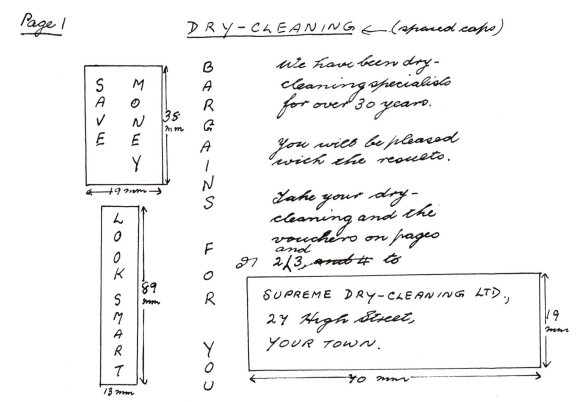

SAVE MONEY 38 mm, 19 mm

LOOK SMART 89 mm, 13 mm

B A R G A I N S F O R Y O U

We have been dry-cleaning specialists for over 30 years.

You will be pleased with the results.

Take your dry-cleaning and the vouchers on pages 2/3, and # to

SUPREME DRY-CLEANING LTD., 27 High Street, YOUR TOWN. 19 mm, 70 mm

Page 4

F O R

S ER V I C E
S A T I S FA C T I O N
V A L U E
SUPREME DRY-CLEANING LTD

Words are sometimes deliberately omitted at the beginning, or end, or in the middle of a sentence. Such omission is indicated by the use of three spaced full stops, as follows: . . . If the omission occurs at the beginning of the sentence, the full stop at the end of the previous sentence is typed as usual, followed by one space after full stop and 3 spaced dots (one space only between each) (as here) . . . . If the omission occurs just before the end of the sentence, the three spaced dots are followed by a fourth dot to show the end of the sentence, as follows: . . . .

13. Practise ellipsis. Read the above explanation, and then type the following on A4 paper in double spacing, centring the main headings. Leave 6 clear spaces at top. Keep your typed copy for future reference in Folder No. 2.

CHAPTER XII

MONEY

The substance chosen for money must have certain characteristics, some of which are given below.

   I. ESSENTIAL PROPERTIES OF SUBSTANCES USED FOR MONEY

       (1) Acceptability

          It must be generally acceptable.

       (2) Portability

          (a) It must be easy to carry.

          (b) The cost of transport must
             not be too great.

       (3) Durability

          (a) It must be hard-wearing.

          (b) It must not deteriorate easily.

       (4) Divisibility

          It must be divisible into smaller
          units . . . in Great Britain pounds
          are divided into pennies.

  II. FUNCTIONS OF MONEY

       (1) Measure of Value

          (a) Money establishes a definite
             standard of value.

          (b) It thus enables the relative
             value of other commodities
             to be compared. . . .

       (2) Medium of Exchange

          It is universally accepted, and
          can thus be exchanged for . . . .

Typist : For easy reference, please arrange the following quotations in tabulated form, using the headings GOODS, SUPPLIER, PRICE, TERMS, DELY. DATE.

Quotation No. 1 from Greenfield + Co. Ltd., 199 Southall Rd., Dundee :

6 gro. Ronson Cadet Lighters . £12.05 per doz.

4 " Rolstar Vanity Flair Lighters £9.40 per doz.

6 " Poppell Gas Lighters £12.30 per doz.

2 " Rolstar Table Lighters £16.60 per doz.

Dely. All ex stock except Poppell Gas Lighters which will be seven days from receipt of order. Terms 5% cash 14 days.

Quotation No. 2 from Carr Bros., 65 W. Regent Str., Glasgow.

4 gro. Rolstar Vanity Flair Lighters @ £9.50 per doz.

2 "   " Table Lighters   £16.75   "

6 " Ronson Cadet Lighters   £12.10.   "

6 " Poppell Gas Lighters   £12.54.   "

Dely. Ex stock . Terms : 7½% in 7 Days.

Quotation No. 3 from MacFarlane + MacClean Ltd., 12 Wheatfield Rd., Edinburgh.

* 6 gro Poppell Gas Lighters @ £18.45 per doz.

* 2 " Rolstar Table Lighters £24.75 "

∓ 4 " " Vanity Flair " £13.65 "

* 6 " Ronson Cadet Lighters £18.62 "

Dely. * Ex Stock ∓ 10 days from receipt of order.

Terms : 33⅓% Trade Discount. Net monthly a/c.

TYPIST : under the heading "SUPPLIER" it is not necessary to type the address of the supplier.

Type the following on A4 (210 × 297 mm) paper in single spacing, with double between numbered and lettered items.

Economic Report (Typist – all words double underscored in closed caps and underscored, please)

Britain earned a record in motor export – 11 per cent higher than last yr. The follwg is a summary of /yr just ended:

I. General

u.c.   stet   1. Early in the new year, prices rose sharply and many articles disappeared from the shops. The reasons given were :—

    (a) Widespread strikes.

    (b) Lack of price controls.

market   2. There was a sharp increase in free quotations for foreign currency.

II. Finance

    1. The %age ratio of gold & convertible

foreign   exchange again improved.

    2. Foreign exchange reserves rose by eight

    # percent.

III. Commerce & Industry

    1. Exports

l.c.   (a) American Market: The demand for all types of motor vehicles increased considerably w. emphasis on:

l.c.   i. Racing models;

l.c.   ii. Saloon cars in the £5,000 range.

(b) European Market: there was little change from / previous month.

2. Imports (a) There was an overall fall in imports

(b) imports of cotton rose as follows: i. Egyptian by 4 per cent. ii. American by 5 per cent.

Typist: Please display

Proposed Dividend (net) (since pd.) 3216 141,496
284,473

Deduct: Amount set aside for
Income Tax 1965/66 31,000

NETT TANGIBLE ASSETS @ 31st ~~May~~ June £253,473

* In the aggregate, the depreciation written off fixtures, fittings & motor vehicles was not materially different from the corresponding ~~expected~~ capital allowances for profits tax purposes. No depreciation has been charged on freehold\ property.

(Excluding investment allowances)

Set out the following in tabulated form, using four headings — Meat, Water to be added, Cooking time, and Remarks.

n.c.

Pot Roast		Water	Remarks
Beef	10-12 mins per lb	½ pint for first 15 mins Cooking time + ¼ pint for ea. subsequent 15 minutes.	Brown all over in hot fat in open cooker before pressure Cooking.
Mutton	10 mins per lb		
Veal	10-12 mins per lb		
Pork	10-15 mins per lb		
Stews		½ pint or more as desired. Be careful not to fill cooker more than ⅔ full.	Cut meat into cubes & brown lightly in hot fat in open cooker
Beef	15 mins		
Irish	20 "		
Chops		½ pint	Brown lightly under grill after Cooking.
Mutton	5-6 mins		
Veal, Pork, Lamb. according to thickness			

TIMETABLE FOR MEAT AT 15 LB PRESSURE *

* Frozen meat should be thawed out before Cooking.

Unit 4

Skill building

Type each exercise (A, B, and C) *once* for practice, *once* for speed, and finally *once* for accuracy.

A. Review alphabet keys

1.   We think it expedient to modernize our works by acquir-
ing an adjacent factory which will at least give more space.

B. Review shift lock

2. UP-TO-DATE, FORTY-ONE, SELF-CONFIDENT, NEVER-TO-BE-FORGOTTEN

3. The COMMANDER-IN-CHIEF was a SELF-CONFIDENT and RELIANT man.

4. CASH IN BANK £1,571; CASH IN HAND £105; GOODS IN STOCK £324.

C. Practise concentration

5. 'Feet' in poetry: (a) The TROCHEE (trochaic rhythm); (b) The
SPONDEE (spondaic rhythm); (c) The TRIBRACH; (d) The IAMBUS;
(e) The ANAPAEST (trisyllabic); (f) The AMPHIBRACH.

Accuracy/Speed Practice

Note: From now on, you must make your own line-endings

Four-minute timing   *Not more than 3 errors*

words

AS.5   As winter draws near, many birds are preparing to leave us and set   13
off on their long flight south in search of sunshine, while some stay   27
behind.   To them a winter of snow and frost will mean a bitter struggle   41
for survival.   Last year hunger and cold drove many to seek shelter and   55
food close to homes, and people who had taken no interest in them before   70
helped them.   Perhaps the most endearing all-the-year round resident is   84
the robin, whose red breast becomes bright in winter-time and who can   98
become very tame.   Sparrows remain with us, so do the starlings.   You can   112
still hear the blackbird singing in the frosty sunshine.   The finches —   126
some so brightly coloured — stay, but they do not often become as tame as   141
the other birds.   The delightful blue tits also are always to be seen.   155
Some of the birds who stay behind in the winter are useful, eating pests   169
which damage the crops, but others do harm.   Harmful or not, they all   183
find surviving the bitter cold a problem.   The ground is hard, and they   198
cannot dig out worms and other food.   There is no fruit, and there may   212
be few berries.   215

    Many of you may want to help them during this bad time.   Food scraps,   228
such as fat, bacon rind, and bits of bread, are always welcome.   Strings   242
of nuts may be hung from the branch of a tree.   Half a coconut provides a   257
wealth of food for the blue tits.   But birds must also drink, so when the   272
ground is frozen, put out water for them.   (S.I. 1.25)   280

Type a copy of the following on A4 paper, making all necessary alterations.

In caps → <u>Minster Trust <s>Ltd</s> Limited</u>

II   <u>Net Tangible Assets</u> ← in caps.

tangible

The following is a statement of net /assets based on the last audited balance sheet at 31st May, after making such adjustments as are deemed appropriate

—

	Cost or valuation £	Aggregate depreciation* £	Net £
FIXED ASSETS			
Fixtures & fittings at cost	145,000	—	145,000
Leasehold property " "	1,500	1,125	375
Freehold " " valuation	10,307	4,825	5,482
Motor vehicles at cost	10,740	5,004	5,736
	£167,547	£10,954	£156,593

CURRENT ASSETS

Trade and other debtors, less provision for doubtful debts, bills receivable & prepayments	166,989
Stock at lower than cost or net realisable value	77,232
Balance at bank & cash in Hand	25,155
	269,376
	425,969

DEDUCT
LIABILITIES

Unsecured Loan (since repaid)	(15,320)
Directors Current a/c	881
Trade Creditors + Accrued Charges	85,519
Current Taxation	36,560

Continued/

Technique development

6. Type a copy of the following in double spacing, paying particular attention to the difference in spacing for hyphens and dashes.

His son was only thirty-one years of age when he was re-elected - by virtue of his far-sighted views - as secretary of the company. The company is moving its factory - now at 9 High Street - to new premises at 30 Broad Street where up-to-date machinery has been installed. The firm is engaged chiefly in the sale of ready-to-wear suits of first-class quality and up-to-the minute style.

Combination characters

When you have to type a symbol which is not included on your typewriter keyboard, you should construct it by combining two characters, i.e., type one character, back-space, and type the other. On some machines it may be necessary to raise or lower the platen before typing the second character, in which case you should use the *interliner* (ratchet release), so that, when you have returned the interliner to its normal position, the platen goes back to the original line of writing. The most common of these combination characters, as they are called, are given below, and an additional list is given in the Reference Manual, page M3.

7. Practise combination characters. Read the above explanation and then type a copy of the following on A5 paper (210 × 148 mm) in double spacing. Keep your typed copy for future reference in Folder No. 2.

COMMON COMBINATION CHARACTERS AND SPECIAL SIGNS

Asterisk	Small x and hyphen	x
Dagger	Capital I and hyphen	I
Degree	Lower case 'o' raised half a space	o
Division	Colon and hyphen	÷
Dollar	Capital S and Solidus	$
Double Dagger	Capital I and another capital I slightly below the other.	I
Equation Sign	Two hyphens — one hyphen slightly above the other	=
Exclamation	Apostrophe and full stop	!
Minutes	Apostrophe	'
Plus	Hyphen and lowered apostrophe	+
Seconds	Quotation marks	"

8. Practise combination characters and special signs. Type a copy of the following in double spacing.

"Hello!", he said. "I am surprised to meet you here again."
Position:- Latitude 21° 12' 15" E. - Longitude 15° 5' 20" N.
240 - 120 ÷ 2 x 3 - 100 + 20 = 300 + 100 - 200 x 2 ÷ 5 + 20.

You are a copy typist employed by Fairfield & Co. Ltd., and you have received the following notes from the Sales Director, Mr. E. K. Reed.

Three of our customers whose names are given below have written complaining about delay in delivering their order. Please write a letter to each as follows:

Dear Sirs, Your Order No. —

We ack. receipt of your letter dated —, & regret

N.P. the delay in despatching your order. [One of our finishing machines has been out of order for a wk & this has the cause of / delay. We hope to have the machine working by Tues. & will then make a point of rushing your order through.

N.P. & [We ~~sincerely~~ apologise for not letting you know about the delay & for any inconvenience we may have caused you. Yrs faithfully.

J.F. MILLER & Sons, LINDA GARDENS, BILLERICAY, ESSEX
Letter dated 14th Feb. Order No. 7/38/64/PUR.

L.A. KINGWOOD & Co. Ltd, KILVEDON, ESSEX.
Letter dated 13th Feb. Order No. HAL/CP/17/64
Typist In this case, omit last sentence of second para. & insert: We are pleased to say that yr. goods will be despatched today

W.M. SIDDONS Ltd., SEAL, SEVENOAKS, KENT.
Letter dated 15 Feb. Order No. Dept.C/PUR/613
Also please type the following memo to the Production Manager (Mr K. Moore)

J.F. Miller & Sons, L.A. Kingwood, W.M. Siddons.
The above-named firms have complained about the

N.P. delay in despatching their orders. [Please do your utmost to get the finishing machine in operation

N.P. immediately. [Kindly report to me tomorrow on this matter.

9. Practise using words and figures. Study rules in Reference Manual, page M7, then type the following in single-line spacing, noting where words or figures are used.

```
There were four or five people in the room at eight o'clock.
There are over nine million inhabitants, but very few voted.
The lunch-time period will be one hour — from 12.30 to 1.30.
We will allow a discount of 5 per cent for cash on delivery.
We hope you can forward the goods within the next five days.
His son arrived on 1st June — on his seventy-fifth birthday.
```

10. Type the following on A5 (210 × 148 mm) paper in single-line spacing, altering words to figures or vice versa, as required.

```
200 children are to spend 1 week's holiday abroad.
It took us almost two hours to walk about 5 or 6 miles.
We shall do our utmost to deliver your order in three weeks.
A trade discount of 25% is allowed on all our goods.
Many of the boys are between 16 and 18 years old.
The box offices are always opened promptly at 11.30 o'clock.
```

Internal telephone index

It is usual to keep a list of names and addresses and telephone numbers which are frequently required. For this purpose use is made of the strip-indexing method, whereby each name and address and telephone number is typed on a separate strip. The strips are usually supplied in sheets, and the details are typed on the strips, which are afterwards separated from the sheet, and then they are inserted alphabetically in devices or frames specially made to take them. These strips can be moved up or down to allow of additional strips being inserted in their correct order, or to remove strips containing obsolete names. The surname is usually typed first, and in upper case letters, followed by the initial(s) and then the address, all on one line if possible. If two lines are needed, these must be in single-line spacing, as the strip is usually not more than 6 mm in depth. In order to carry the eye from the end of the address to the telephone number, continuous dots may be inserted as in the first line of example (leaving one clear space before the first dot and one clear space after the last dot).

NOTE: A comma is typed after surname, and after initials, in an index or alphabetical list.

Example of method of typing strip

```
BROWN, A. J., 46 Thomas Street, Leeds.  LS2 9JT ............ 0532 21375
FISHER, L., & Co. Ltd., 20 Clitton Road, Northampton.  NN1 5BQ 0604 6868
```

11. Practise typing internal telephone index. Read the above explanation; then type the following names and addresses in alphabetical order according to the surname (if a personal name) or the first word of the name (if an impersonal name). Leave double spacing between each name. Left margin: Pica 5 spaces, elite 5 spaces. Right margin to be blocked 5 spaces from right-hand edge of paper.

```
White & Bradbury Ltd., Empire Way, Northampton.  NN1 5BQ  0604 8686
Mardon's Ltd., Green Lane, Wolverhampton.  WV2 4DB  90 20035
Adelphi Ltd., 96 Park Lane, Croydon, Surrey.  CR9 1TP  01-688 3814
Ronaldson, H., Ltd., Broad Street, Liverpool.  L1 6BJ  051-486 1217
Bradley & Bliss Ltd., Kings Avenue, Leeds.  LS1 3AE  0532 21735
MacAndrew Ltd., 31 High Street, Kirby, Liverpool.  LS3 8XF 051-727 2409
G. B. Kent & Sons, 8 Burnett Street, Blackpool.  FYT 3DW  0253 32244
```

HAMILTON : Pop. 42,679 ; M.D. Fri. E.C. Wed ; Hotel - Commercial

KIRKCALDY : E.C. Wed ; Hotels - Victoria, Station ; Pop. 52697

GREENOCK : Pop. 74,607 ; Hotel - Tontine ; E.C. Wed ; M.D. Tuesday

* Shops close Wednesday afternoon or Sat. afternoon

E "   " Tuesday "   " Wed. "

or Sat. afternoon.

Type ~~one~~ an original and one copy of the following advertisement which has to be sent to the printer. Use paper 8" × 6½" / 203 × 165 mm

H
a/   THE GREATEST time & work saver ever offered to the housewife! It is tough, reliable & adaptable sweeper with an amazing selection of inexpensive attachments. These attachments can be changed in a few seconds. This famous sweeper is unequalled for sheer versatility and value for money. An attractive addition to every home — an ideal Christmas present

┌─────────────────────────────┐ 3¼ × 83 mm
│ THE MAGIC SWEEPER   │
│   │
│ Typist: apart from the above │ 1¾"
│ heading, leave this space   │ 44 mm
│ blank for an illustration. │
│ Do not draw the lines.   │
└─────────────────────────────┘

For further particulars complete the coupon opposite

┌────────────────────────────────────
│ TO: Tidy Homes Ltd., 95 Carpet Rd.,
│   SHEPPERTON, Middlesex.
│
│   Please send me free catalogue and price list
│
│   NAME : ———————————————
│
│   ADDRESS : ———————————————
│
│   ———————————————
│
│   ———————————————
└────────────────────────────────────

On the carbon copy, fill in your own name and address.

Production typing

Job 6
Production Target—*10 minutes*

Starting 7 spaces from the top of a sheet of A5 paper (148 × 210 mm), display the following; i.e., centre each line horizontally. List the items in alphabetical order. Type in double spacing with two clear spaces after every third item.

Office ~~Bracts~~ Practice ← caps & underscored

Course Content ← l.c. with initial caps & underscored

14 — Working in a Modern Office
6 — u.c. Getting along w. people
1 — u.c. Automation in the office
3 — Dictating (Machines) & Transcribing
— Internal Communications
4 — (Methods) of Duplicating
8 — u.c Post Office Services
5 — Filing
11 — l.c. / u.c. Sales Office procedure
9 — Purchasing Office "
2 — Cash Handling
13 — Wages Office "
12 — Stock & Stock Control
7 — (Office) Personnel
10 — Reception Work.

Job 7
Production Target—*7 minutes*

Type the following names in alphabetical order, to be used as an internal telephone index, using single-line spacing.

E. M. Hinks Ltd., Chichester Road, Belfast. N.I. BT1 4LA
0232 22957

Maverick & Sons, Gateway, Leicester, LE2 1DL 0533 13147

L.C. CLARE LTD., 21 George Str., Edinburgh. EH 2 2LZ
031-225 1847

Brown & Shell Ltd., Berkley St. London. W7X 6AA . 01-262 5847

Walgarth & Co. Ltd., 39 Hazel Rd., Reading, Berks. RG1 3EZ

Broadway & Co. Ltd., Brook Str., Bradford,
0734 11645
Yorks. BD1 1HZ
0274 51781

J.A. Clarke Ltd.,
1 High Street, Stratford, London. ~~E743~~ E15 4BH
01-794 2114.

From the following information extract towns w. a population over 40,000, and arrange the information about ea. town in tabulated form. Use headings such as: TOWN, HOTELS, etc. List the towns in order of density of population, (*i.e. start with the most densely populated + end with the least populated*).

STIRLING: Population 27,599; Hotels – Golden Lion, Station; Early Closing – Wednesday; Market Day – Thurs.

ABERDEEN: Pop. 185,678; E.C. Wed.,* M.D. Friday; Hotels – Caledonian, Ardoe House.

GLASGOW: Hotels – Central, North British; E.C. Tues; Pop. 1,049,167.

EDINBURGH: E.C. Tuesday‡; Pop. 475,344; Hotels – Caledonian, North British

PERTH, Pop. 40,940; E.C. Wed.; M.D. Mon; Hotels – Royal George, Salutation.

INVERNESS: M.D. Mon. E.C. Wed.; Pop. 29,603; Hotels – Royal, Drumcossie.

DUNDEE: Hotels – Queen's, Royal; E.C. Wed., M.D. Thurs., Pop. 183,560.

AYR: Pop. 44961; E.C. Wed.; Hotels – Savoy Park, Station M.D. Tues.

COATBRIDGE: Pop, 96,670; E.C. Tues.; M.D. Mon.

DUNFERMLINE: Hotel – City; Pop. 48,865; M.D. Tues; E.C. Wed.

KILMARNOCK; Pop 48,027; Hotel – Market; E.C. Wed., M.D. Friday.

MOTHERWELL: (with Wishaw) Hotel – Garrion; Pop. 73,483; E.C. Wed.

CLYDEBANK: Pop. 50,369; Hotel – Boulevard; E.C. Wed.

Type the following on A4 paper in double-line spacing, making any necessary corrections.

ANNUAL REPORT   Caps & underscored

trs / tks   There are 3 noteworthy features of our business for / financial yr. ended on Mar 31st last:

    I. Golden Jubilee: On seventh April our Co. wl

companys celebrate its 50th birthday & to honour / occasion we sh do 2 things / (a) Hold a dinner dance to which all // (Please inset &

n.c. employees & friends wl be invited. (b) Inaugurate a display (a) & (b)

a pension scheme for all employees of more than 5 years service.

    II. Mortgage Loans: The mortgage loans completed during the yr. under review showed a substantial

⊙ u.c. increase / in fact the no. was up by over 100 on / previous yr.

, of course,   III. Interest Loans: It was necessary to adjust our rate of interest on loans to meet the higher rate at which our new issue of debentures was made.

run on   The distribution of our loans is well spread

n.c. over england, scotland & Wales, & / average

slightly amt of loan outstanding is over £3000. During N.P.

H the yr, long term rates moved upwards.

of run on   Our lending has steadily declined from OUR

rate LENDING

6 percent to 5% in accordance w. / general

H fall in long term rates over the past 5 yrs.

_____

Typist - please do not type Roman numerals — ignore them — and type para headings as shoulder headings.

Unit 28

Examination Preview

Production typing

Job 93
Production Target—*20 minutes*

The following letter and credit note are from Morton & Co. Ltd., 197 Stafford Street, Wolverhampton WV2 4DB to Matthew & Gordon Ltd., 14 Broadway Street, Evesham, Worcs. Their Ref. No. NOB/CB. Our Ref. No. CAT/

(a) Type a letter on A5 paper and insert suitable date. Mr. W. Bainbright will sign it. He is the Sales Manager.

letter ↑ Thank you for your memo of 27 April. [etc We have looked at our records + find th. the credit note you mention was posted to y on April 13; however, we have pleasure in enclosing a copy.

(b) Type the following credit note on A5 paper and attach it to the above letter. Mark it 'COPY'.

Credit Note No. 64185 dated 13th April. Return of one packing case £1.50

Job 94
Production Target—*10 minutes*

Type the following memo. from Mr. J. Limmer (A1 Catering Co. Ltd.) to Messrs. R. Bailey, P. Austin, F. Paget. Our Ref. JL/

Please let me ~~know~~ have by Dec. 31 a list of equipment first↑ required during the ↑ half of next year. [You will N.P. remember th. at our last meeting I suggested th. new↑ we limit purchases of ↑ equipment to £200 p.a. for ea. restaurant. Please bear this in mind when compiling yr. list.

Job 95
Production Target—*12 minutes*

Your employer, Mr. R. Flynn, is out all day tomorrow. List the following itinerary in the correct order and type on a postcard.

3.30 p.m. Brown, Jones & Co., Handsworth New Rd., re information on new cos. 12.30 p.m. Lunch reserved for 5 at Grosvenor Hotel, Navigation St., 9.30 a.m. meet Herr M. Hilgeland at Central Station. 9.45 Visit Exhibition at Engineering Centre. 2 p.m. Calthorpe & Gladstone, 319 Handsworth New Rd., re half-yearly figures.

UNIT 28

189

Unit 5

Skill building

Type each line or sentence (A and B) *three* times, and, if time permits, complete your practice by typing each group once as it appears.

A. Review alphabet keys

1.   Much to the delight of the viewers a brilliant question completely baffled the expert quiz jury who quickly retired.

B. Improve fluency

2. Did you buy all the tea and pay the boy the sum you now owe?

3. The man saw the lad was not yet fit for the job you got him.

4. Few can now say why she and her son did not get off the bus.

Accuracy/Speed Practice

Five-minute timing   *Not more than 3 errors*

words

AS.6   When you choose books to read, you should make a point of selecting   13
them as you would your friends. If you constantly read poorly written   27
books, this will have just the same effect on your character and manners   42
as if you mix always with the wrong kind of people. There is no need to   56
be afraid of books which are called great. Much of the best literature   70
is found to be of interest to young and old alike. Some of the famous   84
classics are tales which used to be told to children long ago, such as   98
stories about animals, and tales of goblins and elves and fairies which   112
were said to live in the woods and mountains. Some well-known books,   126
such as, for instance, 'Robinson Crusoe', were not really written for   140
children, but they still remain great favourites with them.   152

      Whatever may be one's taste, there are good books to be found which   165
can satisfy it. One most fascinating book is the 'Arabian Nights', that   180
carries the reader on a magic carpet to the mystic Orient. Some of the   194
great books take us into the world of mythology, to ancient Greece, where   208
Zeus, king of the gods, and Apollo, god of light and music, once dwelt.   223
Reading books of the life story of some great man or woman, or of a hero   237
who achieves something worth while in the face of extreme difficulty, of   251
the deeds of such people and of their human relationship, seems to bring   266
one on intimate terms with the great.   273

      In choosing the right books, it is a help, of course, to seek the   286
aid of some older person who knows what is good, although, in many cases,   301
we can judge for ourselves whether a book is bad or good. To decide if a   316
book is good or bad, you must have some standard to guide you, and the   330
best way to gain such a standard is first to read those books which have   344
proved themselves to be good.   (S.I. 1.27)   350

H and a fine/nibbed pen (preferably not a ballpoint pen). Insert 'B'.

6
to. If any portion of a letter or MS. is reqd. to be inset, see th. the no. of spaces on rt-hand side is equal to th. on the left. The no. indented depends on the longest line of the inset portion.

9
H. When a letter or MS. requires a continuation sheet, y. shd. divide the matter @ a suitable point, w'out, however, leaving too great a space at / foot of the 1st page. At least 2 lines of a para.

(h

97 shd. appear on each at the bottom of /, 1st p. & at the top of a continuation sheet.) The usual

l.c. heading for a Continuation Sheet of a letter is: name of addressee, page no., date, but where a letter is addressed to the manager, or other officials of a firm, the name of the firm must appear in addition to the manager.

8
to. In hyphenated words no space shd. be left before or after the hyphen. Do not separate numerical adjectives, whether in words or figures, from the words to wh. they refer, i.e., six metres,

27 H 6th May, both must be typed on the same line.

27 to. (Words printed in italics shd. be underlined.) Typist: Put this at end of no. 5.

10
H. Enclosures must be indicated in letters & memos.

(A) Headings may be underscored with a single line, never w. a double or treble line.

(B) You shd. also take a sheet of carbon paper w. you, altho' this may be provided.

* It is better to use an eraser rather than eradicators wh. are not always satisfactory.

Technique development

Footnotes

Footnotes are used:

(a) To identify a reference or person quoted in the body of a report.

(b) To give the source of a quotation cited in a report.

(c) For explanations that may help or interest a reader.

Each footnote is:

(d) Preceded by the reference mark which corresponds to the reference in the text.

(e) Typed in single-line spacing.

The reference mark in the text must be a superior character. In the footnote, it is typed either on the same line or as a superior character. In the text NO space is left between the reference mark and the previous character. In the footnote ONE SPACE is left between the reference mark and the first word. The position for the typing of footnotes is explained below.

5. Type the following on A4 paper (210 × 297 mm) in double spacing, and keep your typed copy for future reference in Folder No. 2.

```
                FOOTNOTES IN TYPESCRIPT

     In ordinary typewritten work, the footnote is ALWAYS placed at the
bottom of the page on which the corresponding reference appears and typed
in single spacing.  Care must be taken to leave enough space at the bot-
tom for the footnote, and, if continuation pages are used, a clear space
of 25 mm after the footnote.  The footnote is separated from main text
by a horizontal line across the page from edge to edge of the paper.
This horizontal line is typed by underscore one single-line space after
the last line of text, and footnote typed on second single space below.  The
last line of the footnote(s) must end 25 mm from the bottom of the page,
so that if the text does not occupy the full page, there will be a blank
portion between the last line of the text and the horizontal line.  If more
than one footnote, turn up two single spaces between each.
```

6. Practise typing footnotes in typescript. Type the following on A5 (210 × 148 mm) paper in double spacing, with single spacing for footnotes. Keep your typed copy for future reference in Folder No. 2.

```
     Whether you work in a large or small office, you are

expected to turn out a day's work each working day.*  The

unit cost of typewritten work having risen sharply over the

last few years, all typists must realize the necessity of

increasing their production rate if they are to keep their

jobs.†
```

```
   * In many firms, standards of measurement of typed work have
     been set up, and salaries are paid accordingly.

   † To do this, analyse the whole typing job, and decide on
     the most time-saving way of doing it.
```

Job 92   Production Target—*25 minutes*

Type a copy of the following notes for duplicating, making all necessary corrections.

Examination Hints — (spaced caps., please)

2. Do not be satisfied w. slipshod work. Never overtype. See th. y. hv. a clean pencil rubber & typewriting rubber, & erase all errors neatly.

Run on If h after erasing the error, the letters on either side of the erasure appear faint, type lightly over these

4. If you are not sure how to set out any piece of typing, follow the setting of the test paper wh. is usually a gd. guide as to what is wanted.

N.P. & no. 5 Following carefully the method of paragraphing, i.e., a hanging para. may hv. bn. used for insets. Be consistent in spacing, spelling, etc.

1. Always read carefully all instructions for ea. question before y. start to type.

3. Before starting to type, read thro' to gain an idea of the subject matter, & note any peculiarities of handwriting & special instructions. Be careful w. spelling & punctuation. Use commonsense both in deciphering MS & also in arranging matter.

H

7. Note any instructions given/ regarding headings. Usually words underlined shd. be typed in closed caps, *double* & words treble underlined in spaced caps. (Insert A)

11. Always check thro' yr. work before removing it from the machine.

u.c. 12. Always be in the exam. room in plenty of time to test yr. m/c/ & if anything is wrong w. it, *u.c.* report it to the invigilator before/ start of /exam.

particularly w. words wh. can be spelt in two ways, such as 'realise'

l.c. 13. Take w. y. to the exam. a pencil, ruler, pen pencil rubber & typewriting eraser, also ink for ruling

If typescript which is being prepared for the printer contains footnotes, these should be inserted on the line following that in which the reference appears and *typed in single spacing*. Turn up one single-line space after the line in which the reference occurs, type underscore across the page; turn up two single-line spaces; type reference mark and footnote; turn up one single-line space, and type underscore; turn up two single-line spaces and continue to type from the point reached before typing the footnote. If footnotes appear close to each other, say with only one or two lines of typing between, these may be put together.

7. Practise typing footnotes in matter for printer. Type the following on A4 paper in double spacing, with single spacing for footnotes. Keep your typed copy for future reference in Folder No. 2.

<u>TYPING TECHNIQUES</u>

At the beginning of each Unit in this book you will find drills and reviews on keyboard techniques. It is essential that you practise these until you can type them accurately and quickly without hesitation.

One author[1] puts it like this: 'Even at the expense

---

[1] Jane E. Clem. 'Techniques of Teaching Typewriting,' McGraw-Hill, New York.

---

of textbook requirements, there must be organized teaching for the maintenance and the improvement of techniques for advanced students as well as beginners.'

We agree entirely with the author, and in a recent publication[2] we said: 'Knowledge of display, of word-division,

---

[2] Drummond and Scattergood. 'The Teaching of Typewriting,' McGraw-Hill, London.

---

and of tabulation is USELESS IF THE TYPIST CANNOT OPERATE THE MACHINE EFFICIENTLY.' Therefore the basic need of all typing courses is the development and consolidation of good techniques.

can be typed, set on a machine like a Varityper (wh prints letters of different sizes & types) or even be printed. The finished copy is then photographed and/image either transferred to a sensitized plate th wl be used as a master or transferred indirectly to a copying m/c. This process is suitable for large quantities.

Photo-copying ← all caps

By this method of duplicating an exact copy of an original document can be reproduced ~~produced~~. The basic principle is/action of light on paper wh has ben chemically treated. ~~It~~ This is becoming v. popular in many offices, because of the accuracy & speed w wh/copies can be obtained. This process is not economical for/production of a large no. of copies.

(This process)

Bibliography

A Bibliography is a list of books or magazine or newspaper articles included in footnotes or at the end of a chapter or book to show the source from which information has been taken. It includes the author, the title of the work, place and date of publication, and sometimes the pages to which reference is made. The items are listed alphabetically. If any item takes more than one line, the extra lines are indented ten spaces. The author's name is written first, followed by his Christian name or initials. Titles are usually underscored, or may be typed in capitals. The following specimen will give you an idea of the most common method of typing a Bibliography.

3. Practise typing a bibliography. Read the above explanation. Then type a copy of the following on A5 paper in single-line spacing, with double spacing between each item. List authors alphabetically.

MacLennan, Alexander: Technical Teaching and Instruction
        Oldbourne Book Co. Ltd., 1963

Candlin, E. Frank: A Planned English Course
        University of London Press.

Watcham, Maurice: Gregg Office Practice, pp. 143—145
        McGraw-Hill Publishing Co. Ltd., 1970

Drummond, A. M., and Scattergood, I. E.:
        Gregg Typing, First Course
        McGraw-Hill Publishing Co. Ltd., 1970

Clem, Jane E.: Techniques of Teaching Typewriting
        McGraw-Hill Book Company, Inc., New York

Type the following on A4 paper in single-line spacing with double spacing between paragraphs. Use shoulder headings for paragraph headings. Please leave numbers in figures. Leave 6 clear spaces at top of paper.

TIPS FOR TYPISTS

H Side Margins. When using A4 paper see th. the left-hand margin is not less than 25 mm, i.e. 10 pica, 12 elite. With

stet A5 paper the left margin should be less than 12 mm   noth

l.c. (5 Pica, 6 Elite). No matter what size of paper is used, the rt-hand margin must NEVER be wider than the left-hand mgn.

typing Top Margin. When using headed paper, start three single-line spaces after last line of heading. W. plain paper, leave 6 clear spaces at top.

Bottom Margin. Leave 25 mm or 6 clear single-line spaces.*

Before inserting paper, it is a good plan to put a light pencil mark 25 mm from the btm. edge of the paper as

/h a warning signal. Later, of course, this is erased.Ŧ mark

Spacing. Use single-line spacing for business letters Ŧ & dble spacing f. legal documents, short specifications

l.c. & literary work. draft copies are usually typed in dble spacing, or treble spacing may be used.

Page nos. In typing from MS, the first page is not numbered.
On or pp. the no. is usually placed on the fourth single-line space from the top in / centre of the typing line, with a dash at either side, e.g. -2-

'Indenting revision is necessary,'

stet * This is important when / matter is cont'd on a subsequent page.

Ŧ Many typists use a backing sheet wh. is a little wider than the typing paper.

Ŧ If the letter is short, you may use double spacing & a shorter writing line. When using single-

H line or dble line spacing, leave one clear space

H only between paras.

On the backing sheet make a mark 25 mm from / bottom edge of the typing paper.

2. Type a copy of the following on A4 paper in double spacing. Keep your typed copy for future reference in Folder No. 2.

Spirit Duplicating   all caps.

Indent →

This is another kind of duplicating process, somewhat similar to stencilling, & for up to two hundred copies this method is cheaper than stencilling.

A master copy is prepared by means of a sheet of hectographic carbon (ie. a sheet coated w an aniline dye). The master is typed through an ordinary typewriter ribbon on to the sheet of hectographic carbon being placed @ back of the paper w coated side upwards.

(A special paper having a glossy surface)

Run on This hectographic carbon can be obtained in different colours, so th spirit duplicating can be used when colour work is required

an ordinary pen or pencil being used.

Handwritten copies may also be produced on a spirit duplicator When the master is completed, the carbon sheet is discarded the master is then fitted to duplicating m/c, & as the duplicating paper on wh copies are being made passes through m/c, it is moistened by spirit & print is transferred to sheet of paper.

All th is necessary is to insert a sheet of hectographic carbon of particular colour required, so th part of master sheet may be typed through blue, anor through purple, anor through red, etc, & when copies are run off these appear in the different colours, unlike the stencilling process wh requires a separate stencil to be used for whatever part of the matter is to be in a different colour.

Offset Litho Process   ← all caps

This method of duplicating requires a thin metal or paper sheet on wh matter is typed. A special typewriter ribbon is also necessary, or matter can be written by hand w special pencils. [Where fine quality is needed, masters are usually reproduced by a photographic process. The written copy is

Type the following draft copy for printer in double-line spacing on A4 paper, making corrections indicated.

Erasing – caps

Indent

v.c. The good typist does a minimum of erasing. It cannot
lower / be assumed, th. any human can type a whole day
N.P. w'out making an error now & then. [Erasures must be
l.c. made to correct these occasional errors: But the
erasures* must be well done so th. they cannot be

* Always keep a good rubber within easy reach. If
necessary, tie it to / typewriter w. a piece of string.

of the / detected in casual reading. Move the carriage to the
centre / left or to the right/ so th. the particles from the
u.c. rubber will not fall into the type basket/ insert
a card behind the original copy + in front of the
carbon sheet.

Run on / Erase the error on the original, blow the particles
off the sheet & away from the m/c. Place the
;/ card behind the carbon/ erase the error on the
N.P. carbon copy. Then remove the card, ‡ & return the
carriage

N.P. ‡ If you use ordinary paper, if it is necessary to put
a piece of paper btwn the shiny side of each
carbon sheet + the carbon copy. Remember to
the / remove the pieces of paper before typing/ correction.
carriage to the point on the paper at wh. the error
was made. Type the correction.

Run on / If the typed letters on either side of the correction
are faint, strike over them lightly.

N.P. [note: Although there are a number of eradicating
products (on the market) to correct an error
instead of using an eraser, these methods are not
always satisfactory, & you wl be well advised
to keep to the eraser.

continue on this copy until all copies on erased

(e) Replace m/c cover

l.c. (f) Leave cylinder in correct position (sheet)

after 2
on P.1. (3) Holding / bottom of / stencil + backing in one hand attach the
head portion ✱ of stencil to / cylinder of / duplicating m/c by
placing / perforations, or slots, over / stubbs. or

✱ The face or readable side of / stencil shd fit
H against / drum λ / back of / backing sheet uppermost.

I check copies carefully. If there are any unwanted
spots of ink λ caused by cracks in / stencil λ, (λ) λ
apply correcting fluid. If necessary, a slight tear
can be repaired by use of paper. (gummed)

'A' INTERLEAVING.

Stencil copies are usually run off on paper having
§λ a soft, absorbent surface. Because this kind λ paper dries
(λ up / wet ink λ especially if good quality quick λ drying ink H
)λ is used λ copies can be run off one after the or. w'out danger of
l.c. Smearing. However,
λ Sometimes it is necessary to use bond paper
(or or non-absorbent paper) in order to lend prestige to the
copy. ↗   (duplicating m/c)

Most manfrs. can supply an automatic interleaver or
drying mechanism; otherwise the process must be performed
H by hand + is time + wasting.

When such paper is used, it is necessary to insert
blotting sheets between each stencilled copy to prevent
stet ~~smudging~~ ~~smearing~~. This process is known as interleaving.

Secretarial aid No. 1
Proof-reading

Proof-reading is not easy. Our eyes have a way of passing over the line of typescript and seeing what the mind thinks is there, and not what the fingers actually put there. Moreover, the time devoted to proof-reading is non-productive, and the typist feels it necessary to get on with another job. Yet proof-reading is the sole responsibility of the typist.

There are several common types of errors for which you should look:

1. Spelling, punctuation, grammar.

2. Word substitution—*from* for *form*, *is* for *it*, *as* for *is*, *in* for *on*, *you* for *your*.

3. Transposition of letters—r and t, v and b, i and e.

4. Substitutions that are difficult to detect: n for m, d for s, u for y, or vice versa.

5. Omission of a line or lines which does not outwardly affect the meaning. Check finished work with original.

6. Dates, proper names and place names, and figures.

Composing at machine

Type the following on A5 paper in double spacing, and insert the correct vowel wherever there is a hyphen. *Do not write on this book.*

```
     W- are gl-d t- kn-w th-t it w-ll b- p-ss-bl- f-r you t-
sp--k -t a m--t-ng -f --r Cl-b -n Fr-d-y, 21st N-v-mb-r.  Th-
m--t-ng st-rts -t 6.30 p.m.
     W- -r- s--k-ng th- s-rv-c-s -f a sp--dy -nd -cc-r-t-
typ-st f-r --r s-n--r -ng-n--r.  S-m- pr-v---s -xp-r--nc-
-n th-s typ- -f w-rk -s -ss-nt--l.
```

Review Quiz No. 1

To speed up your production typing, you must be able to apply quickly important details such as spacing after punctuation, correct use of apostrophe, points of typewriting theory, and so on. This is the first of a number of Review Quizzes which you should complete by typing the following in double spacing, and supplying the missing word or words needed to give the correct answer. Do not write on your textbook.

1. There are . . . . . Pica characters and . . . . . Elite characters to an inch (25 mm.)
2. A4 paper measures . . . . . × . . . . .
3. A5 paper measures . . . . . × . . . . .
4. When using A4 paper (except in display and tabulation) the left margin must never be less than . . . . . elite spaces, ... pica spaces.
5. When using A5 paper (148 × 210 mm) (except in display and tabulation) the left margin must never be less than . . . . . elite spaces, ... pica spaces.
6. Divide a word after a . . . . . and before a . . . . .
7. Use the . . . . . to type the Roman numeral one.
8. An inferior character is typed . . . . . the normal line of writing.
9. To type double lines underneath totals use the . . . . .
10. The combination character for a double dagger is . . . . .
11. An example of an ordinal number is . . . . .
12. 'Stet' means . . . . .
13. Always . . . . . your typescript . . . . . removing it from the machine.
14. Type a shoulder heading at the . . . . . margin usually in . . . . .
15. Footnotes in typewritten work are always placed at . . . . . of page.
16. Footnotes in work for printers are typed on the line . . . . . that in which the reference appears.
17. Footnotes in typescript are separated from the main text by a . . . .
18. To show an ellipsis in the middle of a sentence type . . . . . dots, each separated by . . . . . space.

Turn to page 199 and check your answers. Score one point for each correct entry. Total score: 27.

Technique development

Grafting

On occasions it may be necessary to cut out a word, phrase, sentence, or even a paragraph and replace it with a new piece of stencil—this is known as 'grafting', and the following steps should be taken:

1. Place stencil, face upwards, on a piece of cardboard.

2. Cut out the incorrect piece with a sharp knife (or a razor blade) and ruler, cutting as closely as possible to the typed characters.

3. On a spare stencil type the matter, taking particular care not to type beyond the size of the piece cut out.

4. Cut out the piece typed in No 3—it should be slightly larger all round than the piece cut out from the original stencil in No. 2.

5. Place in position and check.

6. If accurate, spread adhesive lightly round edges.

7. Place graft in position immediately, ensuring that the newly typed matter is in correct alignment.

8. Strengthen edges of graft at back and front by applying correcting fluid.

9. Leave to dry for a few minutes.

1. Type a copy of the following on A4 paper in single-line spacing, with double spacing between paragraphs. Keep your typed copy for future reference in Folder No. 2.

When yr stencil is ready for running off, take the follow g. steps:

1. Remove carbon paper.

2. Rotate ~~cylinder~~ drum by means of handle to force a little ink through. *Insert 3* (on the drum)

4. 3 Turn the handle slowly until the stencil falls into position. 6. Inspect stencil & smooth out any creases by gently pushing stencil to outside & bottom edges.

5. Remove backing sheet.

7. 6 Prepare duplicating paper by fanning it. Then place in feed tray.

8. 7 Adjust feed & receiving tray to suit size of paper being used.

9. 8 Raise feed tray. 10 Run off a few trial copies.

11 Adjust position of paper & density as required.

12 11 Set counting device for desired copies. no. of

13. 12 Switch on electricity if an electric machine.

When the required no. of copies has been run off

(a) Drop feed tray & remove paper. unused

(c) (b) Remove stencil by detaching heading.

(d) (c) If y. expect to use the stencil again:

(Insert 'A' here)

i. Remove all excess ink by means of blotting paper or an old newspaper.

ii. When stencil is clean & dry store in an old stencil box

(b) (d) Remove copies from receiving tray.

Contd.

1 first—better put in a heading—RUNNING OFF A STENCIL. Also, please use hanging paras. for numbered items.

Consolidation

Type the following in double spacing on A4 paper, unless otherwise instructed. Paragraphs enumerated (a), (b), etc. should be hanging paragraphs where applicable.

(Typist: first roman numerals outside left margin)

Family Law Reform Act 1969 ← *(Caps + underscore)*
People's Act 1969

(from their eighteenth birthday)

For hundreds of yrs, a person has not become an adult until his/her twenty-first birthday. On 1st Jan., '70 / above Acts came into force + all young people are to be treated as responsible adult citizens. This means th / following points are / right of all persons eighteen + over, instead of 21 + over as previously.

I MARRIAGE

   (a) W. permission fr yr parents or guardian y. can marry after the age of 16.

(sp) (b) At 18 young are free to marry w'out anyone's consent.

   (c) Power to make you a ward of court has bn abolished for persons over 18. *(if you wish to do so.)*

II VOTING

As fr yr 18th birthday y can vote (if you wish to do so.) at Parliamentary + Local Elections.

III PUBLIC OFFICES

H Until y are twenty-one y cannot stand as a candidate for

   (a) Parliament

   (b) Local Elections

IV OWNERSHIP OF PROPERTY + LAND. As fr yr 18th birthday you can

lc/ (Please display these) (a) buy yr own house, property, and land. (b) Take out a mortgage on a hse.

lc/ lc/ V MISCELLANEOUS As fr yr 18th birthday y can (a) hv yr own passport w'out consent of yr parents or guardian; (b) Make a valid will; (c) Inherit money or property; (d) buy gds on H.P. or credit sale.*

VI There has bn a change in / description of persons not of full age. Under Para. 14 of / Family Law Reform Act of '69 a person who is not 18 yrs of age is now described as a minor instead of an Infant.

(sp) * Finance cos. wl no longer hv to insist on an older person giving a guarantee for th payment wl be kept up.

Typist. Lettered items to be indented in single spacing with hanging paras where applicable

Accuracy/Speed Practice
Six-minute timing

Not more than 3 errors

words

AS.32   Someone once said that your face is your fortune. It may not make   **13**
you a fortune, but a well-cared-for face can be a great asset in every   **27**
way. Cleanliness is the foundation of complexion care. Your skin, like   **41**
a flower, grows and changes as time goes by: its multilayered structure   **55**
sheds surface cells as it builds new ones from within. If you do not   **68**
cleanse your skin daily, dead cells and oil accumulate, pores clog, and   **84**
before long your skin ceases to breathe.   **91**

What kind of skin do you have? Dry skin tends to have fine lines,   **104**
looks taut and may flake. Oily skin looks shiny with large pores and   **118**
absorbs make-up. You may be lucky enough to have normal skin — soft and   **132**
just moist enough to look dewy.   **138**

For many years we have had the soap-and-water versus cream-and-   **151**
lotion controversy. Your father will probably say, "You can't beat soap   **165**
and water." He <u>may</u> be right, but, if you are in doubt, compromise. There   **180**
are several light cleansing products on the market that combine creaming   **194**
and washing benefits. However, do not forget the basic rule: cream, wash   **209**
and tissue upwards.   **213**

Now you must choose a suitable freshener because this will make your   **226**
skin feel delightful. It conditions, tightens pores and stimulates circu-   **241**
lation. It also ensures that no make-up or cleanser is left on the skin.   **256**

If you have an oily skin, do not use a moisturizer. Otherwise,   **268**
look for a light cream that sinks into your face. Mist moisturizer is   **280**
good because it works well on normal and most combination skins.   **295**

No matter what type of skin you have, an eye cream is essential.   **308**
Eyes are the focal point of the face and wrinkles start first around the   **322**
eyes. Remember: cleanse, refresh, and moisturize one after the other   **336**
every night and morning.   **341**

If your skin is extremely oily, blemished, or sensitive, you may   **354**
have many problems. In severe cases see a specialist and follow his   **368**
recommendations. A mild case of blackheads or spots can be fairly easily   **382**
dealt with in an old-fashioned way. Boil some water and, with a large   **396**
towel over your head, hold your face over the steaming water for five   **410**
minutes. This treatment helps rid your skin of impurities by opening   **424**
the pores and causing perspiration to flow. Blackheads are not caused by   **438**
dirt but by skin oil which has been oxidized by contact with the air.   **452**

Your face is the first thing at which people look. It will give away   **466**
your age more than anything else; therefore, you must take care of it.   **480**

(S.I. 1.33)

Type the following on A4 paper (210 × 297 mm) in double spacing. Leave 6 clear line-spaces at top of paper. Typing line 60 spaces.

How to start yr. Car Engine   ← caps & underscore

Indent → hand/ First ensure th the / brake is applied & th the gear lever is in / neutral posⁿ. Insert the ignition key into the ignition switch.

u.c.   I   Cold engine

      1. Depress accelerator pedal & then return it to normal posⁿ.

      2. Pull the choke control knob fully out.

      3. (a) Depress clutch pedal & crank / engine by turning the ignition key fully clockwise.

          (b) If the engine does not start . . . return / key to the 'off' posⁿ, pause &

trs.   repeat.

          (c) Keep clutch pedal depressed & the ignition key held . . . until / engine starts.

    II   Warm Engine

      1. Crank / engine by turning / ignition key fully clockwise; keeping / accelerator pedal in /

H   halfway posⁿ . . .

      2. Release the ignition key & the acceleration pedal immediately / engine starts.

Type the following on A5 (210 × 148 mm) paper in double spacing, unless otherwise instructed. Leave 6 clear spaces at top. Centre each line horizontally.

ACCOUNTING   → Leave 2 clear spaces

A first yr course for ONC & professional students

by

rh   Raymond Blockington, B.Com., A.C.A.
Senior Lecturer in Accounting
Wolverhampton Tech College

↕   ←   Typist Leave 38mm here for an insert

Single spacing / Publishers: McGraw-Hill Publishing Co. Ltd., Shoppenhangers Rd, Maidenhead, Berks.

The distribution of the Co's holdings is as follows:—

Typist
Tabulate these
under heading   Net Tangible Assets   No. of Cos.

£200,000
trs

Over £500,000 – 50   £200,001 to £500,000 – 40
£100,001 – £2,000,000 – 9.   Under £100,000 – 7
The accounts and reports were adopted & the Board's proposal referred to above was approved. 'A' — thus continuing the unbroken run of increasing profits since the incorporation of the new Co. 'B' & that the directors recommended the payment of a final dividend

Job 91   Production Target—*20 minutes*
Display the following advertisement as effectively as possible. It is to fit on to a card measuring 178 mm × 229 mm.

For sale by private treaty — New Freehold Semi-detached Houses. Now in the course of erection ~~construction~~ at Grove Lane, Newcastle, Staffordshire by the Newcastle Building Co. Ltd. Situated in the Borough of Newcastle, within walking distance of the Centre of the town.
The Accommodation includes Entrance Hall, Through Lounge, Kitchen & Pantry, two Double Bedrooms, Single Bedroom, and Bathroom. Separate Toilet. Outside: Garage if required, Coal-bunker and Garden to front & rear.
u.c. All main Services will be connected. For further details apply to: Winterton & Sons, 9 High Street, Newcastle. 'Phone: Newcastle 1563'

UNIT 26   **181**

Unit 6

Skill building

Type each exercise (A, B, and C) *once* for practice, *once* for speed, and finally *once* for accuracy.

A. Review alphabet keys

1.   A reasonably-sized bowl of bread and milk is frequently given to children just to relieve their exceptional tension.

B. Review special characters

2. "2" 3/3 4 @ 4/5 £5/£6 7 & 8 '8' (192) (5-4) 8' 2" 6/7 22-15.

3. Credit W. Clare & Co. with 3 lengths of Oak 6' 6" x 3' x $\frac{1}{2}$", @ £3.50 each; on Invoice No. R/79/64 they were charged £5.75 instead of £2.25. Also 12 tins Paint @ 45p each — not sent.

C. Build accuracy on shift key drill

4. Dow-Gow & Co. Ltd., R. & T. Sayers, Ball (U.K.I.) Ltd., Sir,

5. In the High Street at Stratford-on-Avon you will see the Old Tudor House Restaurant Limited owned by Kunzle Catering Ltd.

6. Ask the National Farmers Union Mutual Insurance Society Ltd.

Accuracy/Speed Practice

You should now aim at increasing your speed by 5 words a minute, i.e., if you have been typing at 35 words a minute, your aim is now 40 words a minute.

One-minute timing *Not more than 1 error*

words

AS.7   It has often been said that horses sleep while standing up, which is **14** quite true. Some bigger creatures do the same, and so do birds, for that **28** matter. A horse does not lie down to rest on account of the fact that its **43** heavy body, lying on the hard ground, will make the bones of its ribs sore. **58** Thus Nature has arranged that the joints of its legs should lock, so as to **73** support the body when it is relaxed. **(S.I. 1.19) 80**

AS.8   We are most anxious to keep in touch with all our friends so that we **14** can help them by supplying goods to them at a figure well within their **28** power to pay. With this aim in view, we are sending you a list of questions **43** which we shall be glad if you will answer to the best of your knowledge. **57** We are sure you will have no objection to acceding to this request, and you **72** will certainly find it to your advantage. **(S.I. 1.24) 80**

UNIT 6 29

Job 90

Prepare a fair copy of the following Manuscript, ready for stencilling. Make all necessary corrections. It should be fitted on to one sheet of A4 paper.

Caps —→ <u>Estates Investment Trust Company Limited</u>

Twelfth/ The 12ᵗʰ Annual General Meeting of Estates Investment

Last/ Co. Ltd. was held on the 12ᵗʰ June/in London, the

(ACKLAND) Chairman, Sir Henry Ackland, presiding.

Run on   The following is an extract from his circulated statement :—

⁋   The steady progress of the Coʸ. business has continued during the year under review resulting in a nett increase of the investments by £327,623. Capital Reserve shows an increase on the previous year's figure despite the £200,000 scrip issue made from this a/c.

Caps —→ Higher Income & Dividendᵈ

    Turning to the statement of revenue, the Chairman

trs   said that the income, before tax, for the year, was £358,153 as against £320,477 for the previous

Insert   year/ Allowing for tax, & adding the previous year's

'A'   carry forward, he said that there was an amt. of £504,048 available to cover the dividend/ of   Insert B

dividend/   6%, making, with the 4% interim/ paid last Dec., a total of 10% for the year on the issued and <u>paid-up Share Capital</u>.

Caps —→ Proposed Scrip Issue

    The Chairman also said in his report that a

uc.   <u>resolution</u> was to be put to the A.G.M., which covered the proposal to capitalise the sum of £400,000 by the issue of 400,000 new shares of £1 each, &to distribute the same among the shareholders in the proportion of 2 new shares for every 13 shares held.

Technique development

Vertical centring

To centre material vertically:

1. Count the number of lines (including blank ones) that the material will occupy.
2. Subtract that figure from the number of line-spaces on your paper. On A4 paper there are approximately 70 single spaces. On A5 (148 × 210 mm) paper there are 50 single spaces and on A5 (210 × 148 mm) paper 35 single spaces.
3. After subtracting, divide the remainder by 2 (ignoring any fraction) to determine on what line to begin typing. For example, to centre 8 lines of double-spaced copy on A5 (148 × 210 mm) paper: (a) You need 15 lines, i.e., 8 typed, 7 blank; (b) $50 - 15 = 35$ lines left over; and (c) $35 \div 2 = 17$ (ignore $\frac{1}{2}$). Start to type the matter on the next line (18).

7. Practise display. Read the above explanation; then type the following announcement on A5 (148 × 210 mm) paper, in double spacing, taking steps 1, 2, and 3 above.

NEW EDITIONS
To be Released 10th October
Western European History
Eastern European History
Nuclear Physics
Management Control

Preparing a 'layout' of a notice

Before typing an unarranged notice, prepare a 'layout', i.e., a rough plan in pencil, showing the best arrangement of the matter and the number of lines required. Keep the 'layout' before you as you type the notice.

As a general rule, the following details each occupy one line, and one space at least is left between each.

These details need not be in the same order as that given. 1. Name of advertiser. 2. Nature of notice. 3. Place or address. 4. Any other details (in order of importance). Each line is centred horizontally, and the whole notice vertically. No full stop is used at the end of lines (unless the last word is abbreviated).

8. Prepare a 'layout' for the following notices and then type it on A5 paper (210 × 148 mm).

(a) W. J. Abbey & Co., Caravan Specialists, Delamere, Northwich. Care-free Holidays for years to come. A fine selection of both new and used caravans. Cash or Hire Purchase terms. Open daily for inspection from 8 a.m. to 7 p.m.

(b) J. H. BROADHOUSE & CO. LTD. 21 Scotland Road, Carlisle. CA2 3PU. STAFF VACANCIES. Sec./S'hand-Typist. Asst. Cashier (Grade B). Sales Clerk (Grade C). Progress Clerk (Grade B). Apply in writing, stating qualifications, to: Personnel Officer.

l.c. 9. ⌐ You will be able to see if/ there are /any characters either

⌐ ⌐ /overcut/ or /undercut/, & this w. enable you to

v.c. adjust yr. touch f. future stencils./ by holding
up the finished stencil to the light

3 8. A sheet of this carbon paper,/ coated side upwards,/
is placed betwn / stencil &/ backing sheet wh. is
attached to the stencil. Also place anor sheet
of carbon paper w./ coated side towards / backing
sheet. This wl. give a carbon copy on / backing
sheet & wl. simplify checking.

JOINING A STENCIL

If, near the bottom of a p., y. hv. omitted a few words or
a sentence, it is not necessary to type / whole stencil
again · but / stencil after the last complete para. &
join by anor portion of stencil. Reinforce / join by
N.P. applying correcting fluid. [If y. do not hv. a brief
carriage typewriter, this process is helpful when
stencilling a balance sheet, or similar document,
but the stencil in half & type ea. half separately.
Join them together as suggested above.]

/ which has to be duplicated
on A4 paper lengthwise.

'A' Special stylus pens can also be obtained for
drawing lines or for handwriting.

'B' & this necessitates care being taken to see th.
ea. colour comes precisely in /required position
on / completed document.

'C' The figures shown down ea. side of / stencil
⊢ correspond w. / vertical line /spacing of the
typewriter.

⊥ It is advisable to leave at least 13 mm clear space
⌐ / inside the frame / at the top & sides of the stencil.

⊥ If the fluid in / bottle has become thick, it shd. not
be used.

The horizontal nos. represent pica
⊢ & elite letter /spacing.

by using a special adhesive
sufficient / stencil may.

Effective display

Matter can be effectively and artistically displayed if extra prominence is given to important lines by the judicial use of (a) Spaced capitals (leave three spaces between each word); (b) Closed capitals (one space between each word); (c) Underscore for certain words or lines; (d) Initial capitals and small letters with or without underscore.

NOTE: Take care not to overdo any one of these methods; otherwise no line will stand out more prominently than others, thus detracting from the general appearance.

9. Practise effective display. Read the above explanation, and then type the following advertisement on A5 (148 × 210) paper, using one or more of the above methods.

```
Carpet Mart Ltd., Camden High Street, London, N.W.1.  Special Offer
of Fitted Carpets.  Tomorrow at 9 a.m.  Sale of A.1 Quality
Axminster at less than half price.  Free fitting and free underlay.
Large selection available.  An opportunity not to be missed.
```

Programmes

Programmes can be displayed in various ways. The specimen below is a simple form of a concert programme. Note that the items at the left-hand margin in this particular form start flush at the margin. The items on the right-hand side end flush with the right-hand margin. To ensure that this is the case, bring carriage to one space beyond the right-hand margin, and back-space the number of letters and spaces in the item. Start at point reached. The items in the middle are centred.

10. Practise typing programme. Read the above explanation; then type the specimen programme below on A5 (210 × 148 mm) paper, centring it vertically and following the display precisely. Double spacing between each item. Margins: 12 spaces on each side.

```
                    P R O G R A M M E
Overture          Orpheus in the Underworld          Offenbach
                      THE ORCHESTRA

Song                  The Magic Flute                   Mozart
                      NORMAN ALLIN

Pianoforte          Polonaise in A Flat                 Chopin
                        SOLOMON

Violin              Dance of the Goblins               Bozzini
                     YEHUDI MENUHIN

Song              May Angels Guard Thee                  Verdi
                      ROSA PONSELLE

Selection               Lilac Time                    Schubert
                      THE ORCHESTRA
```

2. Carbon paper is supplied w. / stencils / the object of
wh. is two fold / In the 1st place it helps to
avoid / chipping out of certain characters, &, secondly,
it makes the stencil easier to read f. checking purposes.

First, thoroughly clean / type faces, so th. no
character is clogged. With Elite type ... brush the
type face frequently during / cutting of / stencil.

3. When y. insert the stencil into / typewriter, see
th. the line or scale / is level w. the alignment
scale. If necessary, adjust it in the ordinary
way by means of the paper release lever. Insert
± 'C' here.

4. note the frame of / stencil, & be careful not to
type outside this. [A firm, sharp & even touch (no.6)
is required f. striking / keys, but certain letters need
to be struck more heavily than others / Letters such ⊙ l.c.
as m, w, and / upper / case letters. more open letters such as
o, c, e, underscore, & punctuation marks, need a lighter
stroke, as otherwise / centres may fall out. If this does
happen, type the letters on a piece of spare stencil,
& w. a pin & a speck of correcting fluid insert the
letter in the space.

8. After / stencil has bn. typed, carefully check it before
y. take it out of the m/c.

& Although y. shd. avoid making mistakes, an error can
be rectified by / use of correcting fluid. The procedure
is as follows: —

(a) Flatten the letters to be corrected.

(b) Turn / platten up a few lines.

(c) Put a pencil or flat ruler underneath
the stencil so as to separate it from
the carbon.

(d) Paint out the error w. a very small
quantity of correcting fluid. Leave for a
few seconds to dry, then remove
pencil or ruler, & type in / correct letter(s)
or word(s). ±

Typist — omit the brackets before and after the lettered items
above and leave 4 clear spaces after each letter.

(give above word below the word to be corrected.)

(at the top of the stencil)

Programmes are frequently printed in the form of a folded leaflet, in which case the name, place, and date, etc., are printed on the front page (right-hand side, i.e., with fold to the left), and the items are displayed on the reverse side of the paper as shown below. The word 'PROGRAMME' (unless printed on the front page) will be centred across the two middle pages. Sufficient space must be left between the left-hand and right-hand sides to allow for the fold, as well as for a few clear spaces on either side of the fold. Before you start to type the Programme, mark in pencil the centre of the paper, so that, when the paper is folded, the fold will come in the exact centre.

FRONT SIDE OF PAPER (UNFOLDED)

Front page—right-hand side   Back page—left-hand side

Fold

Back page Left-hand	Front page Right-hand

It is advisable to mark these two pages on your paper before inserting it.

REVERSE SIDE OF PAPER (UNFOLDED)

Page 2—left-hand side of fold   Page 3—right-hand side of fold

Page 2 Left-hand	Page 3 Right-hand

11. Practise typing folded Programme. Read the above explanation; then type the following Programme on A4 paper (folded down centre); follow the layout. Each line is centred horizontally and the whole vertically.

Front page

Y O U T H   C O N C E R T

by the

CITY OF BIRMINGHAM SYMPHONY ORCHESTRA
(Leader: MEYER STOLOW)

at the

TOWN HALL, BIRMINGHAM

on

FRIDAY, 10th NOVEMBER, 19..

at 7.15 p.m.

Conductor: ERIC ROBERTS

Technique development

Manifolding

It is often necessary to make more than one copy of typed material, and there are various processes which may be used, the choice being dependent on the number of copies required. When only a few copies of a letter or document are wanted, these can be produced by Manifolding, i.e. by the use of carbon paper. However, even with light-weight paper and feather-weight carbons, the number of copies which can be obtained is limited—usually six to eight can be made on a manual machine and up to twenty on an electric typewriter. Also a great deal will depend on the hardness of the platen and the clarity of the type face.

If a larger number of copies is required than can be produced satisfactorily by the manifolding method, one of the following processes may be used:
(a) Stencil duplicating.
(b) Spirit duplicating.
(c) Offset litho.
(d) Photo-copying.
These various processes are described briefly in the following notes.

2. Type a copy of the following on A4 paper in double spacing. Keep your typed copy for future reference in Folder No. 2.

STENCIL DUPLICATING. (spaced caps. & underscored)

By this process

l.c. [A master copy or stencil is prepared, the required matter being typed on a stencil sheet wh. is made

H of special wax-like paper.

Run on When / stencil has bn prepared, it is attached to a drum on a rotary m/c, of which there are many different

stet ~~types~~ makes, but all of these work on more or less / same

/h principle. The paper used for the copies / which is

/h called duplicating paper / presses against the drum, & ink

H is forced thru the cut / out forms of the characters. [When   N.P.

// a stencil is / cut / by typewriter, the ribbon is switched out of action, so th. / type face strikes on to the stencil

H w'out passing thru the ribbon, thus producing a clear / cut character. Insert 'A' here.

/h colour work can be produced on rotary duplicators

/h This entails having a different drum for each colour / [In

/g this case / however / a separate stencil ~~has to~~ must be prepared

f. ea. colour instead of / whole of / matter being typed

or on one stencil / Insert ~~HH~~ 'B' here.

When a stencil is to be cut, the followg. points / shd be noted:

Before proceeding with pages 2 and 3 below, note the following:

1. Calculate the number of vertical lines required, allowing for the spacing to be left between items. (In specimen below, we suggest leaving two clear spaces.)

2. The margins at the extreme left of page 2 and the extreme right of page 3 should be equal, and the number of spaces before and after the fold should be equal. The left and right margins should be a minimum of 13 mm and a maximum of 25 mm. The space on either side of the fold should be a minimum of 7 mm and a maximum of 13 mm.

3. If the carriage of your typewriter is long enough,

then put the paper in lengthwise, and in typing the table below, the margin and tab. stops would be set at the points indicated. However, if you have a short carriage, then each page will have to be typed separately, and in that case your left margin will be 12(10) and the right margin 63(55) for the first page, and 7(4), 58(49) for the second page.

4. With a short carriage you will have to type the heading PROGRAMME so that it runs across the two pages without a break, half on page 2 ending close to the right-hand edge of that page. The other half is typed on page 3, starting close to the left edge of the paper. Before you start to type page 3, make a light pencil mark to show the exact point at which the heading is to be continued.

Fold 70(59)

(Page 2)   (Page 3)

P R O G R A M M E

12(10)	63(55)	77(63)	128(108)
1. Bohemian Festival		6. Marching Song	Holst
Picturesque Scenes	Massenet	ORCHESTRA	
ORCHESTRA			
2. My Name is Mimi		7. None Shall Sleep	
La Bohème	Puccini	Turandot	Puccini
MARION SMYTHE-WILKES		CHARLES WEST	
Soprano		Tenor	
		RICHARD GREY	
3. Introduction and Rondo		Baritone	
To the Spring	Grieg		
ALFRED SADLER		8. Spring Song	Mendelssohn
Piano Solo		ALFRED WOODS	
		Flute	
4. Toreador Song		WILLIAM CLARKE	
Carmen	Bizet	Piano	
GEORGE GIBSON-BROWNE			
Baritone		9. One Fine Day	
		Madame Butterfly	Puccini
5. Hungarian Rhapsody		JOAN ELLIS	
No. 6	Liszt	Soprano	
ORCHESTRA			
		10. March of the Toys	
		Babes in Toyland	Herbert
I N T E R V A L		ORCHESTRA	
(Refreshments on Sale)			
		* * * * *	

Unit 26

Skill building

Type the alphabetic review *once* for practice, *once* for speed, and finally *once* for accuracy.

Review alphabet keys

1.   The secretary realized that the question as to the kind
of performance to be given next June is awaiting a decision.

Accuracy/Speed Practice
Five-minute timing   *Not more than 3 errors*

	words

AS.31   The general tone of business during the year has, on the whole, **13**
been satisfactory.   There are, however, straws in the wind to which it **26**
is desirable to draw attention.   During the war and post-war years, **39**
failures in business were infrequent.   Many failures are largely due **53**
either to fraud or folly, or a combination of both.   In the period **67**
in question there was no particular object in indulging in the former, **81**
and no great opportunity of displaying the latter.   Markets would **94**
absorb anything that was offered, even ill-made rubbish, and the art **107**
of salesmanship was superfluous.   This era shows signs of drawing to **121**
a close, and the less intelligent and less efficient will find it **134**
harder to survive. **138**

In some trades capacity to produce is still the only limiting **150**
factor to the volume of sales, but this is by no means universal.   In **164**
many others there is evidence of increasing stocks and a sense of **177**
selectivity, both as regards price and quality, which did not exist **190**
before.   There is no longer the same insatiable appetite. **201**

So long as this tendency does not go too far it is no bad thing. **214**
It is salutary that the value of salesmanship should be realized, and **228**
that good workmanship and efficient and economic production should **241**
come into its own.   There is no doubt, however, that in a world where **255**
appreciation of the realities of the situation is conspicuously absent, **269**
there will inevitably be casualties. **276**

The export position is not unsatisfactory and it is time that some **290**
tribute was paid to those who are working continuously to maintain **303**
existing and to expand new markets.   Appreciation of their efforts **316**
will not make them lie down on their jobs: their portion hitherto has **330**
more than frequently consisted of reproof for unattained ideals. **343**

Those with the maximum amount of information on the subject pro- **355**
fess to see the elimination of the overall adverse balance by the end **369**
of the year.   It is to be hoped that they are correct.   While it would be **384**
unwise to question these conclusions, it would be equally unwise to **397**
be complacent.   (S.I. 1.50) **400**

Production typing

Type the following in double spacing on A5 paper, using a 60-space typing line.

NP/ Please send us 6 1-kg tins Colourless Lacquer, 5 2-kg tins Thinners, & 5 1-kg tins Weather-Resisting Enamel. [The above-named shop is holding in ten days' time a one-week sale of shop-soiled ladies', men's & children's wear of high-

NP/ grade quality. [Two days ago he said he was starting in two weeks' time on a fortnight's cruise, but we are now told he is taking his daughter's youngest child abroad in his son's car, instead of using his daughter's, as hers is being overhauled.

Display the following as effectively as possible on A5 paper and insert a suitable border.

uc/ The Canterbury Singers present Bless the Bride by A.P. Herbert music by Vivian Ellis by kind permission of Samuel French Ltd. Stage Manager: Harry Vincent. Wardrobe mistress: Mary Brown. Dances arranged by Susan James. The Opera produced by F. Faulkner.

Type the following Programme on A4 paper as a folded leaflet, displaying it as effectively as possible.

Sports Day, Boldmere Jnr school, Sat., 20th May, @ 2.30 p.m. Proceeds in aid of the Library Fund. Programme 5p Events 1. Boys 7-8 yrs Hoop Race 50 yds. 2. Girls 7-8 yrs Potato Race 50 yards 3. Boys 8-9 yrs Sack Race 50 yds 4. Girls 8-9 yrs Egg & Spoon Race 50 yds. Dance Display 5. Boys 9-10 yrs. Wheelbarrow Race 60 yds. 6. Girls 9-10 yrs Three-Legged Race 60 yds. 7. Boys 10-11 yrs Skipping Race 60 yds. 8. Girls 10-11 yrs Obstacle Race 60 yds. Distribution of Prizes.

Type the following circular letter ready for stencilling on A4 paper.

Ref. AH/JC. Date as Postmark. Dear Sir or Madam,
Gas Council Films and Filmstrips I h. pleasure in enclosing
u.c. of the Council's latest catalogue of films/trips. (of films &
"Please note that our two latest productions, "Piping Hot" all caps
and "WINDOW TO THE SKY" will not be available until the end
N.P. of next month. [Any enquiries relating to the booking of films
u.c. should be made direct to / film library.)
run on The Council does not provide projection facilities, but,
u.c. if required, your local gas Showrooms may be able to assist. fres/
N.P. [All films are ~~now~~ available to approved borrowers on/loan.
N.P. Filmstrips are sold outright. [A booking form is enclosed for
your convenience, and we hope to ~~hear~~ hear from you. Yrs ffthy.
J.H. NICHOLSON, Film Officer, SWIZZLEWICK GAS COUNCIL.
Typist In first para. after word "filmstrips", insert — a list u.c.
of subject headings has now been included, and pp. are
numbered for easy reference.

You are asked to prepare a form letter ready for duplicating on A5 paper containing the following wording. Type this suitably. It will be signed by the Manager.

all caps Dear Sir (s), Repair Replacement under Guarantee.
We shall be pleased if you will (a) Supply advance
replacements) for or (b) Exchange or repair the
H undermentioned defective articles which are
being forwarded by separate post, together
with a copy of this letter. Description.
Reason for return. Yours ffthy. JOHNSON
T/ ELECTRICAL SUPPLIES LTD.

Unit 7

Skill building

Type each line or sentence (A, B, C, and D) *three* times, and, if time permits, complete your practice by typing each group once as it appears.

A. Review alphabet keys

1.   When dazzled by the headlights of the many passing cars
the expert driver just pulls to the kerb and quickly brakes.

B. Review shift key

2. Milan Luton Wales Genoa Perth Turin Irish China Japan Newton

3. Miss E. Newton visited China, Japan, Milan, Genoa and Turin.

4. 'The Plane Makers' — Reginald Marsh, J. Watling, D. Sherwin.

5. Your London Palladium Show — Cliff Richard with The Shadows.

C. Practise common letter combinations

6. he when them hear held then other where heard either reached

7. Either one or both may reach the valley where they are held.

8. When they reach there, they will hear about the bad weather.

9. All other helpers were then compelled to seek shelter there.

D. Build speed on common phrase drill

10. they are, they must, they have, they would, they should not.

11. They must leave now if they are to catch the next train out.

12. They should not call unless they have a late train to catch.

13. They will be late for the play which they are hoping to see.

Accuracy/Speed Practice
Two-minute timing   *Not more than 2 errors*

	words
AS.9 The sun shone brightly as the car slid smoothly through the leafy	13
lanes, and the passengers' talk ceased for a while. Shortly they would	27
reach their goal, and all of them were anxious that the first glimpse	41
of it should not be marred by the fact that they were not looking out	55
of the windows. Suddenly, they came round the last corner, and before	69
them lay the village, with its grey stone houses along a street lined	82
with trees, a wonderful view of hills for a background, and a quiet	96
river flowing gently along. The car rolled to a stop. They strolled	110
for a time through the quiet street, past the gardens, so full of	123
flowers, and on to the church. Once or twice a dog barked. Otherwise,	137
all was peace. A day to remember, they thought, as, turning for a	150
last glance, they slowly went back to their car. (S.I. 1.20)	160

Typist — The following will be eventually printed at the foot of the previous exercise, but in the meantime I would like to see what it looks like, so please type it on a separate sheet.

To: Business Education World Reprint Dept.,
   330 West 42 street,
   New York, N.Y., 10036. U.S.A.
   I am enclosing $____ for wh. pl. send me:
   — Copies of HOW TO MEET THE CHANGING NEEDS IN TYPEWRITING
          @ $1.00 ea.
   — Copies of ELECTRIC TYPING @ 75¢ ea.
      (Typist continue to list / titles given in / previous exercise)
PAYMENT FOR FULL AMOUNT MUST ACCOMPANY ALL ORDERS.

Name _____
     (Please print).
School _____
Address _____

Please type the following letter ready for signature. Use suitable date.
In addition to / file copy, make a copy for Miss J. Banks.
J. White, 427 Pershore Rd., B'ham. B5 2PO
Dear Mr White   Yr letter of Apl 8 has done me a favour th I appreciate v. much
N.P. Thank y. for taking the trouble to write me [Before yr letter was received one of
stet these errors had bn discovered t was ~~amended~~ corrected in our first reprint [As I am sure N.P.
I need not tell y., we make great efforts to keep errors out of our publications.
N.P. Yet an occassional error still slips through. [I hope y. will continue to let us
know about any errors y. may find in our books in future. I hope also,
of course, th there will not be any for y. to find !
   Yours very sincerely, John James, Commercial Editor

mentioning 2 errors that y.
h. found in one of our books

The other one will be corrected
in the next printing.

Technique development

14. Review use of dash. Type a copy of the following in double spacing. Remember to leave one space before and after dash, but no space before or after hyphen.

It is some twenty – no, more like thirty – years, since we saw him. The new secretary – Mr. H. Smith-Jones – takes up his duties on Monday. Some passers-by – and there were quite a few – stopped to listen. He said, "To be or not to be – that is the question." The visit of my new-found friend – if I may be so bold as to call him that – has given me great pleasure. We can supply up-to-date models of those chairs.

Menus

The following specimen will be a guide to the general display of a Menu. Note that the courses are separated from one another by extra spaces, and by a few dots or asterisks.

15. Type the following menu to fit on a card measuring 210 × 148 mm. Keep your typed copy for future reference in Folder No. 2.

T H E   B E L L   H O T E L

WORCESTER

<u>Saturday, 16th August, 19..</u>

LUNCHEON

Tomato Soup
or
Grape Fruit

* * *

Fried Fillet of Plaice — Sauce Tartare
Roast Chicken, Sausage and Stuffing
Bread Sauce
Roast and Creamed Potatoes
Spring Cabbage
Garden Peas

* * *

Peach Melba
Fruit Tart
or
Cheese and Biscuits

* * *

Coffee

* * *

Display the following. All matter underscored to be typed in closed capitals—do not underscore.

Reprints Available

(Typist - please put in order indicated by the nos. at the left-hand side. Do not type nos.)

① How to ~~make~~ meet changing needs in typewriting — A 9-part series by John L. Rowe covering such topics as correct touch, writing nos. & symbols, electric typing, development of speed & accuracy.

32 pages $1.00 per copy

⑤ Data processing: An introduction for students — A four-part series by Merle [MERLE] W. Wood & Robert G. Espergen [ESPERGEN] th. introduces data processing to High School students in language they can understand.

16 pages   50¢ per copy

in which she discusses skill & production techniques in electric typing.

② Electric typing — The columns written for Business Education by Marion Wood

H ③ The typing teacher as a technician / A series by Alan C. Lloyd on development, protection + refinement of basic typing skill.

24 pp.   75¢ per copy
16 pp.   50¢ " "

④ How to teach transcription — a series of 4 articles th. constitute a detailed outline for a transcription course.

⑦ Effective teaching techniques for general business — A nine part series by Dr. J. David Satlow that offers suggestions for arousing student interest.

20 pp.   45¢ per copy
[SATLOW]
12 pp.   35¢ per copy

⑥ Shorthand Dictation Laboratory — A report on schools th. h. installed electronic equipment for dictation. [shorthand]

16 pp.   75¢ p. copy.

⑧ General Business: Student projects th. w. intensify learning — By Alan C. Lloyd.

8 pp.   25¢ p. copy

⑨ Handling the business management of extra curricular activities — J. David Satlow's just concluded 14-part series.

52 pp. $1.50 per copy

through classroom discussion, group projects, etc.

Taking messages

You will sometimes have to take telephone messages or messages from a caller on your employer's behalf when he is out. Do not trust to your memory, but immediately type the message, and put it on your employer's desk. Many firms have printed message pads, in which case you will simply fill in the details. If, however, no printed pad is provided, you should type your message, which should contain the following details:

1. Message for . . . .

2. Date and time . . . .
3. Name of firm, caller and address
   . . . .
4. Phone No. . . . .
5. Details of message . . . .
6. (At foot) Your signature . . . .

NOTE: A good plan is to use any spare time you may have to type out or stencil a supply of a suitable form, so that you may have this ready for use when needed.

16. Practise typing messages. Type the following on A5 (148 × 210 mm) paper, using double spacing for the headings and single spacing for the body of message. Leave a margin of 13 mm on each side. Keep your typed copy for future reference in Folder No. 2.

```
                  Date: 5th March, 19..   Time: 2 p.m.
Message for: Mr. H. Brown
Name of firm and caller:  Mr. J. Smith,
                          of J. Smith & Co. Ltd.
Address: Bennetts Hill, Birmingham.   Phone No.: 236 4607
```

```
Message: Mr. J. Smith called with regard to your enquiry
about office furniture, and would like you to phone him
as soon as you return.

                          Taken by: A. W. Burton
```

Appointments itinerary

If your employer has appointments outside the office, an itinerary may have to be prepared for him which will enable him to know exactly where he should be at any given time. This schedule of a day's appoint-ments should be typed on a convenient size of paper or, preferably, on a card which he can carry about with him.

17. Practise typing appointments itinerary. Type a copy of the following itinerary on postcard size paper or on a postcard (148 × 105 mm). Keep your typed copy for future reference in Folder No. 2.

```
                    I T I N E R A R Y

        Mr. P. T. Reade's schedule for 8th May, 19..

   9.30 a.m.   Lewis's Ltd., High Street
               Buyer — Mr. L. F. Wood.
  11.00 a.m.   L. C. Marcell & Co. Ltd., Broad Street
               Buyer — Miss M. H. Moyers.
   2.30 p.m.   A. M. Bushell & Son, Victoria Street
               Buyer — Mr. S. F. Morrall.
   3.30 p.m.   R. Young & Co. Ltd., Hagley Road
               Buyer — Miss B. Swann
               Return to office to sign letters.
```

Care of the typewriter

To aid you in the production of first-class work, it is essential that your typewriter is kept in good working order. To do this you need a cleaning kit comprising:

1. A hard type-brush.
2. A long-handled soft dusting brush.
3. A duster.

Every morning you should:

(a) Brush the type with the hard brush. Brush outwards from back to front—never from side to side.

(b) Clean mechanism inside frame with soft brush.

(c) Use the duster for the outer casing, the platen, and cleaning underneath the machine.

Always keep your typewriter covered when it is not in use, and, if you have to move it

(a) lock the margins;

(b) lift it by the base *from the back*.

Great care is necessary when oiling a typewriter, and it is preferable to leave oiling to an experienced mechanic.

Composing at machine

The following letter is written in abbreviated longhand. Type it on A5 paper, spelling all words in full.

```
    We wr deltd to hv yr nws this a.m. and esp. to lrn that
all yr effts drg the 1st fw mnths hv bn rewd in sch a satis.
mnr.  We shl nw lk fwd to hrg yr vce on the Rdio Prog. on the
ausp. day in Jan.  It wll be a grt joy to the whl fam. & I nd
nt tell you hw prd we fl ovr hvg sch a tlntd reltv.  My own
princ. cse for plsre ls in the fct that it ws I who frst
sgstd yr tkg up brdcstg.  Ths gvs me a tny shr in yr scess.
```

Review Quiz No. 5

Type the following on A4 paper in single-line spacing, with double spacing between each item, filling in the correct word or words in the blank spaces. Do not write on your textbook.

1. When typing tabular work remember to mark . . . . . and . . . . . of vertical lines.
2. In tabular work with subdivided columns type the . . . . . headings first.
3. Leader dots should preferably be in groups of . . . . . dots . . . . . spaces.
4. Leader dots should always be typed . . . . . each other.
5. Always leave . . . . . space before the start and after the end of leader dots.
6. No word or letter must extend . . . . . the last leader dot.
7. When ruling by underscore, turn up . . . . . before and . . . . . after horizontal lines.
8. When a printer's dash is inserted instead of a column heading, type . . . .
9. A reference sign in the body of tabulation or manuscript has . . . . . space before it, but . . . . . space after it in the footnote.
10. Reference signs should be . . . . . slightly in the body of text.
11. In wide tabulation work space can be saved in the . . . . . or in the . . . . . column.
12. In marking scale-points for diagonal headings, mark the top of the diagonal line at the same point as the . . . . . vertical line.
13. When the Particulars Column of a tabulation is narrow, ... leader dots may be used.

Turn to page 199 and check your answers. Score one point for each correct entry. Total score: 18.

An itinerary will also have to be prepared for your employer if he plans to be away from the office on business for a few days. This will list: arrival and departure times of trains, planes, etc.; hotel accommodation booked; names, addresses, telephone numbers of people on whom he has to call. It should contain complete details with dates and times of his programme for any particular trip.

18. Practise typing travel itinerary. Type the following on A4 paper in single-line spacing, using 25 mm margins. Keep your typed copy for future reference in Folder No. 2.

<u>I T I N E R A R Y</u>

<u>Mr. J. C. Washington's visit to BRISTOL</u>

<u>8th — 10th June, 19..</u>

<u>Monday, 8th June</u>

1325		Taxi from office to New Street Station, Birmingham.
1405	depart	New Street Station (platform 7) on The Devonian. ← *(Refreshment car available.)*
1620	arrive	Bristol (Temple Meads).
		*one night*ʌ Accommodation booked ʌat the Grand Hotel, Broad Street, 0272 21645.
1930		Dinnerʌwith Mr. J. Smythe *at Grand Hotel*ʌ (Gloucestershire Rep.✓) *Typist: Please type in full*

<u>Tuesday, 9th June</u>

1000		Town Clerk's Office, Council House, *1175*⊙ Tel: 0272 ~~21715~~, re site for new factoryʌ *u.c.* correspondence in file No. 1.
1130		Appointment with Mr. F. Squires, Manager, Secure Building Society, 7 Temple Gate.
Insert A		Tel. 0272 21715. Correspondence in file No. 2.
1700	depart	Grand Hotel. Mr. Smythe will collect your luggage and drive you to Weston-Super-*Mare.*
1745	arrive	Weston-Super-Mare.
	m	Accomodation booked at Grand Atlantic Hotel, Beach Road, Tel: 0934 6543.
1930	#	Dinnerʌat Grand Atlantic Hotel with Mr. and Mrs. Partridge & Mr. Smythe.

<u>Wednesday, 10th June</u>

0930	depart	Weston-Super-Mare (Refreshments on train).
1232	arrive	New Street, Birmingham.

Ⓐ *1400 Bristol Aeroplane Co. Ltd., Filton House, Tel: 0272 31476 Correspondence in file No. 3.*

Type a copy of the following Hire Purchase Agreement on A4 paper.

AGREEMENT No. _____

Dated the _____ day of _____ 19 - -

Name of Purchaser _____ (Mr./Mrs./Miss)

Address of Purchaser's Premises _____

The purchaser I/, being the occupier of the premises specified, hereby agree to purchase from BARKER, JENKINS & Co. LTD. (thereinafter referred to as the "Seller") the goods, appliances and/or apparatus ~~(hereinafter)~~ (herein referred to as/the apparatus) set out below on the terms and conditions described in the schedule overleaf.

Signature of Purchaser _____ Occupation _____

Witness _____ Address of Witness _____

Signed on behalf of Sellers _____

List Price Total	Purchase Tax Total	Description of Apparatus – Maker, Model, and serial number.

Total Purchase Price	Initial Payment	Amount Remaining	Interest on amount remaining	Total Amount Remaining

Production typing

Job 17

Production Target—*6 minutes*

Type the following Menu on A5 paper, centring it horizontally and vertically.

Soup – Chilled Fruit Juice – Melon Cocktail
Roast Turkey, Chipolata Sausage, Cranberry Sauce,
Parmentier and Duchess Potatoes, Garden Peas and
Sprouts.
Peach Flan with fresh cream – Ice Cream –
Cheese Board – Coffee

> Typist – treble – line spacing
> between courses, please

Job 18

Production Target—*5 minutes*

Type a suitable message form containing the necessary details and complete the form by making up a message for your employer to the following effect.

Caller Mr J Smith of Smith, Jones & Co Ltd. Is Mr Griffiths free to have lunch with him on Wednesday when he could discuss purchase of midget recorders for travelling executives

Job 19

Production Target—*10 minutes*

Type the following Travel Itinerary for Miss W. J. Wilkinson's visit to London, 22nd January, 19..., in the correct form on A5 paper.

08.00 Report Air Terminal St. Enoch Square, Glasgow. 08.50 Dep St. Enoch Square by BEA Coach for airport. 09.35 dep. Renfrew Airport (Flight No. 5023) 10.55 arrive Ldn. (Heathrow) 11.55 arrive West Ldn. Air Terminal 02.30 Reception Dorchester Hotel, Park Lane, Ldn, W6. 03.00 Display of Christian Dior Spring Collection 18.00 Report to West Ldn. Air Terminal 18.35 Dep. W. Ldn. Air Terminal for airport 19.40 dep Ldn (Heathrow) (Flight No 5064) 21.00 arrive Renfrew Airport. 21.35 arrive St. Enoch Sq.

Production typing

Job 82
Production Target—*20 minutes*

Type a fair copy of the following Will which has been drawn up for Mrs. Janet Hay Honeybourne, 17 Russell Square, London, W.C.1. Her executrix is Miss Andrea Ward, 19 Edgware Road, London, W.2.

just/ *All Caps* → This **is** the last Will and Testament of me . . . . of . . . .

First I direct the payment of all my/debts funeral and testamentary expenses

All Caps → I appoint . . . . of . . . . . . to be my executrix

I give, devise & bequeath the following legacies

To my brother William Geo. Powell the sum of £5,500. As to all the rest residue and remainder of my real and personal estate or any other estate at the time of my ~~death~~ **decease** (over which I have **dispos**disposing of power×) I give and bequeath the same to the said Andrea Ward of . . . . . . as her absolute property

All caps → I hereby Revoke all former Wills and other testa-mentary writing and declare this to be my last Will and Testament (hereto made by me)

All caps In Witness whereof I have hereunto set my hand this . . . . . day of . . . . one thousand nine hundred and . . . .

Caps *of* *of hereunto/* Signed by her last Will (as the testator) in the presence of us present together who in her presence and in the presence of ea. other have/L subscribed our names as Witnesses

Job 83
Production Target—*5 minutes*

A Write the following letter and encl. a copy of the above. To– Mrs. Honeybourne, ~~15 York Rd, Leeds 9.~~ (address as above)

Dear Mrs Honeybourne, I enclose a fair copy of the Will you suggested when you called here last week. If you agree with the contents, perhaps you would be good enough to call, as arranged, at this office on Monday next at 2 p.m.

Skill building

Type each exercise (A, B, and C) *once* for practice, *once* for speed, and finally *once* for accuracy.

A. Review alphabet keys

1.   On the card table with the green baize top six men were playing a game of bezique, and they looked extremely jovial.

B. Improve control of figure keys

2. 2929 3838 4747 5656 1920 1930 1940 1950 1960 1970 1980 1990.
3. Dates to remember: 1066, 1215, 1603, 1707, 1815, 1918, 1945.
4. For this year, £1,850,000 has been allocated for residential building; £974,640 for houses; £760,230 for other buildings.

C. Improve control of shift lock

5. FIRST-CLASS, FORTY-FOUR, HIT-OR-MISS, PAY-AS-YOU-GO, 60-WATT
6. Were the FORTY-FOUR books in FIRST-CLASS condition when they were sent to you? I <u>must</u> say I do NOT like <u>your</u> PAY-AS-YOU-GO policy and HIT-OR-MISS methods. Buy <u>seven</u> 60-WATT bulbs.

Accuracy/Speed Practice
Three-minute timing

Not more than 3 errors

words

AS.10   In presenting the accounts for the past year, we very much dislike   **13**
having to put before you something that is not very bright. At the out-   **28**
set I would like to say to you that this is due to a change in policy on   **42**
the part of your Directors.   **47**

    As you know, there have been changes in the directorate. The idea   **61**
of the old Board was to save the Company's cash without having regard   **74**
to what the new Board think is the most essential point of our policy —   **88**
namely, that of keeping the plant, etc., at the maximum point of good   **102**
repair. I do not mean to say that these assets of the Company had been   **117**
allowed to fall into a bad state, but what I do mean is that we now see   **131**
that, in order to make the best return to our members, we must bring   **144**
ourselves up to date.   **149**

    I am not holding out any strong hopes of reaping a benefit from   **161**
these changes at once — even when we have our plant in order it will   **175**
still take some time before the full effect will be felt. However, I   **189**
can assure you that, with the new plant, and by keeping a very careful   **203**
watch on our expenses, we are full of hope, provided that trade improves,   **217**
or, at any rate, does not fall off. As you know, we are trying hard to   **231**
gain orders from abroad, and this will help.   **(S.I. 1.28) 240**

At the top, usually printed, appear the words 'THIS IS THE LAST WILL AND TESTAMENT', starting at 15. A Will is usually typed on double paper, both sides of each sheet being used, and in double-line spacing.

Certain words must be capitalised in the text of a Will, such as the following:

NAME (of testator); AND; I APPOINT; I BEQUEATH; I DEVISE; I DEVISE AND BEQUEATH; I GIVE AND DEVISE; I GIVE AND BEQUEATH; I DIRECT; I GIVE; I REVOKE; IN TRUST; IN WITNESS WHEREOF; SIGNED.

Wills are folded and endorsed in the same way as Agreements.

9. Practise typing, folding and endorsing a Will. Type the following on A4 paper, in double spacing; then fold and endorse.

THIS IS THE LAST WILL AND TESTAMENT

— of me —

ELSIE CARTER of 25 Old Road Solihull in the County of Warwick the Wife of JAMES CARTER. ------------------------------------

1.   FIRST I DIRECT the payment of all my just debts funeral and testamentary expenses by my Executors hereinafter named.

2.   I APPOINT my Husband the said James Carter and my Son JOHN CARTER to be the JOINT EXECUTORS AND TRUSTEES of this my Will. ------------------------------------

3.   I GIVE all my clothing and apparel my personal jewellery trinkets and articles of personal use or adornment UNTO my Daughter JANE CARTER absolutely. ------------------------------

4.   I GIVE AND BEQUEATH UNTO my Brother TOM DAVIES the sum of ONE HUNDRED POUNDS if he shall be living at my death. --------

5.   I GIVE DEVISE AND BEQUEATH all my real and personal estate whatsoever and wheresoever not hereby or by any Codicil hereto otherwise specifically disposed of and of which I can dispose by Will in any manner I think proper (hereinafter called 'my Residuary Estate') UNTO my Husband the said James Carter for his own use and benefit absolutely. ----------------

6.   LASTLY I hereby REVOKE all former Wills. -----------------
IN WITNESS whereof I have to this my Will set my hand this Thirty-first day of December One thousand nine hundred and sixty-four. ------------------------------------

ELSIE CARTER

SIGNED by the said ELSIE CARTER as and for her last Will in the presence of us both being present at the same time who in her presence at her request and in the presence of each other have hereunto subscribed our names as witnesses. -------------------

B. Johnson,
The Manor House,
Solihull, Warwickshire.
Company Director.

I. Wilkins,
12 Falstaff Road,
Shirley, Solihull,
Secretary.

Technique development

Notice of meetings

For formal meetings, such as General Meetings, Extraordinary General Meetings, and Committee Meetings, written notices are sent to those entitled to attend. The notice, which is prepared by the sec-retary, should contain details of the date, place, and time of meeting. The salutation and complimentary close may be omitted.

7. Practise typing Notice of Committee Meeting. Read the above explanation. Then type the following notice on A5 (210 × 148 mm) paper in single-line spacing. Left margin 25 mm, right margin 13 mm.

THE CHAMPION LAWN TENNIS ASSOCIATION
73 High Street
NORTHAMPTON

Chairman:
W. B. Sykes

Secretary:
Miss P. Clarke

12th February, 19..

A meeting of the committee of The Champion Lawn Tennis Association will be held in the Committee Room at 73 High Street, on Friday, 27th February, at 7 p.m.

Pauline Clarke
SECRETARY.

8. Type the following in single-line spacing on A4 paper, and keep your typed copy in Folder No. 2 for future reference.

7. Type the following Agreement in double spacing, copying and noting the display.

AN AGREEMENT made this First day of December One thousand nine hundred and sixty-four BETWEEN JOHN BERK of 22 Water Street in the City of Liverpool (hereinafter called "the Licensor") of the one part and CHARLES PAGE of 37 Bogmoor Road, in the City of Glasgow (hereinafter called "the Licensee"), of the other part.
WHEREBY IT IS AGREED as follows:

1. IN CONSIDERATION of the royalties hereinafter stipulated the Licensor grants to the Licensee a sole licence to manufacture the washing machine in accordance with the patent of invention No. AB 824,568 filed on the Tenth day of May One thousand nine hundred and sixty in the United Kingdom and to sell the said machine within the United Kingdom during the continuance of the aforesaid Patent.

2. THE LICENSEE agrees to pay to the Licensor an annual royalty of Two per cent on the nett selling price of the machines made by the Licensee and invoiced by him to his customers, the said royalty to be payable on the Fourteenth day of July and the Fourteenth day of January of each year for the entire duration of the said Patent.

3. THE LICENSEE shall keep proper books of account in regard to the said washing machines manufactured and sold by him under the aforesaid Patent, which books shall at all reasonable times be made accessible to the Licensor for inspection by him or his agent.

AS WITNESS the hands of the parties the day and year first before written.

SIGNED by the said JOHN BERK   )
in the presence of:—   )   JOHN BERK
(Name of witness)   )
(Address)   )
(Occupation)   )

SIGNED by the said CHARLES PAGE)
in the presence of:—   )   CHARLES PAGE
(Name of witness)   )
(Address)   )
(Occupation)   )

8. Practise folding and endorsing a legal document. Study instructions for folding and endorsing legal documents on Page M4 of Reference Manual. Then fold your typed copy of the above Agreement in the correct manner and type the endorsement.

9. Practise typing Notice of Committee Meeting and Agenda. Type the following Notice of Meeting and Agenda on A4 paper, with margins of 25 mm on left and 13 mm on right. Use single-line spacing for the notice, and double-line spacing between the numbered items in the Agenda. Keep your typed copy in Folder No. 2 for future reference.

THE CHAMPION LAWN TENNIS ASSOCIATION
73 High Street
NORTHAMPTON

Chairman: Secretary:
W. B. Sykes   Miss P. Clarke

                                                    12th February, 19..

A meeting of the Committee of the Champion Lawn Tennis Association will be held in the Committee Room at 73 High Street, on Friday, 27th February, at 7 p.m.

A G E N D A

1. Apologies.

2. Secretary to read the Minutes of last meeting.

3. Matters arising out of Minutes.

4. Correspondence.

5. Additional cloakroom facilities. Sub-committee to submit three quotations for consideration.

6. Any other business.

7. Date and time of next meeting.

                                             PAULINE CLARKE
                                                Secretary.

10. Type a copy of the following Notice of Annual General Meeting and Agenda. Use A4 paper, with margins of 25 mm on left and 13 mm on right. Notice to be in single-line spacing, and double spacing between numbered items in the Agenda.

Highfield Youth Club
Bromley Lane, Chislehurst, Kent.

Chairman: Secretary:
H. Wilkes   R. W. Hall

Notice of Annual General Meeting

The Annual General Meeting of the Highfield Youth Club will be held in the Club Hall, Bromley Lane, on Friday, 15th Jany., 1972, & it is hoped tt all members will be able to attend.

Agenda

1. Apologies. 2 Minutes of last Annual General Meeting. 3. Matters arising. 5 Chairman's Report. 6. Treasurer's Report. 4. Correspondence. 7. Election of Officers & Committee. 8 Any other Business.

R. W. Hall
Secretary

In addition to the main rules on the previous page, you should note the following:

Certain words, such as the following, are typed in spaced or unspaced capitals, to make them more prominent:

SPACED CAPITALS: A N   A G R E E M E N T
                           B E T W E E N
                           A L L   T H A T
                           A L L   T H O S E
                           A N D   W H E R E A S
                           T O   H O L D

CLOSED CAPITALS: TOGETHER
                           PROVIDED
                           PROVIDED ALSO
                           IN WITNESS

Also Names of Parties the <u>first time these appear</u>, ~~for~~ the first words or words of each recital, and ~~for~~ the words: SIGNED SEALED AND DELIVERED, also money items, such as THREE HUNDRED POUNDS.

There are 2 clauses which appear at the end of all legal documents, viz.

<u>Testimonial Clause</u> — This appears at end of wording of document and reads: "IN WITNESS whereof the said parties to these presents have hereunto set their hands and seals the day and year first above written." (Note: In the Draft this clause may be abbreviated to: "In witness, etc.").

<u>Attestation Clause</u> — This starts in the margin at 5, and is bracketed at 40 as follows:

SIGNED SEALED AND DELIVERED   )
by the within named (Name in   )
capitals)   )
in the presence of (Name in   )
capitals)   )

(Witness's signature and address
and occupation)

NOTE: The wording of the Attestation Clause may vary slightly in the different documents, but the typist in a solicitor's office always has a copy to guide her.

Insert at 'A' The first word of each paragraph commences at the 20th degree of the scale (or 51 mm from left edge). If numbered, type the figure at the 15th degree (or 38 mm from left edge).

Staff meetings are informal, and the notice of a meeting and agenda are usually sent out in memo. form.

11. Practise typing Notice of Staff Meeting. Type the following memo. on A5 (210 × 148 mm) paper, using margins of 25 mm. Keep your typed copy for future reference in Folder No. 2.

M E M O R A N D U M

To: All Sales Representatives   Date: 17th August, 19..

From: Sales Director

SUBJECT: Sales Meeting

A meeting of Sales Representatives will be held in the Sales Director's office at Head Office at 9 a.m. on Monday, 31st August.

A G E N D A

1. To discuss new lines to be offered next month.

2. To consider the question of discounts.

3. To consider the activities of competitors.

4. Any other business.

12. Type the following notice on A5 paper, using 25 mm. margins.

To: All Directors   Date: 21st August, 19..
From: Co. Secretary

Subject - monthly meeting
A Directors' meeting will be held in the Board Room at 10 a.m. on Tuesday 30th August.
AGENDA
1. Sales figures for August.
2. New office extension
3. Appointment of cost accountant
4. A.O.B. —

Chairman's agenda

The Chairman's Agenda may contain more information than the ordinary agenda. The right-hand side of a Chairman's Agenda is left blank, so that he can write in the decisions reached on the various points. The word AGENDA is centred (in closed capitals) in the left half of the writing line, and the word NOTES is centred (in closed capitals) in the right half of the writing line. The numbers start at the left-hand margin and are repeated at the centre of writing line.

Technique development

6. Type a copy of the following notes in single spacing, with double spacing between paragraphs. Use A4 paper. Keep your typed copy for future reference in Folder No. 2. Make all necessary corrections.

LEGAL WORK

Although you *may* ~~will~~ not be required to type legal documents unless you are employed in a solicitor's office, you should have a general idea of the way in which the most common of such documents are typed and endorsed. A legal document is usually typed 3 times. The first typing is a rough copy, *u.c.* known as a /draft/ The second typing is a /Fair Copy/ which is a neatly typed copy of the rough corrected draft for submitting to a solicitor or client. The final copy is the 'Engrossment' for signature by all the parties concerned. *different* *stet*

There may be slight variations in form in ~~various~~ legal offices, but there are certain basic rules which apply to the typing of all legal documents, the most important of which are as follows:

1. A black ribbon is generally used.

2. A wide left-hand margin is required. *(Insert 'A')*

3. ¹ The Draft is typed in treble spacing to allow room for corrections. This copy may contain abbreviations, & numbers, sums of money and dates may be in figures instead of in words.

4. ³ Punctuation marks are usually omitted to avoid possibility of a double or ambiguous meaning being conveyed, which might lead to lawsuits.

5. All pages are numbered at bottom in centre.

6. ⁴ If the matter contains numbered clauses, a full stop appears at the end of each clause.

7. ⁶ In certain documents, such as a Will or Engrossment of a deed, a red ink line is ruled to fill in any long blank spaces at end of clause, or sometimes a series of unspaced hyphens may be used (----------).

8. The Fair Copy is typed in double spacing and must not contain any abbreviations, alterations or erasures. Figures, money items and dates must be in words.

9. The Engrossment is typed in double spacing and on both sides of the paper. Here also no abbreviations, alterations or erasures are allowed. No words may be divided at line-ends. All figures, money items & dates must be typed in words (House nos. may be in figures).

10. The last page is left blank, as this will bear the Endorsement when the document is folded.

Continued on next page

13. Practise typing Chairman's Agenda. Read the explanation at foot of page 43; type the following on A4 paper in single spacing, with double spacing between numbered items. Left margin 25 mm and right margin 13 mm.

THE YORKSHIRE MOTOR RACING CLUB
105 Bradford Road
YORK

The ANNUAL GENERAL MEETING of THE YORKSHIRE MOTOR RACING CLUB will be held in the Grosvenor Room of the Grand Hotel, York, on Wednesday, 24th August, at 7.30 p.m.

AGENDA   NOTES

1. Ask the Secretary, Mr. Jones,   1.
       to read apologies.

2. Ask Mr. Jones to read Minutes   2.
       of last Annual General
       Meeting.

3. Matters arising. It is antici- 3.
       pated that questions will be
       asked about

       i.   Cancellation of Rally   i.
              last August.

      ii.   The delay in amending   ii.
              the Regulations.

4. Chairman's Annual Report (copy   4.
       attached).

5. Ask Treasurer, Mr. Moss, to   5.
       submit his annual report.

6. Ask members if they have any   6.
       questions.

7. Election of   7.

       i.   Officers   i. (See attached list)

      ii.   Committee   ii.

     iii.   Honorary Auditor.   iii.

8. Any other business   8.

9. Chairman to declare meeting   9.
       closed.

Unit 25

Skill building

Type each line or sentence (A and B) *three* times, and, if time permits, complete your practice by typing each group once as it appears.

A. Review alphabet keys

1.   The child just spent his pocket money buying five dozen extra special fireworks which very quickly went up in smoke.

B. Build speed on common words

2. He has not said when he will send us his bill for the house.
3. Please supply the ten we ordered at the beginning of August.
4. You will remember that that particular item is not required.
5. It seems to me that the sound came from the other direction.

Accuracy/Speed Practice
Five-minute timing

Not more than 3 errors

words

AS.30   A good rule to follow for a kitchen or for any place in which   12
practical work has to be done is the old saying "A place for every-   26
thing and everything in its place." Different people, however, will   39
have different views as to what is the best place for anything, but   53
an important thing to remember is that utensils and food containers   66
should always be put back in precisely the same place after they have   80
been used. Taking and replacing containers should be an automatic   93
procedure. Many people prefer to keep their kitchen saucepans in   106
cupboards instead of on open shelves, probably because they are out of   120
sight, and so the kitchen looks tidier, but other people like to keep   134
their pans on open shelves because they are easy to see, quick to get   148
hold of, and less likely to be damaged. If you prefer to keep your   161
saucepans in cupboards, it is well worth while to have sets so that they   175
will fit into each other. A lot of time can be wasted if you keep your   190
saucepans in one place and the lids in another, so if you cannot put the   204
lids on top of the saucepans, they may be kept on hooks or racks.   217

   The extent to which work in the kitchen can be done more easily and   230
more efficiently is somewhat limited, but it is possible to arrange   244
working surfaces and storage places in such a manner as to suit individual   259
needs and methods. A row of hooks for small cooking tools saves waste of   273
time in searching, particularly if it is near the kitchen stove. Wall   287
cupboards or shelves are also very convenient. These should be low   301
enough to be within arm's reach without being so low that you run the   314
risk of bumping your head. Colanders should also be kept within reach   328
of the sink or cooker.   333

   Moreover, the preparation and mixing of food can often be made less   346
tiring by having a kitchen stool which is adjustable in height and with   361
a rail or step for one's feet. Many kitchen operations can be made less   375
arduous if a little thought is given to them, but these depend on the   389
individual, as no two persons operate in the same way.   (S.I. 1.38) 400

14. Type the following on A4 paper in double-line spacing with margins of 25 mm on left and 13 mm on right. Keep your typed copy for future reference in Folder No. 2.

Notice of Annual General Meeting

As l.c. (?) You wl see from the specimen below there is difference in the display of a notice of meeting & agenda for the Annual General Meeting of a Limited Company, the wording being much more formal. Note the following: /s

Caps. (a) Notice of Meeting is in spaced capitals (three spaces between words) & starts at the margin.

(b) NOTICE IS HEREBY GIVEN is in closed caps., & is indented five spaces from left-hand margin – set tab stop for subsequent lines.

(c) Numbers are typed 3 spaces in from tab. stop. (d) The address of the firm & the date are put at the bottom left-hand side flush with margin. (e) BY ORDER OF THE BOARD, etc., and level w. rt-hand margin.

(one space only between words)

Typist Please display lettered items.

15. Practise typing Notice of Annual General Meeting of Limited Company. Type the following on A4 paper in single-line spacing, with double spacing between numbered items. Margins 25 mm on left and 13 mm on right. Keep your typed copy for future reference in Folder No. 2.

THE BOLTON FURNISHING COMPANY LIMITED

N O T I C E   O F   M E E T I N G

NOTICE IS HEREBY GIVEN that the Tenth Annual General Meeting of the Company will be held at the Queen's Hotel, Bolton, on Friday, 28th April, 19.., at 12 noon, to transact the following business:

1. To receive and consider the Directors' Report and Accounts for year ended 31st December, 19..

2. To confirm the recommendations of the Directors as to the payment of a final dividend.

3. To re-elect one Director.

4. To transact any other business of an Ordinary General Meeting.

Any member entitled to attend and vote at the Meeting whereof notice is hereby given may appoint one or more proxies to attend, and, on a poll, to vote instead of him; a proxy need not also be a member.

The Parade Works,
Summer Hill,
Bolton, Lancashire.

6th April, 19..

BY ORDER OF THE BOARD

A. THOMPSON

SECRETARY

Typist: Mrs. C. W. Robertson of 1231 Bristol Rd., South, Birmingham. B31 12AJ wrote to us last Tuesday about our Save-As-You-Earn Scheme. Please type the follow₃. reply for despatch today.

Dr. Madam, Th. y. f. yr. letter dated . . . . abt our SAYE scheme.

N.P. [SAYE is a five-year contract between y. & the Building Soc. You must agree to save a regular amt ea. month for 5 yrs. Provided y. complete the contract, y. are not paid interest but an equivalent bonus to one year's savings, & on this bonus y. do not pay any income tax. The bonus wl. be equivalent to a compound rate of interest of abt 7%

N.P. n.a. [If y. leave all the money invested for a further 2
H years, y. w. at the end of seven yrs. have a tax free
N.P. bonus doubled. [Unfortunately, there are penalties for stopping before the 5 years are up, although y. always
W.P. get back at least as much as y. hv. pd. in. Please write to me again if y. require further information. Yrs. ffy., EVERLASTING BUILDING SOCIETY LTD., J. MILLS, MANAGER.

representing a gross rate of 12% p.a. to those paying income tax at the standard rate.

(margin note, right side:) representing £1 & £0.

(lower panel)

Here are examples of how yr. savings will accumulate₃

(margin note, top right:) Typist - please display this before last para of letter.

SAVINGS		REPAYMENTS			
		at 5 years		at 7 years	
Monthly	Total for 5 years	Bonus	Bonus plus savings	Double Bonus	Double bonus plus savings
£1	£60	£12	£72	£24	£84
£2	£120	£24	£144	£48	£168
£3	£180	£36	£216	£72	£252
£4	£240	£48	£288	£96	£336
£5	£300				
£10	£600				

(Typist - please complete these columns)

Typist Please prepare the notice and agenda for a Committee meeting of the Mods Club, 196 West George Str., Glasgow C2 which is to be held at the ROYAL HOTEL, Sauchiehall Str., Glasgow, at 8 p.m. on Thursday, 15 July 19—
Please insert appropriate date. Use suitable size paper. The Chairman is Miss L. McLeod. Sec. Miss D. ASHBURN. Items on agenda are I Apologies for absence II Minutes of last Meeting III Matters arising. IV Correspondence V Sub-Committee's report on outing planned for Sept. VI New L.P. Records VII A.O.B. VIII Date and time of next meeting. // Please change Roman to Arabic figures

Please type the notice & Chairman's Agenda for a meeting of the directors to be held in the Board Rm. at 10 a.m. on Fri. 17th Nov. Insert appropriate date. Use paper of suitable size and leave 51 mm at top. Items: Monthly Sales; Appointment of agent in Lancs; Apologies; Any other business; Minutes of last meeting; Matters arising; Resignation of Co. Secretary.
Note: Please put items in correct order & number in Arabic figures

Will you please type a memo. to be circulated to all Heads of Depts. from the Man. Director who wishes them to attend a meeting in the Board Room on Wednesday, 20th Dec. at 10 a.m.
Items (No. in Arabic, please): Need for better time-keeping; Fall in Sales; New Central Filing System; Increase in Canteen prices; Any O.B.

Type the following tabulation with diagonal column headings, and rule.

AVERAGE FAHRENHEIT TEMPERATURES

MONTH.	Athens	Barcelona	Florence	Gibraltar	Lisbon	Marseilles	Milan	Moscow	Naples	Rome	Seville
January	48	43	46	55	51	44	35	8	48	45	52
Feb.	49	48	49	57	54	50	46	18	52	51	60
March	52	50	44	56	52	46	38	9	49	47	56
April	59	52	56	61	58	55	55	30	57	57	64
May	66	58	63	65	60	61	63	41	64	64	70
June	74	69	72	70	67	68	70	53	70	71	78
July	80	74	76	75	71	71	73	56	75	76	85
Aug.	80	73	77	73	70	72	75	66	76	75	86
Sept.	73	69	70	72	68	66	66	46	70	70	78
Oct.	66	62	62	67	62	59	56	34	63	62	68
Nov.	57	58	52	60	67	51	46	22	53	53	60
Dec.	52	54	46	56	62	46	40	12	47	46	54

Type the following abbreviations in alphabetical order, giving their meanings. Set out in 2 columns headed 'Abbreviation' and 'Meaning'.

e.g., viz., ad. val., etc., P.S., N.B., MSS.,
E. & O.E., B.O.A.C., O.B.E., Et seq., M.O.H., V.C.,
B.R.S., C.O.D., E.F.T.A., R.S.V.P., x.d., NUT,
TUC, NATO, NALGO, LEA, C.B.I., D.E.P.,
A.E.U., T.G.W.U., Ph.D., M.A. (cantab), c.i.f.

Unit 9
Skill building

Type each line or sentence (A, B, and C) *three* times. If time permits, complete your practice by typing each group once as it appears.

A. Review alphabet keys

1. The lights of the oncoming bus quite dazzled this weary driver, and the extra jerking probably caused this accident.

B. Build speed on common prefixes

2. convenience, confident, condition, consider, concern, confer
3. We are concerned about the condition of the conference hall.
4. I feel confident that you will confirm the present contract.

C. Build speed on common suffixes

5. settlement, equipment, agreement, shipment, payment, moment.
6. I am in agreement that payment for the shipments is now due.
7. At the moment we have yet to experiment with that equipment.

Accuracy/Speed Practice
Four-minute timing   *Not more than 3 errors*

words

AS.11   One chore which is an essential part of household routine, but which   14
can be a burden if not tackled rightly, is the weekly wash. Badly washed   28
clothes need more frequent replacements, and this means an enormous rise   43
in household expenses.   47

It may be found difficult to recognize the many new textiles on the   60
market today and to know how these should be washed. So, when buying   74
garments, always see that they have a label showing the washing instruc-   89
tions — otherwise you should not buy them.   Then again, there is the   102
question of shrinking, which may happen with such materials as cotton or   117
wool unless they bear a label to the effect that they have been pre-   130
shrunk.   132

Before washing coloured articles, it is advisable to cut off a small   146
piece of the material from a seam or a belt and wash it in the normal way.   161
Then place it between two pieces of white cloth, and press it with a hot   175
iron.   If you find that the colour has run into the white cloth, the   190
garment should not be washed.   194

You should not allow articles of clothing to become too dirty. If   207
you do, drastic methods must be used to clean them, and these may help to   222
destroy the fabric. The sorting of dirty laundry is of the utmost impor-   236
tance. Lightly soiled articles should be passed through two lots of suds,   251
so as to save rubbing. Very dirty garments should be left until last;   265
then the dirt can be loosened in the first lot of suds and afterwards   279
passed into the second suds. Woollen articles should be washed in luke-   293
warm water. On most packets of soap powder or soap flakes the washing   307
temperatures advised for the various types of fabric are shown.   (S.I. 1.34)   320

Display the following tables on A4 paper and rule.

WEST MIDLAND AIR TRANSPORT LTD.

Flights – Birmingham/~~Dublin~~   ← Closed caps. + underscored

minimum check-in-time : 40 mins.   Coach Transport: Public
before take-off   Transport to + from airports

Frequency	Depart	Arrive	Aircraft	Flight No.
Monday, Tues, and Thurs.	1200	1255	Viscount 1-11 jet	WM 827
Wed. — — — —	1500	1555	Viscount 1-11 jet	WM 843
Sat. — — — .	0900	0955	"	WM 933

(Typist. Please transpose these two columns. Aircraft / Flight No.)

Connecting Flights :

West Midland Airway connect at Dublin w. flights to USA + Canada

Fares between Birmingham + Dublin		
Normal Tourist Single Fare Valid one Year	Tourist Excursion Return Fare - Valid one month	
	1st July - 30th Sept.	1st April - 30th June
£9.55	£13.80	£12.75

Technique development

Fractions

Where fractions are not provided on the typewriter, you should use ordinary figures with solidus, e.g., 1/12. Where such fractions are used all other fractions *in the same work* must be made by the use of the solidus, e.g., 5/16, 1/2, 3/4.

If whole numbers appear with fractions of this kind, leave a space between the whole number and fraction, e.g., 1 1/12.

8. Practise fractions. Read the above explanation, then type one copy of the following in double spacing.

We thank you for your letter, and are pleased to inform you that we can supply from stock various dies with bores of 5/32", 3/16", 7/32", 9/32", 5/16", 11/32", as well as larger sizes of 1 1/12", 1 5/12", 1 5/16", 1 7/16", up to 1 13/16".

Minutes

Details of any decisions or resolutions or business discussed at a meeting are recorded and preserved. These are known as Minutes. They are either written in a Minute Book or typed on loose sheets and kept in a Loose Leaf Minute Book. Each Minute is numbered, and a wide margin should be allowed for marginal headings. The Minutes should be written up as soon as possible after the meeting, and the third person and past tense are used. The numbering of the Minutes facilitates indexing.

9. Type the following on A4 paper in single-line spacing with double spacing between numbered items. Keep your typed copy for future reference in Folder No. 2.

ORDER OF MINUTES

1. Description of meeting, including time, date and place.

2. Names of those present — Chairman's name appearing first, followed by the names of the officers.

3. Apologies received.

4. Reading of Minutes of last meeting.

5. Matters arising.

6. Correspondence.

7. Reports of Officers.

8. General business discussed — with details of any resolutions taken.

9. Any other business.

10. Place, date, and time of next meeting.

11. Place for Chairman's signature.

12. Date on which Minutes are signed.

Job 77

Type the following in tabulated form. Use vertical headings and rule.

all caps → Sales Meeting
Underscore headings   January – December 1964 (Attendance Record)

Salesmen	January	February	March	April	May	June	July	Aug:	Sept.	Oct.	Nov.	Dec.	Totals
G. A. LIGHT	X	X	X	X	–	X	X	X	–	X	X	X	10
D. O. WILLIS	X	–	X	X	X	X	X	X	X	X	X	X	11
H. COMPTON													
L. NICHOLSON													
C. HOBART, Jnr.													
C. HOBART, Snr													
A. BOSWELL													
J. GILL–PARSONS													
M. LOMAX													
P. ELLSWORTH													
A. St. John BROWN													
F. SINCLAIR													
~~K. KINGSTON~~													
L. CHARTER													
K. KINGSTON													

Typist Please put names in alpha. order, listing surnames first. I have not completed the attendances, but they were as follows:— Kingston, Compton, Nicholson + Hobart Jnr. were absent in Jan + Nov. Kingston was also absent in Aug. Charter, Boswell, Hobart Snr. & Brown were absent in Feb. Lomax, Gill-Parsons, Ellsworth + Sinclair were absent July, Sept + October. Lomax & Ellsworth were also absent in December.

10. Practise typing Minutes. Type the following on A4 paper in single-line spacing, with double spacing between the numbered Minutes. Set margins and tab stops at points indicated.

<u>MEETING NO. 52</u>

<u>MINUTES</u>

Tab stop 40(35)→A committee meeting of THE CHAMPION LAWN TENNIS ASSOCIATION was held in the Committee Room at 73 High Street, on 27th February, 19.., at 7 p.m.

Present:

Tab stop 45(40)→Mr. W. B. Sykes (Chairman)
Miss G. J. Brown
Miss P. Clarke
Miss J. Coley
Mrs. A. Rigby
Mr. R. C. Sadler

Tab stop 12(10)　　　　Margin 35(30)

1.	Apologies	Apologies were received from Miss H. Cook and Mr. J. Crowe.
2.	Minutes	The Secretary read the Minutes of the meeting held on 22nd November, 19.. These were signed by the Chairman as being a correct record.
3.	Correspondence	There was no correspondence.
4.	Cloakroom facilities	It was proposed by Miss Brown, seconded by Mrs. Rigby, and agreed nem. con., that the quotation from E. Clements Ltd. for £1,250 should be accepted. The Secretary was asked to see that the work was put in hand as soon as possible.
5.	Any other business — Standing Orders	Miss Coley raised the question of a revision of the Standing Orders. RESOLVED: That a sub-committee consisting of Mr. W. B. Sykes, Mrs. A. Rigby, and the Secretary should examine the Standing Orders and submit a draft of any amendments.
6.	Next meeting	It was agreed that the next meeting should be held on 20th April at 7 p.m.

Chairman's Signature

Date

Diagonal headings

The headings of a table are sometimes typed diagonally, as in the table below. This can best be done if the figure columns are all made the same width, which will be the width of the longest line in any of the figure columns. To type such headings the paper will have to be inserted diagonally, and the headings must be typed parallel to the diagonal lines and centred between the two. It is advisable to rule the diagonal lines after the table has been completed, and, when the paper is reinserted to type the headings, the diagonal lines should be aligned with the alignment scale.

The scale-points for these lines must be marked in pencil, and the following procedure should be adopted:

1. Find in the usual way the horizontal spaces required for the column items and spaces between the columns (making all the figure columns the same width). Rule by underscore or ink the top horizontal line, or mark the beginning and end as usual.

2. Find the number of vertical line-spaces required for the headings in the same way as you did for vertical headings (see Page 158). Turn the paper up this number of spaces, and rule or mark the second horizontal line.

3. Along this second line mark in pencil the scale-points for the vertical lines between columns (which will also be the scale-points for the *bottom* of the diagonal lines) and set tab. stops for the start of each column as usual.

Mark the scale-points for the *top* of the diagonal lines as follows: The top of the first diagonal line should be marked at the same scale-point as the second vertical line, the top of the second diagonal line at the same scale-point as the third vertical line, and so on. For the top of the last diagonal line tap the space-bar once for the number of spaces required for the longest line of the column plus 3 extra spaces (to allow for spaces between columns) and mark the top of the last diagonal line at the point reached.

9. Practise typing diagonal headings. Type the following table in double spacing on A4 paper.

MILEAGE CHART

TOWN	Aberdeen	Birmingham	Bristol	Edinburgh	Exeter	Glasgow	London	Liverpool	Manchester	York
Aberdeen	—	403	480	115	555	142	488	326	326	299
Birmingham ..	403	—	88	288	163	289	110	90	80	127
Bristol	480	88	—	365	75	366	116	159	161	215
Edinburgh ...	115	288	365	—	440	44	373	211	211	184
Exeter	555	163	75	440	—	441	170	235	236	290
Glasgow	142	289	366	44	441	—	394	212	212	207
London	488	110	116	373	170	394	—	197	184	145
Liverpool	326	90	159	211	235	212	197	—	35	97
Manchester...	326	80	161	211	236	212	184	35	—	64
York	299	127	215	184	290	207	145	97	64	—

11. Type the following on A4 paper in single-line spacing, with double between the numbered items. All paragraphs, other than the first, should be hanging paragraphs where applicable. All numbers to be copied as written. Keep your typed copy for future reference in Folder No. 2.

LITERARY MATTER

For / typing of work such as short stories, books, theses, lectures, etc., ~~there are~~ the follow'g will be a guide:—

1. Size of paper : A4 - one side only is used.

2. Spacing : Double - to leave room for corrections or additions.

3. Margins : Left-hand / wide, usually 38 mm so th. sheets can be bound or fastened together. Right / hand 13 mm to 25 mm. Top & bottom margins equal - first line of matter starting 25 mm from top & last line ending 25 mm from bottom. [To ensure uniform top + b'm margins on ea. sheet, adopt one of the follow'g methods :

Insert 'A' here → (a) Rule a heavy line on backing sheet (wh is usually (b) wider than the typing ~~line~~ paper) across / complete width of sheet 25 mm from the top & at a point 25 mm from bottom.

4 Pagination (h numbering of pages) : First page is not numbered, second & subsequent pp are numbered 13 mm from top in Arabic figures & in / centre of / page; viz. - 2 - (dash, space, number, space, dash. Numbering is continuous throughout / Prefaces are usually numbered in small Roman numerals.

7 ¶ Throughout the whole work, the layout for chapter headings, use of capitals, numbering, etc., must be consistent.

5 ¶ Chapter headings + numbers : The 1st page of a chapter may be in the form of a "Dropped Head", i.e., the chapter no. is typed 51 mm to 76 mm from / top edge in roman numerals or

not separately for ea. chapter

7. Type the following on A5 paper. Use vertical headings and rule.

RETAIL PRICES IN THE EEC + THE UK   (In full please)

	milk	Butter	cheese	Sugar	Bread
	£*	£‡	£‡	£‡	£‡
Belgium	0·08	0·87	0·64	0·16	0·09
France	0·07	0·81	0·79	0·12	0·15
Germany	0·09	0·80	0·81	0·13	0·13
Italy	0·10	1·05	1·38	0·17	0·14
Netherlands	0·08	0·82	0·65	0·13	0·09
U.K.	0·09	0·37	0·39	0·18	0·09

* Price per litre
‡ Price per kilo

Rearranging tabular matter

1. It is often necessary to rearrange the matter. Before starting to type it is essential that you make a rough plan of what has to be done.

2. When columns in tabulation are very wide, it is necessary to consider where space can be saved. The following hints will be of help to you in such cases.

(a) If the longest lines of the columns are in the headings, additional lines may be taken for these, so as to reduce the width required for the columns.

(b) If the longest lines are in the descriptive column, the length of these lines may be reduced by taking extra lines for lengthy items. If this is done, allowance must be made for these extra lines when calculating the number of vertical lines required.

(c) As a last resort, you may have to leave two spaces instead of three between columns, or even to omit spaces before and after the vertical lines.

(d) To save vertical spaces, it may be necessary to omit spaces before and after horizontal lines, or to use half-spacing before and after these lines.

8. Display the following in tabulated form and rule.

SEA PASSENGER MOVEMENT BY PORTS

In thousands

Port	January to September		
	To U.K.	From U.K.	Total

Column 1 - Dover, Folkestone, Harwich, Hull, London, Newhaven, Southampton, Tyne Ports.
Column 2 - 1132, 336, 271, 8, 32, 175, 58, 59
"   3 - 1130, 362, 288, 7, 31, 174, 63, 61
"   4   2262, 698, 559, 15, 63, 349, 121, 120

Arabic nos. The heading is typed on the 3rd single-line space below / chapter no. in capital letters & centred.

N.B. *Footnotes*: Typed as explained on p.22 in single-line spacing.

stet

lc

8. Correction of errors: The Typist is expected to correct errors in spelling, grammar, or punctuation. Where a word can be spelt in two ways, the same spelling must be adopted throughout.

9. Words to be printed in italics must be under-scored.

Insert at 'A'

(a) Put a light pencil mark 25 mm from top A bottom edge of sheet before this is inserted in machine

12. Practise typing literary matter. Type the following chapter of a story in double-line spacing. Make all corrections indicated, and also correct any spelling, punctuation, etc.

caps → { OUR FARM. Chapter I }   Please type as dropped head

uc   Winter had arrived at the farm. Conditions were /
lc   same all over / country, but the fact was of little
⊙   importance to Ethel & myself. We were for it, & it
⅄   made us proud to think th we, at least, were prepared
NP   for the worst. [We had always made plans for the
      winter wherever we had bn, but this yr it was
      different.

Runon   We were not so concerned for ourselves, we   ℅
      had frost & suffered (together) many winters, but now
stet /   our principle thoughts were centred concerned on our little
⅄   stock of cattle, & we wondered how it wd be affected
NP   if the winter were a severe one. [Being responsable
tousp   for a heard of cattle was something new, &, although

Vertical column headings

To find the number of line-spaces to be left between the first and second horizontal lines to allow for the vertical headings, count the number of characters and spaces in the longest line of the heading and add two extra spaces (i.e., one space before and one space after the heading). Then convert this number into single-line spaces as in the following example:

Assuming the longest line of all vertical headings takes up 16 horizontal spaces, the total number of horizontal spaces required is 16 plus 2 = 18. As there are 6 single-line spaces in 25 mm (1"), there are 9 single-line spaces in 38 mm (1½"). You should therefore turn up 9 single-line spaces after the first horizontal line, then turn up one more space and type the second horizontal line.

Another method of finding the amount of space required for vertical headings is to type the longest heading on a piece of paper and measure the space needed. When the paper is reinserted for the headings to be typed, see that the alignment scale is level with the vertical line already ruled (or marked) and arrange the heading in such a way that it is spaced equally between the 2 vertical lines. Also when typing the headings, remember to leave one clear space before and after.

NOTE: With vertical headings it is better for each heading to start at the point fixed for the longest line of the heading.

6. Practise tabulation with vertical headings. Type the following on A4 paper in double spacing. Rule in ink.

SHARE INDICES

Groups and Sub-Sections	Monday March 9	Friday March 6	Thursday March 5	Wednesday March 4	Tuesday March 3
Capital Goods					
Aircraft	106.08	106.00	106.53	106.90	106.62
Building Material	140.66	141.75	141.98	143.27	143.20
Engineering	109.70	109.91	110.16	110.33	110.62
Machine Tools	93.73	94.01	93.04	92.75	92.62
Miscellaneous	98.50	98.16	98.25	98.40	97.76
Consumer Goods	102.53	102.62	102.60	102.93	103.07
Electrical	105.44	104.86	105.19	106.10	106.17
Household Goods	124.81	125.61	124.95	125.00	125.54
Rubber Goods	101.43	101.43	101.63	101.48	102.67
Other Groups					
Chemicals	115.42	115.41	115.61	115.41	115.93
Oil	151.63	152.25	152.89	152.77	153.17
Shipping	141.79	142.44	142.54	142.96	143.96

le we had managed fairly well in the summer & Autumn, we
had no experience of safeguarding a heard through/cold
more winter days, +/ especially, the cold nights.

    I decided th I shd have to hv a vehical of
some kind, whether car or tractor I must decide f.
c/skf myself/ I did not mention this to Ethel ~~partly~~ particularly because
I did not want to worry her, but I must admit
th /\ I was afraid she wd make up my mind for me.
I/ N.P. ~~That was~~ (my principle reason was). [During one of my
a friend/ jaunts to / village, I asked/ for his advise. He
prs. tried to persuade me th a car was / only (thing possible).
I argued against it, but when he pointed out th
we could use it for going into / village to do our
shopping, I allmost agreed, but there still remained
a doubt in my mind.

    I almost wished I had confided in Ethel, &
asked/ /\ her for her advise, but / obstinasy of / male
prevailed against it. How, I thought, wd a
H/ second/hand car, even w special tyres, cope w.
H/ ?/ / mud & slush of / country/side in / winter time/
Surely a tractor wd be a better proposition, but /\
our beingh how cd we, in the 1st flush of/ landowners go
P/ shopping in a tractor/ & this weighed heavily on
my mind —
rumor It wd be better than a bicycle, wh I / at present, used/
fs. but did not seem to fit [very well in] w our ideas
of a simple country life. Then again, I thought,
what wd our new neighbours think/ when we (h and say)
parked our tractor at the market alongside
?/ NP their sometimes gleaming cars/ [In the end
for me/h Ethel solved the problem/ by suggesting th we shd
buy a tractor for / farm & a bicycle for shopping.

Unit 24

Skill building

Type each exercise (A and B) *once* for practice, *once* for speed, and finally *once* for accuracy.

A. Review alphabet keys

1.   The Fair was a blaze of light, and many youths and boys
even queued to join in the exceptional fun on the cake-walk.

B. Improve control of figure keys

2.   tie 583 row 492 you 697 eye 363 wit 285 your 6974 tire 5843.
3.   Add 7,578, 4,600, 1,250, 8,543, 839, 795, 124, 120, 109, 99,
94, 83, 74, 62, 54, 37, 26, 9, and the total will be 24,496.
4.   1122, 2233, 3344, 4455, 5566, 6677, 7788, 8899, 9900, 01234.
5.   2345, 3456, 4567, 5678, 6789, 7890, 8901, 9012, 0123, 12345.

Accuracy/Speed Practice
Four-minute timing   *Not more than 3 errors*

		words

AS.29   Which is better: to be an expert — a specialist — in some one   **12**
direction, or to be a good all-rounder?   **20**

   In our modern world we need both. We could not do without the   **32**
services of specialist physicians and surgeons, and in the sciences we   **46**
owe much to specialists in research. It has been said that specialists   **61**
are persons who know more and more about less and less, so that the time   **75**
may come when they know everything about nothing.   **85**

   For beginners in business or those preparing for business, we feel   **98**
that they should aim at good all-round knowledge, ability, and skill.   **112**
Get the best accuracy and speed you can in typewriting and, at the same   **126**
time, give proper attention to office practice, business arithmetic, and,   **141**
above all, to that basic study without which all else is of little or no   **155**
value — English.   **158**

   You may say that you have been 'doing' English for the past ten   **171**
years or so, and this is no doubt true. However, as you have worked   **184**
through the manuscript exercises in this book, you will have realized   **198**
that, without a good knowledge of the use of words, you cannot expect to   **212**
be an accurate and fast typist. By English we mean ordinary, practical   **226**
English, which covers such matters as knowing when to write 'there' and   **240**
'their', or 'here' and 'hear'; knowing with reasonable certainty where   **254**
to put in commas, semicolons, and full stops; where to start a new para-   **269**
graph, where to use a capital letter, whether to use words or figures.   **283**
In brief, you should be sure of those simple conventions of written   **296**
English which you must know when you are typing a letter which your   **310**
employer will sign without feeling ashamed of it.   **(S.I. 1.37) 320**

Production typing

Job 23 Production Target—*8 minutes*

Type the following Manuscript in the correct form on A4 paper, making all necessary corrections, both those indicated and any errors you may find.

CHAPTER II

Centre in all caps → Enquiry into the cost of Industrial Movement

Today we are all cost conscious. Much study has bn. devoted to ~~lowering~~ increasing costs & increasing / productivity of british industries. But / most investigations have concentrated of on methods of management, little has bn. said abt the effect on costs of the location of the factory. In recent years, however, interest in location has quickened. The board of trade has therefore indicated research into a number of aspects of industrial location. The National Institute of Economic & social research* has undertaken the most ambitious study of this question.

This has bn. made possible by the co-operation of a no. of firms who ~~has~~ have voluntarily supplied confidential information to the National Institute. * "The Cost of Industrial Movement" by W. F. Luttrell (Cambridge Univ. Press)

[and production]

Job 24 Production Target—*6 minutes*

Type the following Menu on A5 (148 × 210 mm) paper, arranging the Courses in the correct order, and making corrections as marked. Insert date.

The White Horse Hotel Painswick Gloucestershire

~~Dinner~~ Luncheon

Cream of Tomato Soup or Honeydew melon Lemon Meringue, Fresh Fruit Salad, Sherry Trifle. Grilled Fillet of Plaice or Roast Duckling ~~with Apple Sauce~~ Red Currant Jelly Orange Salad Roast and Creamed Potatoes Garden Peas. Coffee. Cheese & Biscuits

Production typing

Job 76   Production Target—*35 minutes*

Type the following table on A4 paper in single spacing. Rule all lines in ink.

TURNOVER OF WORLD TRADE

World Trade Turnover*

	1938	1950	1962	1963	1964‡
in milliards of U.S. dollars					
Industrial countries:					
Western Europe —					
E.E.C.	10.5	20.5	47.4	45.7	49.5
E.F.T.A	10.5	21.7	36.7	35.1	37.1
Other Countries "	1.4	4.1	6.7	6.4	6.8
Total for Western Europe ..	22.4	46.3	90.8	87.2	93.4
United States‡ and Canada	7.3	26.2	47.0	43.1	46.1
Japan	1.5	1.8	7.1	5.9	7.1
Total for industrial countries	31.2	74.3	144.9	136.2	146.6
Non-industrial countries					
Latin America	3.2	12.4	18.0	16.7	16.5
Other Countries	10.0	30.4	46.6	44.1	44.7
Total for non-industrial countries	13.2	42.8	64.6	60.8	61.2
World trade turnover ..	44.4	117.1	209.5	197.0	207.8

* Excluding trade between the U.S.S.R., eastern European countries + mainland china.
‡ Preliminary.
‡ Including military aid shipments.

UNIT 23   156

Type the following Minutes of Meeting in the correct form, making all corrections. Use A4 paper. All Roman numerals to be changed to Arabic numbers.

I
uc.
trs

Board Meeting No. 35. Minutes. A meetg of the Board of ~~present~~ directors was held at the registered office of the Co. on (March) 17th 19—— at 10 am. Present: Mr. C. H. Fullard (Chairman) Messrs. F. Chamberlain, B. J. Round, ~~F. Budge~~ Mrs. J. Watkins (Directors). In attendance: Mr. A. Randle (Auditor) Mr. C. Sanders (Sec.) I Apologies — Mrs. F. Budge regretted that she was unable to attend III Matters arising II Minutes — the Sec. read the minutes of the Board Meeting held on 16th April Feb. Mr. Round said that the new factory at Barry, Glam. wd. be ready by June of next year. IV Subscriptions — It was decided to cease membership of the British Institute of Marketing and that the Sec. should give notice. V A.O.B. — Sick Pay: It was proposed by Mr. Fullard, seconded by ~~Mr. Budge~~ Mrs. Watkins, and agreed unanimously that the instructions about deductions of National Health Sick pay from salary paid during sickness, as outlined in Minute No. 33/6, shd. be circulated to monthly-paid staff only. VI Next meeting — as the date of the next meeting wd. fall on Good Friday, it was agreed that the Board shd. meet on 10th April at 10. a.m.

immediate

lc.

<u>Note to Typist</u> In No. II after 16th Feb. insert: After approval by the meeting, the Chairman signed the Minutes.

Type the following ticket as effectively as you can on post card-size paper.

Youth Ball at the Locarno Ballroom Friday 27th April. Novelty prizes. Dancing 8 pm. to one am. Tickets 30p. Holder will be required to show ticket on entering or leaving the balcony area.

Job 75

Type a copy of the following table in single-line spacing on A4 paper (297 × 210 mm); i.e., insert lengthwise in machine. All underscored headings in the first column should have a clear line-space above and below them. Rule all lines in ink and insert leader dots.

Analysis of Vacancies Notified & Filled

All districts *and districts*

Group	All districts				Centre	
	Notified		Filled		Notified	Filled
	Boys	Girls	Boys	Girls	Total	Total
Practical / Constructional						
Indoor						
Designing, making or repairing in						
Metal	1,357	2,165	2,709	685	7,133	3,394
Wood	288	7	196	2	295	198
Or materials	4,968	2,060	679	920	3,417	1,599
Outdoor						
Building & Civil Engineering	1,203	—	751	—	1,203	751
Agriculture	86	6	55	4	92	59
Scientific & Medical						
Laboratory & Scientific Jobs	188	60	38	8	248	116
Medical, Nursing, etc.	33	108	—	80	141	80
Personal Service						
Sales Work	1,395	2,084	639	833	3,479	1,472
Hotel & Catering	110	205	57	59	315	116
Clerical / Administrative						
General Office	1,200	2655	433	1053	3855	1486
Shorthand - Typists	—	356	—	136	356	136
Office Machines	152	750	64	236	902	300
TOTAL	10,980	10,456	5621	4016	21,436	9,637

Unit 10

Skill building

Type the alphabetic review *once* for practice, *once* for speed, and finally *once* for accuracy.

Review alphabet keys

1.   A junior executive of the firm was asked to explain the
question raised by a young man who seems very hazy about it.

Accuracy/Speed Practice
Five-minute timing   *Not more than 3 errors*

words

AS.12 Science fiction is a term we link with weird creatures from outer	13
space or strange objects flying through the shadowy night. Should we	27
not have more respect for science fiction? I think we should, because	41
so many of the tools used in science and space travel are things that	55
I read about in science fiction.	61
I remember reading that strange story about a ship that could travel	75
beneath the oceans of the world and it was powered by energy from the	89
sea. In my young days the author was laughed at for writing such fan-	103
tasy. Today there are submarines that stay submerged for as long as a	117
year and they are powered by atomic energy. Then there was that tall	130
tale about a visit to the moon — at a time when the only means of flight	144
was a balloon. Today, man has landed on the moon on three different	158
occasions and returned safely.	164
I also enjoyed reading that tale about a machine that could take a	177
person forward or backward in time. As far as I know, such a machine	191
has not been made, but, at this very moment, some genius may be hard at	205
work on such an invention. Would it be wise to look into the past? Or,	220
what is more to the point, would it be a good thing to look ahead to the	234
year 2001 and see what is in store? I often look back with joy, but the	248
thought of looking forward frightens me.	256
Of course, science fiction was not confined to story books. There	270
have been many motion pictures that dealt with this subject and showed,	284
for the first time, the strange objects described in books. The men	298
from outer space always had a ray gun as part of their standard equipment,	312
and what a useful weapon it was — to the space men at any rate. Now earth	327
men have harnessed a ray called the laser beam. It is used as a cutting	341
tool.	342
Which came first, fiction or fact? Did scientists read the fiction	356
books and make up their minds to invent the things described in them?	370
Or were the writers of the books prophets who could predict what would	384
take place in the future? Will the present fictitious flying submarine	398
become fact? **(S.I. 1.28)**	400

Tabular work frequently has footnotes to explain some reference to the figures or details in the table. The same rules apply to these footnotes and their corresponding reference signs in the body of the table as those already explained for manuscript work, i.e., the footnotes are typed underneath the table in single-line spacing, with double spacing between each. The reference sign in the body is typed immediately after the item to which it refers without a space being left. In the footnote the reference sign is typed (usually as a superior character) and one space is left after it.

13. Type a copy of the following table in double-line spacing, and rule in ink on the typewriter. Insert leader dots.

DEVELOPMENT AREAS

The following table gives the numbers of persons registered as unemployed and the percentage rates of unemployment in each of the Development Areas at 16th November, 19 . .

Development Area	Number of unemployed persons on registers at 16th November, 19 . .			Percentage rate of unemployment*	
	Males	Females	Total	Males	Females
North-Eastern	28,653	9,125	37,778	3.8	3.0
West Cumberland	1,540	591	2,131	3.7	3.7
Scottish	40,796	15,117	55,913	5.3	3.6
South Wales and Monmouthshire	14,946	6,606	21,552	2.9	3.5
Wrexham	947	529	1,476	3.3	5.2
South Lancashire	2,337	1,726	4,063	2.3	3.3
Merseyside	672	682	1,354	1.3	1.8
North-East Lancashire	19,329	5,793	25,122	3.0	3.2
Total, all Areas	109,220	40,169	149,389	4.1	3.2

* Number registered as unemployed expressed as percentage of the estimated total number of employees (employed and unemployed).

Technique development

Poetry

The following rules are a guide to the typing of poems:

1. *Positioning:* The longest line of the verse must be centred on the page horizontally, with uniform margins all round.

2. *Spacing:* Single-line spacing, double between verses.

3. If alternate lines rhyme, these usually begin at the same scale-point (unless they are of irregular length, when they are centred). The first line and all lines rhyming with it are written at the margin, while the second and all lines rhyming with it are indented two spaces from the start of the first, third, etc., lines. (Short lines may be indented more than two spaces.)

(b) In blank verse (i.e., where no lines rhyme), all lines also start at margin.

(c) When lines are of approximately equal length, and when successive lines rhyme, these start at the margin, i.e., there is no indentation.

(d) If all lines rhyme, these all start at the margin.

4. Each line starts with a capital letter.

2. Practise typing poems. Read and study the above explanation, and then type each of the following poems on A5 paper. Keep your typed copies for future reference in Folder No. 2.

(a) Alternate lines rhyme

The Brook

```
I chatter over stony ways,
   In little sharps and trebles,
I bubble into eddying bays,
   I babble on the pebbles.

              Alfred Tennyson
```

(b) Blank verse

```
To be, or not to be — that is the question:
Whether 'tis nobler in the mind to suffer
The slings and arrows of outrageous fortune,
Or to take arms against a sea of troubles,
And by opposing end them?  To die — to sleep:
No more; and, by a sleep, to say we end
The heart-ache, and the thousand natural shocks
That flesh is heir to — 'tis a consummation
Devoutly to be wish'd.  To die — to sleep:
To sleep! perchance to dream: ay, there's the rub.

                     William Shakespeare
```

(c) Successive lines rhyme

To the Daisy

```
With little here to do or see
Of things that in the great world be,
Sweet Daisy! oft I talk to thee
      For thou art worthy,
Thou unassuming commonplace
Of Nature, with that homely face,
And yet with something of a grace
      Which love makes for thee!

                     W. Wordsworth
```

Apart from the use of the underscore, on most modern typewriters provision is made for the speedy ruling of both horizontal and vertical lines. On the alignment scale you will find two small notches or round holes. Place the point of a pencil or suitable ball pen in one of these notches or holes and hold it in position against the paper with the right hand. With the left hand on the carriage release, by running the carriage along you will obtain a continuous horizontal line. To avoid running the carriage too far, it is advisable to stop about two spaces before the scale-point at which the horizontal line is to end, and then tap the space-bar until the scale-point is reached.

To make a vertical line, instead of running the carriage along you release the platen ratchet by means of the interliner and turn the platen up with the left-hand knob. If the vertical lines extend almost to the bottom of the page, it is better to rule these by hand after the paper has been removed from the machine, to avoid the paper slipping when the platen is turned down for the start of the next line. After you have had some practice in ruling in this way, you will find that it saves a great deal of time, particularly if carbon copies are being taken.

12. Practise ruling on the typewriter. Read the above explanation, and then type the following in double-line spacing on A5 paper. Rule all lines as explained above.

FINANCIAL MANAGEMENT

Average Salaries according to age group

Age Group	Average Emoluments £	Range		Recent Annual Percentage Increase %
		Lowest £	Highest £	
25-29	1500	900	1700	21
30-34	1700	1000	1800	13
35-39	1800	1100	2300	14
40-44	2000	1500	3000	11

1. Where the 'Particulars' or 'Description' column has no heading, but has a long dash to represent the printer's dash, five consecutive hyphens should be typed centrally. One hyphen only is not sufficient. The underscore may also be used to represent the dash, but as this necessitates the use of the interliner to ensure that the underscore is centrally typed, it is better to use hyphens instead of the underscore.

2. In figure columns, where the figures run into thousands, three consecutive hyphens should be typed to represent a blank; one hyphen is not sufficient in this case.

3. No abbreviations, apart from those words which are always abbreviated, should appear in tabulation work. An exception is made in column headings when it is necessary to save horizontal spaces.

The following rules will be a guide to you if you are called upon at any time to type a play.

1. *Size of paper:* A4.

2. *Spacing:* Single-line spacing. Double after each actor's words.

3. *Margins:* Left-hand: Wide (63 mm) to allow room for typing of names of characters and for binding. Right-hand margin: 13 mm to 25 mm.

4. *Names of characters:* In capitals and underlined, starting 25 mm from left edge of paper; set tab. stop here and use margin release when typing names of characters in left margin. If long, abbreviate these.

5. *Speeches:* Start at margin. Indent first line of each speech 5 spaces.

6. *Stage directions:* Short stage directions typed in middle of typing line between margins. Long ones start at margin set for body. All unspoken words of any kind typed in red in brackets, or typed in black and underlined in red ink.

7. *Numbering of pages:* Pages numbered consecutively throughout—generally at foot in centre and in Arabic numbers.

8. *Introductory pages:* The usual arrangement of these is as follows:
Page 1: Title page—Title and type of play, and author's name in capitals.
Page 2: Synopsis of Acts and Scenery—Acts and numbers of Acts in capitals.
Page 3: List of characters in capitals and cast in small letters. Also sometimes list of costumes.

3. Practise typing play. Read and study the above explanation, and then type the following on A4 paper, using separate sheets for each of the first three introductory pages, and displaying these correctly. Keep your typed copy for future reference in Folder No. 2.

Title page:
(Centre vertically and horizontally)

Margin
12(10)

35(30)

Page 2

40(35)

Page 3:

Page 1 of play

30(25)

Leave 76 mm at top

<u>ONE-ACT PLAY</u>

Period — Ca. 1910

I M P R I N T   F O R   M U R D E R

by

P. C. PRATT

SCENE: The Superintendent's Office at a
        London Police Station.

        The Superintendent's desk is sited right
centre with window behind, right. Door, left
centre. Chairs at both sides of desk, and at back.
Hatstand upper left. Bookcase back centre.

                    CHARACTERS

SUPERINTENDENT
A GENTLEMAN
POLICE CONSTABLE
LUCY BRANT (Wife of Harry Brant)
STAN. LEWIS (A 'mobster')
MRS. ALLEN (Mother to Lucy)
HARRY BRANT (First Suspect)

        <u>I M P R I N T   F O R   M U R D E R</u>

<u>DISCOVERED</u> <u>The Superintendent working at his desk.</u>
<u>He looks up as, following a knock, the door</u>
<u>opens. Enter a gentleman of some fifty years</u>
<u>of age. He is wearing a full-skirted frock</u>
<u>coat and carries a top hat. The Superintendent</u>
<u>springs to his feet.</u>

Leader dots

Leader dots (full stops) are used to guide the eye along lines of figures from one column to another. There are four methods of grouping which can be used, viz.

1. One dot three spaces .   .   .   .

2. Two dots three spaces ..   ..   ..

3. Three dots two spaces ... ...

4. Continuous dots ....

The best grouping is the second, i.e. two dots three spaces. It is not advisable to use continuous dots, unless the column containing leader dots (usually the first descriptive column) is only narrow, and then not more than six continuous dots should be used.
Type leader dots lightly and evenly.
If any item in the column takes more than one line, the leader dots should be typed only on the last line of the item.
Care must be taken to see that the groups of dots come underneath one another in all lines. To ensure this, you should adopt the following procedure: Bring the carriage to the first tab. stop set for the first column of figures; back-space once for every space between first and second columns plus an extra two spaces. At this point set tab. stop. Back-space 5 from the tab. stop just set, and set another tab. stop. Continue in this way until you have approximately reached the last word of the shortest line in particulars column. Bring carriage back to margin and type first line, using tab. bar to insert leader dots if and when required.

NOTE: There must always be at least one space between the last word and first group of dots or the last dot and the vertical line, i.e. leader dots must never be typed right up to preceding or following word or line, and no word or letter must be allowed to extend beyond the last leader dot on the line although leader dots may extend beyond the last word.

11. Practise typing table with leader dots. Read the above explanation, and then type a copy of the following table in single spacing on A5 paper.

PRESCRIPTIONS BY MEDICAMENT CLASS

Medicament Class	Estimated Total		Average Net Ingredient Cost per Prescription in pence
	Number of Prescriptions in millions	Net Ingredient Cost £ millions	
Tablets, capsules, lozenges ..	109.9	42.3	93
Mixtures, linctuses, etc. ..	53.4	8.3	38
Eye, ear, nasal drops, etc. ..	5.7	0.8	36
Injections, etc.	2.6	2.1	193
Other liquid preparations ..	8.5	2.2	62
Ointments, pastes, etc. ..	15.5	4.4	67
Other solids, etc.	3.4	1.2	87
Trusses and hosiery	0.8	1.1	325
Total	199.8	62.4	——

12(10) <u>SUPER</u>.   30(25)   Well, well, sir! Come in, come in! Delighted
to see you after this long time. Take this chair,
sir.

<u>GENTLEMAN</u>   (Seats himself at end of Superintendent's desk)

Nice to see you, Superintendent. I have been
visiting an old servant who lives close by — and
won't be living here or anywhere else very long, I
fear. Couldn't miss the chance to have a word with
you. I hope you are not too busy?

<u>SUPER</u>.   I'm very glad you did call, sir. I'm not all
that busy. The only important matter at the moment
is a local murder. All straightforward and cut-and-
dried. Nothing to interest you, I'm afraid.

<u>GENTLEMAN</u>   I'm easily interested, Superintendent. Do tell
me about it.

<u>SUPER</u>.   Very well. The murdered man was a rather
unsavoury character, a money-lender by the name of
Solly Isaacs. He was also strongly suspected of
being a 'fence', and not above a spot of blackmail
if opportunity offered.

<u>GENTLEMAN</u>   H'm! A very promising subject for murder.

<u>SUPER</u>.   Yes, indeed! He was found in his office by
the cleaner first thing this morning with a bullet
in his head, and the murder weapon, a revolver, on
the floor near by. An anonymous communication put
us on to a local lad named Harry Brant; so we
picked him up, and, sure enough, his prints are
all over the weapon, while his only alibi rests on
the evidence of his wife.

<u>GENTLEMAN</u>   It sounds almost too cut-and-dried.

<u>SUPER</u>.   Well, the gun is his, and he can't explain
its presence on the scene of the crime. I've sent
it, with the bullet the surgeon recovered, to
Scotland Yard for matching up.

<u>GENTLEMAN</u>   Of course, Superintendent, you won't need me
to tell you that, if a man owns a gun, the fact of
his finger-prints being on it is less remarkable
than if they were not. And would any murderer today
leave his gun behind complete with prints?

<u>SUPER</u>.   There is that, of course, sir; but Brant is only
a young chap and may well have lost his head.

Technique development

Tables with subdivided columns

Tabular statements sometimes have columns with subdivisions, each of which has a main heading which has to be centred right across the subdivided columns, and also separate headings for each subdivision. In such cases, it is advisable to type these headings first. The specimen below is an example of such a table, and the steps explained under the table will give you an idea of how to proceed.

10. Practise typing table with subdivided columns. Type the following table on A5 paper (210 × 148 mm) in double spacing.

SINGLE-SUBJECT EXAMINATIONS

Subject	Number of Papers Worked	Results		
		1st Class	2nd Class	Failed
Arithmetic	5,400	900	1,800	2,700
Commerce	1,456	35	485	936
Economics	1,858	22	619	1,217
English Language	14,120	706	6,956	6,458
Office Practice	132	11	63	58
Typewriting	28,760	2,771	9,586	16,403

1. Proceed as usual as far as marking the beginning and end of first horizontal line.

2. Along this line mark as usual the scale-points for the vertical lines which extend to the top, and set the tab. stops for the start of each column including the subdivided columns.

3. Bring carriage to tab. stop for start of column with subdivisions, and centre the heading above the subdivided columns.

4. Mark in the beginning and end of the horizontal line underneath this heading, and along this line mark scale-points for the vertical lines of subdivided columns.

5. Type the headings of each of these columns, starting at the tab. stop already set for each, as these headings are the longest lines.

6. Turn up one single-line space and mark beginning and end of second horizontal line.

7. Then proceed to type headings of the remaining columns, bearing in mind that these must be centred vertically between the top horizontal line and the bottom line above the column items. This is done by finding the number of single spaces between the two horizontal lines and then typing the headings halfway between them.

8. When ruling the vertical lines for the subdivided columns, see that you do not extend them right up to the top.

GENTLEMAN	And how about motive?
SUPER.	Isaacs' records show that Brant had borrowed a sizeable sum to start a small business, and was behind with the repayment. Isaacs was not a pleasant chap when one of his victims couldn't pay up. He may well have goaded Brant beyond endurance.

(Knock at the door)

Ah! This may be Scotland Yard's report on the revolver. Come in!

(Enter a constable with a box)

CONSTABLE	From Scotland Yard, sir.
SUPER.	Right, let's have it.

(He takes box and removes lid)

Exit constable

Single actor's parts

Single-part copies are the parts of a single actor separated from the remainder of the play to help memorising. Note the following rules:

Size of paper: A5.

Spacing: Double (single-spacing for stage directions).

Margins: Left-hand 13 mm, right-hand 13 mm.

Speech: Indent first line 5 spaces. Set tab. stop. Subsequent lines start at margin.

Stage directions: As for complete play (see No. 6 on page 57).

Cues: To enable the actor to know when it is his turn to speak, the closing words of the previous speaker are given as cues. These start about the middle of the line, and are preceded by continuous leader dots. All cues and unspoken words are either typed with red ribbon, or they are typed in black underlined in red ink.

4. Practise typing single actor's part. Read and study the above notes and then type the following on A5 paper. Keep your typed copy for future reference in Folder No. 2.

GENTLEMAN

.... Take this chair, sir.

Nice to see you, Superintendent. I have been visiting an old servant who lives close by — and won't be living here or anywhere else very long, I fear. Couldn't miss the chance to have a word with you. I hope you are not too busy?

...........to interest you, I'm afraid.

I'm easily interested, Superintendent. Do tell me about it.

.... if opportunity offered.

H'm! A very promising subject for murder.

.... on the evidence of his wife.

Unit 23

Skill building

Type each line or sentence (A, B, and C) *three* times. If time permits, complete your practice by typing each group once as it appears.

A. Review alphabet keys

1. The big garden adjoining a quaint cottage was kept very trim and the gaily-coloured azaleas were exceptionally fine.

B. Build speed on common word drill

2. please happy leave given paper money cause begin out say the

3. I am happy to say that he has given some money to the cause.

4. Before I begin to hand out the papers, ask her for her book.

5. Please tell her that I will leave here in about three hours.

C. Build speed on fluency drill

6. They said that they must plan each week what they must sell.

7. Last year that same call came when they were away from home.

8. Each must hear what that girl will talk over with Jill Wood.

9. This plan from some club made both boys very busy last week.

Accuracy/Speed Practice
Three-minute timing   *Not more than 3 errors*

AS.28   words

We can well understand your concern over the increased rate for our insur- 15
ances. It is natural that you should want to know why this increase has come 30
about. We hope that the following information will be of help. 42

There are no longer any low-priced cars. As a result, we are now insuring 57
greater values, and a person who is insured wants to be compensated for the 73
financial loss that he has sustained. 80

All costs today are far above those which we have been accustomed to pay. 95
Repair costs on cars used by our policy-holders average over one hundred per 110
cent more for each claim than in 1950. Similar increases which have occurred 125
in all other items must be included in the cost of insurance. The costs of 140
labour have increased in proportion to the cost of living. The prices of 154
everyday necessities have increased. In comparison with these prices, we 169
still believe that the cost of your protection is very reasonable. 182

There is no doubt that car insurance rates could be much less if only we 197
would be more careful. We have it within our power to reduce the rate of 211
insurance to any point we see fit if we would reduce accidents to a minimum. 227
If we all work together, we shall again bring insurance rates down.   (S.I. 1.40) 240

Production typing

Job 27   Production Target—*25 minutes*

Type in correct form on A4 paper the following portion of play.

Bloggs' Big Day by Hilary Dorman   Time – Present. The scene is laid in a boarding house parlour. The furniture is drab, but clean. There are varied ornaments, pictures, etc., & there is no colour scheme. <u>Characters</u>: Mr. Bert Bloggs, Lodger; Annie Bloggs, his daughter; Mr. Arthur Slye, another lodger; Mrs. Siddells (Lily), Landlady; Miss Cora MacDunit and Miss Zela Moviedrone, Two ladies from the Matrimonial Agency. The scene opens with Mr Bloggs sitting at the table, which is in the centre of the room. He is a middle-aged man, very quiet, & a widower. He has always longed for his freedom, but on becoming a widower, he wishes to re-marry & have a 'nice little home' again. He is a retired railway clerk. He is alone. The door opens & Mrs Siddells enters with a tray, on which are balanced a teapot and a plate of bread and butter.

<u>Mr. Bloggs</u>: Morning, Mrs Siddells

<u>Mrs Siddells</u>: Morning, Mr Bloggs. Sorry about the breakfast, but the gas is off again and I've had to use the primus. I only managed to boil some water, though – as the 'blinkin' thing ~~went~~ konked out. Do you mind just plain bread and butter? I 'aven't anything else to offer.

<u>Mr. Bloggs</u>: No, I don't mind. I just 'ope nothing else fades out. There h'ain't much left as it is.

<u>Mrs. Siddells</u>: (She is rather <u>reefined</u>, a widow with a tendency to over-dress & make-up): So do I. I'm sick of trying to run a boarding – er – guest house, as things are today. I reelly think I'll have to close down, not havin' a man about the place to ~~teld~~ 'elp. Ah! well, I'd better go & see if the post's come. (Exits) (She collides with Annie Bloggs in the doorway; they say 'sorry', ~~etc.~~)

Type the following circular letter for signature by the Managing Director to be sent out tomorrow.

Our Ref. Mr G K/MO

Dear Madam,   <u>Shopping simplified!</u>

NP/

over/
olc

stet/

NP/

NP/
with our
compliments
NP.

NP

you are under no obligation
whatsoever to buy, but

We are approaching you direct by post, as we feel sure th you wl wish to be among the 1st to know all a special offer we are making. [Enclosed we are sendg you an advance copy of our latest catalogue, wh contains details of a hundred worth-while gift articles , We wd strongly recommend you to look thro' the exciting & interesting pp & select those items wh appeal to you most.

All our gds are guaranteed, but if for any reason they do not gv you satisfaction, we ~~undertake~~ guarantee to refund yr money so th there is no risk whatever as far as you are concerned. Many of the lines we are offering are unique. [If you wish to order, just write out yr reqs on / form below & send us a P.O. or cheque for the cost, plus postage. [If yr order amts to £3 or over, we shl send you a special free gift [If you hv no immediate use for any of the lines offered, we suggest th you keep the cat. in a convenient place in yr home.

Run on   Some of yr friends may ever be glad of an opportunity to browse thro' it, & it wl certainly provide you or them w an ideal solution to yr gift problems. In this way you can shop @ yr leisure, & we hv no doubt th you wl be pleased w yr purchase. Yr money wl be refunded if you are not fully satisfied, provided th you return yr purchase in gd condⁿ within 7 days of rect.

Our offer of free gifts holds gd for / current yr. [Why not make a trial purchase?

Yrs ffy,
Mr G King Ltd.

To: Mr G King Ltd. Spinhill Drive, Sheffield. S13 8FD
Please send me the followg gds on trial:
Cat. No.   Quantity   Description   Colour   Price
                   Typist ↑ leave 38 mm here.

Cheque/Postal Order enclosed fd ——————
Name (Mrs./Miss) ————————————
Address ————————————

Annie Bloggs: Morning, Dad. Sorry I can't stop. I'm late already. Let me have that bit of bread, will you? (Takes Mr. B's piece of bread & butter, gulps his tea and goes). So long! (Dashes out)

Mr. Bloggs: Well, I'm blessed. Young people rush round like 'blinkin' grasshoppers these days. There h'ain't much peace for us old 'uns. (Mr. Slye enters). He is slick — and sly).

Mr. Slye Good morning, Bloggs. (Sits at table). Pass the bread & butter, please. Thanks. Would you pour me a cup of tea, please?

Job 28 Production Target—*5 minutes*

Type in correct form a copy of Mr. Bloggs' part in the above play.

Job 29 Production Target—*3 minutes*

Type each of the following verses in correct form on A5 paper.

She is not fair to outward view
As many maidens be;
Her loveliness I never knew
Until she smiled on me.
O then I saw her eye was bright
A well of love, a spring of light
                    H. Coleridge

To Anthea

Bid me to live, and I will live
Thy Protestant to be;
Or bid me love, and I will give
A loving heart to thee.
                    R. Herrick.

Production typing

Job 72

Production Target—*15 minutes*

Type the following table in double spacing, centring it both horizontally and vertically. Rule all lines by underscore.

STATISTICAL RECORDS

Choice of Employment Conferences

Type of School or College	Number of Schools	Number of Conferences	Number of First School Reports Received	No. of First Vocational Guidance Interviews
Grammar, Technical + Commercial	36	45	8784	3673
Comprehensive + Bilateral	5	17	1267	1157
Independent + Private Schools	110	345	13481	12478
Other Sec. Schools	10	7	179	161
Approved Schools	2	9	85	33
TOTALS	163	423	18796	17502

Job 73

Production Target—*15 minutes*

Type the following table in double spacing, centring it both horizontally and vertically. Rule all lines in ink. List trades alphabetically.

NUMBER OF EMPLOYEES AT 31ST DECEMBER 1970

Trade	Males	Females	Total
Rubber goods + materials	78000	35800	113800
Cardboard Boxes, Cartons, etc.	23,000	31,400	54,400
Wood Containers + Baskets	18600	5600	24200
Brushes + Brooms, etc.	13300	8300	16500
Linoleum, Leather Cloth, etc.	8200	4200	17500
Furniture + Upholstery	95000	35200	130200
Games + Sports Requisites	11400	19000	30400
TOTALS	247500	139500	387000

Secretarial aid No. 2

Stationery

The job you are doing will determine what kind of paper you use, so that you must choose the quality which is suitable. You should ask yourself: How much handling will the paper receive? How long will it have to last? How many carbon copies are wanted? The process by which paper is made results in the fibres running in one direction—called grain. The longer the fibres, the stronger the paper in the direction they run. When the grain is horizontal the paper bends more easily round the platen and is less likely to slip. When the grains run vertically, it is easier to make neat erasures. In any case, erasing strokes should always be made in the same direction as the grain.

The most commonly used paper in business for original copies is bond. The appearance of bond paper is a bright non-fading white, combined with an opaque and uniform finish.

Some paper has a watermark, i.e. a sketch or wording which can be seen when the sheet is held to the light. Its chief value is that it identifies the right side of the paper. When you can read the watermark, you are looking at the side of the paper on which you should type.

Composing at machine

Type the following on A5 paper, replacing the words underscored by another word without altering the meaning.

We must endeavour to comfort that small child who, I hear, has lost some coins with which she intended to purchase a present in the city for a person living near her home. She is very much troubled as she fears her mother will be angry.

Review Quiz No. 2

Type the following on A4 paper in single-line spacing, with double spacing between each item, filling in the correct word or words in the blank spaces. Do not write on your textbook.

1. There are . . . . . single-line spaces to an inch. (25 mm).
2. On A4 paper there are . . . . . vertical lines.
3. On A5 paper (148 × 210 mm) there are . . . . . vertical lines.
4. Display is more effective by the use of . . . . . or . . . . . capitals.
5. A notice of a meeting is generally accompanied by an . . . . .
6. Records of business discussed at a meeting are called . . . . . and are entered in a . . . .
7. . . . . . spacing and . . . . . paper are used for typing stories, books, etc.
8. First page of manuscript is . . . . . numbered, but subsequent ones are usually numbered at . . . . .
9. When the first page of a chapter starts lower down than the remaining pages, this is called a . . . .
10. Prefaces are usually numbered in . . . . numerals.
11. Unspoken words in a play are typed in . . . . .
12. Single actor's parts are typed on . . . . . paper in . . . . . spacing.
13. Names of characters in a play are typed in . . . . . in . . . . . and . . . . .
14. The closing words of a speaker's speech in a Play are known as . . . . .
15. In typing poetry each line begins with a . . . . . letter.
16. Minutes of a meeting are written in . . . . . person and in . . . . . tense.
17. If all lines of a poem rhyme, there is no . . . . .
18. Short stage directions are typed in . . . . . of line.

Turn to page 199 and check your answers. Score one point for each correct entry. Total score: 26.

Ruling in ink

If horizontal and vertical lines are to be ruled in ink, follow the same procedure as for ruling by underscore, but in this case the beginning and end of each horizontal line must be marked in pencil, as well as the vertical lines. When table has been completed, remove paper from machine and, with a fine nib, rule lines carefully and neatly to scale-points marked, using red or black ink. Always wipe edge of ruler after ruling each line to prevent smudging. It is essential that vertical and horizontal lines meet exactly.

Sub-headings in tabulation

Sub-headings in tabulation are always typed in lower case with initial capitals. They are also centred horizontally and vertically as in the example below.
Note: If column headings take more than one line, they must be typed in single spacing.

12: Practise centring sub-headings. Type the following table in double spacing on A4 paper. Rule all lines in ink. List industries in alphabetical order.

TREND OF INDUSTRIAL PROFITS

Monthly Table of Company Profits

(£000's)

Industry	Number of Companies	Profits	Depreciation	Tax
Aircraft & Components	7	31550	8876	8423
Paper & Packaging	43	67193	20693	22809
Building Materials	100	97825	25292	33619
Iron & Steel	23	144699	54071	38524
Electricals (Light)	60	86750	27150	26627
Motors, Cycles & Components	31	70979	25582	21025
Electricals (Heavy)	13	69854	19959	21613
Breweries, Distilleries & Soft Drinks	49	115622	(47554	13695)
Clothing & Footwear	417	32215	7032	11245
Machine Tools	20	12870	1720	5252
Engineering & Metal	262	194388	44400	66543
Chemicals & Allied	73	315282	89581	101588
Rubber Manufacturing	13	33665	11292	11920
Construction	41	29496	9423	8660

Job 30 Production Target—*10 minutes*

Type the following on A4 paper using appropriate display. Use double-line spacing for the main text.

The following 2 verses are from "A Red, Red Rose" written
u.c. by the great _scottish_ poet Robert Burns.

O, my luve's like a red, red rose   [LUVE'S]

That's newly sprung in June;

O, my luve's like the melodie

That's sweetly play'd in tune.

As fair art thou, my bonnie lass,

So deep in luve am I;

And I will luve thee still, my dear,

Till a' the seas gang dry.

Robert was born in Alloway, Ayrshire, in the yr.
1789. His father was a peasant farmer.

Run on Education in Alloway was of a high standard &
N.P. in his youth he eagerly read every book on wh. he
could lay his hands. He began writing (poetry) in his early
teens & by / age of 25 his genius as a poet was
beginning to show in / mass of poetry wh. he had
written

One of his most famous poems depicts an
Ayrshire peasant's household. The scene is
similar to th. of the home into wh. he was born
& he vividly describes / end of the week's labours
N.P. & / gathering of the family on a Sat. evening. All
his works give a clear picture of the beauty of
nature; tender sentiments & his spontaneous &
inborn genius.

His poems so appealed to people th. many of his
long poems were repeated by them & / even today
if every printed copy of his works were lost, the
majority of his poems could be written down from
memory by many people all over the world.

, although they might not have read poetry,

(marginal inserts: H "evening these early days"; / "the bitter's Saturday night" —)

Technique development

Ruling of tabulated statements

Tabulated statements are sometimes made more effective and clearer by ruling horizontal and/or vertical lines. Although it is assumed that you have already learnt how to rule up tabulated work, the following notes will serve as a reminder.

1. If horizontal lines only are ruled, use the underscore and let the lines project two spaces beyond the margins on either side.

2. Always turn up one single-line space before a horizontal underscore and two single-line spaces after.

3. If both horizontal and vertical lines are required, rule these (a) either by underscore, in which case the paper has to be removed from the machine after the table has been typed, and reinserted sideways for the ruling of the vertical lines; (b) or by ink; (c) or a combination of the two, e.g., horizontals by underscore, verticals by ink.

4. The vertical lines between the columns must be ruled exactly in the middle of each blank space. It is therefore advisable to leave an odd number of spaces between the columns—one for the vertical ruling, and an equal number on either side of the ruling.

The points on the scale at which the vertical lines are to be ruled should be marked by light pencil marks at the top and bottom of the columns.

5. To find the point at which to mark the vertical line, proceed as follows: (a) Move to tab. stop following vertical line. (b) Divide number of spaces between columns by 2 and take next highest figure, e.g., 3 spaces between columns—divide by $2=1\frac{1}{2}$, call it 2; 5 spaces between columns = $2\frac{1}{2}$, call it 3. (c) From tab. stop back space 2 (or whatever the figure is), and put a pencil mark.

NOTE: Do not extend the vertical lines above or below the horizontals—see that they meet exactly.

11. Practise ruling. Read the above explanation, and then type a copy of the following table in double spacing on A5 paper (210 × 148 mm). Rule horizontal lines by underscore and vertical lines in ink.

ROBINSON & CO. LTD.

Report of Tenth Record Year

Year to 31st December	1964	1963	1962
	£	£	£
Group profit before tax	308,146	356,601	404,581
Taxation	159,905	157,643	179,693
Group net profit	148,241	198,958	224,888
Ordinary dividend			
(Less tax)	55,125	55,125	60,637
Revenue reserves and			
unappropriated profit	801,289	923,438	1,069,247

Tabulation with columns of figures

When columns in a table contain figures, care must be taken to see that units come under units, tens under tens, etc.

If you do not use the comma to separate thousands from hundreds, etc., figures must be set out as explained on page 132. However, if any number in any column of a table contains six or more figures, all groups must be in threes even though the column may contain items of less than six figures.

Display the following on A4 paper.

(Typist - please draw
rectangles to sizes
indicated, but do not
type in sizes)

GREGG NEWS LETTER.

VISUAL AIDS

Free Charts:

Education Service,
10 Lombard Street, London, E.C.3

British Insurance Association,
Queen Mary Street, London, E.C.4

The Public Relations Officer,
Westminster Bank Ltd.,
41 Lothbury, London, E.C.2

Free Films:

The Public Relations Officer,
The Stock Exchange,
Throgmorton Street, L/n, EC4

Sound Services Ltd,
Wilton Crescent, L/n, S.W.19

(left margin, vertical): Typist: If you can, would you please reproduce the district too, with the postcodes.

51 mm

BASIC BUSINESS
ARITHMETIC
by
R. Watson

64
mm
b.c.

Price 80p

A Basic Textbook
for students preparing
for elementary level
examinations

102 mm

TAKE A LETTER   A—Z
It is very much regretted that booking
for this film cannot be accepted until
the beginning of next yr.

32
mm

COMMERCE FOR SCHOOLS
by
W. Outhwaite

Price 63p

A balanced course
for CSE pupils

51 mm.

NEW EDITIONS

SECRETARIAL TRAINING
D. M. Sharp & H. M. Crozier

COMMERCE: STRUCTURE AND PRACTICE
T. A. C. Shafto

EXPLORING LOCAL BUSINESS
Maurice Watcham

ENQUIRIES TO:

McGraw-Hill Publishing Co. Ltd.,
Shoppenhangers Road,
MAIDENHEAD, Berks.

BOOKS FROM AMERICA
Write to us for books
on the following
subjects:

51
mm

Business Subjects
Typewriting
Office Practice

Skill building

Type each exercise (A, B, C, and D) *once* for practice, *once* for speed, and finally *once* for accuracy.

A. Review alphabet keys

1. It was a hazardous task that the steeplejack performed, but owing to his vast experience he could now do it quickly.

B. Build accuracy on shift key drill

2. You Must Always Check All Work Before Removing From Machine.

3. The Forty-Second Annual General Meeting of Johnson & Wilkins Ltd. was held on Friday, 14th April, the Chairman presiding.

4. Tours to Belgium, France, Holland, Italy, Majorca and Spain.

C. Build accuracy on shift lock drill

5. OUR ORDER No. 8681/116.10/EX/2, of 16th AUGUST, is EXTREMELY URGENT. Delivery MUST be made by 31st OCTOBER without fail.

6. EXETER (Devon): LONDON 170; BODMIN 64; PLYMOUTH 42; BUDE 50.

7. NEWCASTLE-UPON-TYNE; OGMORE-BY-SEA; SOUTHEND-ON-SEA; LANARK.

D. Build accuracy on concentration drills

8. U.S.S.R.: Novo-Nazyvayevskoye; Dnepropetrovsk; Ilovlinskaya.

9. Thailand: Nakhon Ratchasima; Ukraine; Mezhizichi-Koretskiye.

10. Wales: Crib-y-Ddysgyl; Bwlch-cum-Orthin; Nant Ffrancon Pass. Llanfairpwllgwyngyllgogerychwyrndrobwllllandysiliogogogoch.

Accuracy/Speed Practice
Two-minute timing

Not more than 2 errors

words

AS.27   The Thames Valley is a district well known to thousands of people, 13
not only from this country but from every part of the world. The 26
scenery is lovely, while the winding river is frequented by fishing and 40
sailing enthusiasts. However, it is the history of the district which 54
chiefly appeals to visitors. There is Runnymede, where King John signed 69
the Magna Carta in 1215. Kingston still has the "king's stone", on 80
which were crowned seven Anglo-Saxon monarchs. The town, granted a 95
first charter by King John in 1199, is a busy market town in these days. 110
Richmond, in early times called Shene, meaning brightness, is also popu- 124
lar. It was Charles I who enclosed the Great Park and stocked it with 138
deer, but it was not until the reign of Charles II that the public were 153
allowed to go into the royal park. (S.I. 1.33) 160

Unit 11

Skill building

Typing line:
60 spaces

Type each line or sentence (A, B, and C) *three* times. If time permits, complete your practice by typing each group once as it appears.

A. Review alphabet keys

1.   Dick was extremely delighted to be requested to play in the Junior Festival Concert, held at the Zoological Gardens.

B. Build speed on fluency drill

2. Next week they will have some more pens from that nice shop.

3. Some boys whom they know must have gone home late last week.

4. This girl says they will soon have read that book once more.

5. They will come past that road when they walk home from work.

C. Build speed on common letter combinations

6. although discount thought amount should about doubt your our

7. I thought the amount of discount you allow us is not enough.

8. I am anxious that you should quote for this particular work.

9. We thought we should like to open an account with your firm.

Accuracy/Speed Practice

Note: You should now aim at increasing your speed by 5 words a minute.

One-minute timings   Not more than 1 error

words

AS.13   We thank you for your note, and regret to inform you that we do   **13**
not stock the particular type of case for which you are now asking,   **26**
but we can make these up for you if you would like us to do so. Unfor-   **40**
tunately, at this stage we are unable to quote you a definite price,   **54**
but we will look into our costs and let you know by the end of the   **67**
present week the price we are able to quote and the delivery date.   **80**

(S.I. 1.25)

AS.14   When you have to type envelopes from cards or lists, it is a good idea   **14**
to turn each card or list, with the envelopes you have already completed,   **29**
face downwards on the desk, so that, after you have finished all of them   **43**
and turned them back again, you will find that they are in the right order   **58**
ready for checking. This method will greatly simplify your work and save   **73**
time. Why not try it for yourself?   **(S.I. 1.27) 80**

Display the following Application Form, using A4 paper and taking a carbon copy. Leave sufficient space for applicants to fill in details.

Caps.& centre | NewTown Technical College
Dept. of Business Studies & General Education

Principal:.
L.A. Johnson
B. Sc. (& Eng., M.I.Mech.E.

Head of Dept.
K.L. Phillips
M.A. B.Com.

Caps.& underscore & centred. | Application Form – Full-time Secretarial Courses
For applicants under 18 yrs of age.

l.c. &c.
1. SURNAME (Block letters) – – – – – –
2. Christian Names (in full) – – – – –
3. Date of Birth – – – – –   Phone No. – –
4. Full address – – – – – – –

5. Full name and address of Parent or Guardian
    – – – – – – – – – – – – – – – –

6. Name and address of last school attended
    – – – – – – – – –

stet 7. ~~Examinations passed~~
    – – – – – – –
8. Qualifications for which studying – – – –

all wording underscored to be in closed caps. But NOT underscored.

DECLARATION

I wish to enter NewTown Technical College & I hereby undertake (1) to attend at the college for the full period of the Course; (2) to pay the appropriate fee; (3) to purchase the necessary books; (4) to attend all lectures; (5) to abide by the rules set forth by the college.

Signature of Applicant: _____

Signature of Parent or Guardian: _____

Date: _____

FOR OFFICE USE

Date received – – – – –   Interview Notified – – – – –
Date interviewed – – – –   Result of interview – – – – –
admitted – – – – – –   Result notified – – – – – –

Technique development

Typing decimals

1. Always use full stop for decimal point.
2. Leave NO space before or after decimal point.

3. No punctuation is required at end of figures, except at the end of a sentence.

10. Practise typing decimals. Read the above explanation, then type a copy of the following in double spacing.

For your guidance, we give you below, as requested, the measurements in the metric system (to three decimal places). 0.990 x 1.371 x 1.219 metres.   3.353 × 3.048 × 2.743 metres. 3.657 x 2.590 x 1.524 metres.   2.108 x 5.100 x 1.890 metres.

Typing sums of money in context

1. If the sum comprises only pounds, type as follows: £5, £10, or £5.00, £10.00.
2. If only pence, type: 10p 7p
   NOTE: *no* space between figures and letter p, and no full stop after p (unless, of course, it ends a sentence).
3. With mixed amounts, i.e., sums comprising pounds and pence, the decimal point and the £ symbol should always be used, but *not* the abbreviation p.
   Example: £7.05. The £ sign and p should *never* appear together.
4. If the sum contains a decimal point but no whole pounds, a nought should be typed after the £ symbol and before the point. *Example:* £0.97.

11. Practise typing sums of money in context. Read the above explanation and then type a copy of the following in double spacing.

Our invoice of the 6th May was for a total sum of £10.55, whereas the cheque we have received is made out for £10.00 only, so there is a balance due of £0.55 (55p), which please remit by return.

Typing decimals in columns

1. When typing decimal figures in columns see that the decimal points come under one another.
2. There must be the same number of decimal places in each line of the column, so that where necessary the figure 0 is used to make up the required number of decimal places. For example, if there are two decimal places, type 6.00, 6.60, 6.66. If three decimal places, type 6.000, 6.600, 6.660, etc. If there is no whole number, type 0 before the decimal point, e.g. 0.66.

3. If pounds and pence are typed in columns, the £ sign is typed over the unit figure of the pounds. No sign appears over the pence or decimals of a pound.
4. If the column contains whole pounds only, the £ sign is typed over the longest item, e.g.,

£	but	£
200.55		240

12. Practise typing columns of decimals. Type the following on A5 paper (148 × 210 mm), using a left margin of 20 and setting tab stops for the second, third and fourth columns at 35, 51 and 64 respectively.

		£	£
1,240.52	1,505.125	101.45	101
4,668.24	3,242.150	25.50	25
3,101.50	4,925.500		
9,010.26	9,672.775	126.95	126

Production typing

Job 69 Production Target—*20 minutes*

Type in correct form on A5 paper an Income and Expenditure Account for the Stockfield Social Club for the twelve months ended 31st July, 1971.

Handwritten manuscript:

Expenditure

Donations to Charities	£21·35
Printing, Postage & Stationery	24·77
Heating & Lighting	30·50
Dance Band	15·25
Sundry Expenses	7·22
Excess of Income over Expenditure	
£	
£	

Income

Sale of Badges	£5·25
Proceeds from Dances	10·77
Subscriptions	123·00
Arrears of Sub- scriptions	10·50
Conference Fees	21·00
£	

(Typist—please calculate, and put in totals)

Job 70 Production Target—*20 minutes*

Type the following Balance Sheet in correct form on two separate sheets of A5 paper.

Handwritten manuscript:

BALANCE SHEET OF ROBINSON & SONS LTD.
AT 31ST DECEMBER 1971.

Liabilities

Capital
1000 Shares of £1 fully paid — £1000
General Reserve — £1095
Current Liabilities
  Trade Creditors — £975
  Inland Revenue (Staff Income Tax) — £30 — £1005
  Balance for Distribution — £277
    £3,377

Assets
Fixed — £869
  Fixtures — £869
  Less Depreciation — £122 — £747
Investment (Lloyds Bank) — £500
  Accrued Interest — 55 — £555
Current
  Stock-in-Trade — £1487
  Trade Debtors — £4988
  Cash at Bank & in hand — £90
    £3377

UNIT 21 143

Lay-out of business letter

Letters can be displayed in various ways, the styles most commonly used being illustrated below. In deciding which to use, you should follow the method adopted by your firm. For information concerning the typing of business letters, see 'Parts of a Business Letter' and 'Steps in writing a letter' on pages M2 and M3 of Reference Manual.

Fully blocked	Blocked	Semi-blocked	Indented
	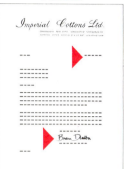		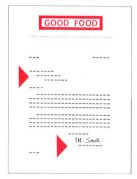

Take particular note of the differences between these styles.

Every line starts at left margin.

Date ends at right margin. Complimentary close and signature start in middle and are blocked.

Indented paragraphs in body. Otherwise same as blocked form.

Inside address, paragraphs, and signature indented.

Fully blocked letter

13. Study the layout of a fully-blocked letter as illustrated above, noting that *every* line starts at the left margin. Then type the following letter on A5 paper (148 × 210 mm) in single-line spacing with double spacing between paragraphs. Use a 50-space typing line (Margins: Elite 12/62, Pica 5/55). Keep your typed copy for future reference in Folder No. 2.

Turn up 3 spaces →
Our Ref. ABC/DEF

3 spaces →
15th August, 1971

Remember: All lines start at left margin.

3 spaces →
Miss M. K. James,
40 Broadmeadow Close,
BIRMINGHAM 30.

3 spaces →
Dear Madam,

2 spaces →
This letter is to announce our Annual Sale which will be held in two weeks' time.

2 spaces →
We understand from our Sales Manager that you paid us a visit last year, when we had the pleasure of supplying you with various household goods at considerably less than the usual retail prices.

2 spaces →
In a fortnight's time we shall have an even wider range of sale goods, the prices of which will compare favourably with any in the country. It will certainly be worth your while to pay us a visit.

2 spaces →
Yours faithfully,

1 space →
THE BARGAIN STORES

5 spaces →
A. B. Coates

1 space →
Manager.

UNIT 11

67

14. Practise typing two-page Balance Sheet. Type the following Balance Sheet, using two separate sheets of A4 paper. Use double spacing between the items. Note that two money columns are needed on both sides. After completion of the typing, join the two sheets together.

F. W. WILKINSON & CO. LTD.

Balance Sheet as at 31st December, 19..

	£	£
CAPITAL		
Authorized		
6% Cumulative Preference Stock (in £1 Units)	300,000	
Ordinary Shares and Stock (in Units of 5p)	480,000	
4,400,000 Shares (unclassified) of 5p	220,000	
	£1,000,000	
Issued and fully paid		
6% Cumulative Preference Stock (in £1 Units)	300,000	
Ordinary Stock (in Units of 5p)	480,000	780,000
RESERVES		
Capital		
Share Premium		486,790
Revenue		
Contingencies	12,000	
Profit and Loss Account	54,429	66,429
PENSION FUND	32,225	
Deduct payments	7,913	24,312
CURRENT LIABILITIES AND PROVISIONS		
Bank Overdraft	371,956	
Creditors and accrued charges	450,998	
Purchase Tax	2,724	825,678
		£2,183,209
FIXED ASSETS		
Freehold Land and Buildings as valued at 31st December,		
19.. with additions at cost .	260,549	
Less Depreciation and amounts written off	144,886	115,663
Plant, Machinery, Fixtures and Fittings, with additions since 31st December, 19..	505,659	
Less Depreciation	341,530	164,129
Tools, Patterns, Dies and Designs		124,725
Trade Investments at cost		16,000
CURRENT ASSETS		
Stock on hand and work in progress	1,355,473	
Debtors, Bills Receivable, and Prepayments		
Less Provision for Doubtful Debts	401,427	
Bank Balance and Cash in hand	5,792	1,762,692
		£2,183,209

'Attention' line

It is the custom with some firms to have all correspondence addressed to the firm and not to individuals. If, therefore, the writer of a letter wishes it to reach a particular person or department, the words 'For the attention of Mr. . . .' are typed at the left margin on the second single-line space after the address and before the salutation. This wording is also typed on the envelope two single-line spaces above the name.

NOTE: The salutation will, of course, be in the plural, i.e., Dear Sirs.

Enclosures

When any enclosure is to be inserted in a letter, this should be indicated in one of the following ways:

(a) By typing: Enc., Encs., Encl., or Encls. at left margin at bottom of letter (at least 4 single-line spaces below signature), or the word 'Enclosure' may be typed in full. In both cases lower case letters (with an initial capital) or upper case letters may be used, with or without underscore.

(b) A printed and/or numbered label may be affixed at foot of letter. Some firms also state what the enclosure is. Example: Enc. Invoice.

14. Practise typing letter with 'Attention' line and enclosure. Type the following letter on A4 paper, using a 60-space typing line. Margins: Elite 20/80, Pica 12/72.

Turn up
3 spaces → Our ref. GHM/JKL

3 spaces → 15th October, 1971

H. W. Jones (Drapers) Ltd.,
47 Leicester Road,
COVENTRY.   CV1 5RS

2 spaces → For the attention of Mr. W. Frost

2 spaces → Dear Sirs,

As we have not had any acknowledgment of our previous letter, with which we sent samples of various floral designs which we have brought out for the present season, we are now writing to impress upon you the advisability of placing your order without loss of time if you wish to secure any of these new materials.

Lest the previous samples should not have reached you, we are enclosing further samples of the designs in question.

Supplies are becoming short as the season advances, and our stocks are being rapidly exhausted. Moreover, we shall not unfortunately be able to repeat these particular designs.

We look forward to hearing from you at your convenience.

Yours faithfully,
H. G. CAMPBELL LTD.

Min. of
4 spaces → Sales Manager.

Enc.

NOTE: Leave 6 spaces between town and postcode and 1 space between two halves of code.

UNIT 11   **68**

12. Practise typing single-page Balance Sheet. Type a copy of the following on A5 paper (210 × 148 mm).

WILLIAM WOODHOUSE

BALANCE SHEET
as at 30th June, 1971

LIABILITIES	£	ASSETS	£
Sundry Creditors	700.62	Leasehold premises	1,000.00
Expenses out-standing	52.00	Fixtures and Fittings	456.50
Reserve Account	500.00	Stock-in-Trade	550.62
Capital Account	2,300.90	Sundry Debtors	845.88
		Cash in hand	50.00
		Cash at Bank	650.52
	£3,553.52		£3,553.52

13. Type a copy of the following Balance Sheet on two separate sheets of A5 paper (148 × 210 mm). Note that two money columns are needed on both sides. After completion of the typing, join the sheets together.

W. J. BRIDGWATER & CO.

BALANCE SHEET AS AT 31ST MARCH, 1971

	£			£
Capital as at 1 April	3,000	Fixed Assets		
Add Profit for the yr	1,085			
	4,085	Freehold building		2,500
		Plant & machinery		1,000
Less Drawings	1,000	Motor Vehicle		500
	3,085			4,000
Current Liabilities	£	Current Assets	£	
Bank Overdraft	525	Stock	750	
Creditors	1,800	Debtors	500	
	2,325	Cash	160	1,410
	£ 5,410			£ 5,410

Subject heading

In a fully blocked letter the subject heading (if any) is typed at the left margin and underscored if in lower case. The subject heading may be typed in closed capitals without the underscore.

Displayed matter in fully blocked letters

When matter is to be displayed in a fully blocked letter, all lines start at the left margin, one clear space being left above and below the displayed matter.

NOTE: If definite instructions are given for the matter to be 'inset', then it must be 'inset' even in a fully blocked letter. For method of display see page 73(3).

15. Practise typing fully blocked letter with subject heading and displayed matter. Type the following letter, in fully blocked style, using A4 paper and margins of 20/80 Elite, 12/72 Pica. Insert date.

```
Ditta A. Di Giorgio,
Via di S. Martino,
Rome, Italy.

For the attention of Sig. G. Luciano

Dear Sirs,

Contract No. 1456/9/70

Please note that we have today drawn on you the three drafts
mentioned below, covering the goods ordered by you in accord-
ance with the above contract:-

1.   £120.25 at 30 days' date
2.   £80.50 at 60 days' date
3.   £50.75 at 120 days' date.

We trust these will have your acceptance in conformity with
the terms arranged with you on the occasion of your visit to
our factory.

Despatch of the first consignment has already been made
(invoice attached), and the other two shipments will follow
on the dates specified.

Will you kindly acknowledge receipt of this letter, confirm-
ing your acceptance of the drafts in question.

Yours faithfully,
H. S. MITCHELL (EXPORTERS) LTD.


A. B. Scott
Secretary.

Enc.
```

Income and expenditure account and profit and loss account

There are two other accounts which you may have to type, both of which have two sides like the Receipts and Payments Account.

1. *Income and Expenditure Account.* This is used by a non-trading concern or non-profit making institution, such as a club, society or other charitable institution.

The right-hand side contains details of income received during a given period, and the left-hand side shows the expenses incurred. The difference between the two sides represents either a deficit (if expenses exceed income) or a surplus (if income exceeds expenses).

2. *Profit and Loss Account.* This is used by a trading or profit-making concern. The right-hand side contains details of profit, and the left side details of expenses.

The rules applying to the typing of an Income and Expenditure Account and a Profit and Loss Account are the same as those applying to a Receipts and Payments Account.

11. Practise typing Income and Expenditure Account. Type the following on A5 paper (210 × 148 mm).

<u>FAIRHURST SPORTS AND SOCIAL CLUB</u>

<u>Income and Expenditure Account for the year ended 31st December,1971</u>

<u>Expenditure</u>		<u>Income</u>	
	£		£
Rent	30.00	Subscriptions	105.00
Cleaning	13.50	Dances	8.37
Heating and		Refreshments	5.13
Lighting	39.12		
Stationery	5.25		
Postages	13.32		
Printing (due)	3.52		
Excess of Income			
over Expenditure	13.79		
	£118.50		£118.50

Balance sheets

A Balance Sheet is a statement of the Liabilities and Assets of a firm or company, and shows the financial position at a given time. There are two sides—the Liabilities on the left-hand side, Assets on the right-hand. If possible, a long-carriage machine should be used for typing a Balance Sheet, so that it can be typed across the full width of brief paper. If a long-carriage typewriter is not available, the Balance Sheet usually has to be typed on two separate sheets of A4 paper, one sheet being used for Liabilities, and the other sheet for Assets.

The rules applying to the typing of Balance Sheets are the same as those already explained for Receipts and Payments Accounts. To ensure sufficient space being left for money columns (a Balance Sheet usually has at least two money columns on both sides), it may be necessary for the wording of an item to be taken on to more than one line.

If two separate sheets are used, the heading of the Balance Sheet should run right across the two sheets without a break, half being typed on the Liabilities side, and ending close to the right-hand edge of the sheet. The other half is typed on the Assets side, starting close to the left edge of the sheet.

The side containing the larger number of items should be typed first, and, before starting to type the second sheet, you should make a light pencil mark to show the precise point at which the heading is to be continued, to ensure that the two parts of the heading are in line with each other. Also mark lightly in pencil on the second sheet the line on which the £ sign appears, the line on which the first item is to be typed, and the exact position for the total, so that the two sides may coincide exactly.

When the typing is completed, the two sides may be joined together by a strip of Sellotape or other adhesive affixed to the back, care being taken to see that the edges just meet.

Type the following letter on A4 paper. Mark it for the attention of D. F. Grant, Esq.

JARRETT, GRANT & Sons
27 Dunham Way,
Stockton-on-Tees,
Teeside. TS19 7LE
　　　　　　　　　　　　　　　　　Suitable date.

Dr Sirs,
　　Advertisement in the Agricultural Journal

We hv. recd. yr. ltr. of /16 March w. regard to /above
advert & thank y. for yr. offer of services for our (as agents)
N.P.① products [We are quite ready to take yr. offer into
consideration, but we would like to hv a reply to/
following points in order to give us some idea of yr. selling capacity.
　　a) The extent of / territory y. feel capable of covering satisfactorily
　　b) The display facilities at yr. disposal.
　　d) The approx min. turnover y. anticipate for the 6 months
　　　of /agency.

[insert this portion + use following paras.]

[before fixing an appointment to discuss this matter,]

For yr. guidance we encl. a catalogue of our main
N.P.w.c. products. [When we hv. had an opportunity of considering
stet　/above informn., we shall be pleased to arrange an
interview to suit yr. convenience/ when/ question of commission
+ terms of payment can be discussed.
Yrs ffy,
W.B.A. Thompson Ltd.　R.L. Moss.　Man. Dir,

Typist — Sorry I omitted (c) it should read.
　　How you propose to introduce our products.
　　On yr. market.

Technique development

Receipts and payments account

There are certain accounts which you may be asked to type for your employer, such as a Receipts and Payments Account, which is used by clubs and societies. The purpose of this account is simply to show in summarized form the cash received and the cash paid out during a given period, and the amount of cash in hand. There are two sides to the account. The left-hand side shows the amount of cash in hand at the beginning of the period and the money received during the period, while the right-hand side shows the payments made. The difference between the two sides is the balance in hand at the end of a given period.

Guide to typing Receipts and Payments Account
1. Allow equal space for the Receipts and Payments sides.

2. The left and right margins must be equal.

3. Leave at least 5 spaces between the end of the money column on the left side and the start of the items on the right-hand side, so that, after completion of the typing, a thin red ink line may be drawn down the centre to divide the two sides, with equal spaces on both sides of the ink line.

4. Type the longer side first.

5. Use double spacing between each item. If any item requires more than one line, type the item in single-line spacing, indenting two spaces the second and subsequent lines.

6. The totals on both sides must be typed opposite each other. This may mean leaving a blank space on the shorter side before inserting the total.

7. The horizontal lines above and below the total and the total itself are typed in the same way as in invoicing.

10. Practise typing Receipts and Payments Account. Type the following on A5 paper (210 × 148 mm). Rule red line down the middle.

FAIRHURST SPORTS AND SOCIAL CLUB

Receipts and Payments Account
for the year ended 31st December, 1970

Receipts	£	Payments	£
Cash in hand	9.33	Rent	30.00
Cash at bank	30.50	Cleaning	13.50
Subscriptions	105.00	Heating and Lighting	39.12
Profit from Dances	8.37	Stationery	5.25
Refreshments	5.13	Postages	13.31
		Cash in hand	7.15
		Cash at Bank	50.00
	£158.33		£158.33

Type the following letter on A4 paper. Insert suitable date and subject heading 'Agency'.

R. L. Moss Esq.,
Man. Dir.
W. B. A. Thompson Ltd.,
7 Birmingham Rd.,
Wolverhampton. WV2 4DB.

Dr. Mr. Moss,

Thank y. for yr. ltr. of .... about my firm acting as agents for yr. products.

(:) The following are the answers to/points raised in yr. letter ∧

(:) (a) We wd be prepared to cover the follow^g counties/ Northumberland, Durham Cumberland, Westmorland + Yorks.

facilities ∧ (b) Our display/ at the above address are ~~limited~~, but we could set aside one room∧ for this purpose. (measuring 5m x 6m)

(c) At present we have two field reps. covering the counties mentioned and∧ i.e. in (a) ∧ If we were appointed yr. agents, we wd consider ~~appointing~~ engaging another 2 reps.

; ∧ (d) Anticipated turnover is difficult to assess ∧ however, as yr stet ∧ ∧ products are ~~in demand~~ popular ∧ we estimate orders in the region of £12,000 per annum.

I wd be available to discuss these points w. you any day next wk. Perhaps y wd like to visit us + meet my two partners✱ + myself as well as our two reps. mentioned in (c). If not, I shall be pleased to call on you. Kindly let me know which will be convenient to you.

Yrs sincerely, D.F. Grant

Typist — please use block paras for (a) – (d)
   also at ✱ please insert :(John E. Jarrett and
                                    Michael J. Thorrowgood).

Unit 21

Skill building

Type each line or sentence (A, B, and C) *three* times. If time permits, complete your practice by typing each group once as it appears.

A. Review alphabet keys

1.   The calves grazing in the field jerked their heads with fright when alarmed by the explosions at the near-by quarry.

B. Build speed on common letter combinations

2. very here over cover refer other there better orders service

3. I refer to our order which must be delivered here next week.

4. We must give credit for the very good service on all orders.

5. Her other insurance policy is much overdue and must be paid.

C. Build speed on common phrases

6. for the, for these, for them, for their, for that, for this.

7. But for them, we would have no excuse for this visit to you.

8. For the time being, we are happy for that to remain dormant.

9. Thank them for their good wishes and for all these presents.

Accuracy/Speed Practice

Note: You should now aim at increasing your speed by 5 words a minute.

One-minute timings   *Not more than 1 error*

words

AS.25   Everyone should have a hobby. It is healthy and can lead to a   12
longer and happier life. The choice of the hobby is not so important   26
as how you make use of it. If your job is one that necessitates your   40
sitting down at a desk for hours at a time, you should choose a hobby   54
that will enable you to unwind your muscles or one that will help you   68
to relax. It will also bring added interest into your life. (S.I. 1.30)   80

AS.26   In these modern times, scarcely a month goes by without some   12
well-known and well-loved building being demolished and replaced   25
by concrete and steel. This is the case all over the country, and   38
if we are to have new towns and cities, it must, we know, be done,   51
but how sad it is to see some renowned building disappearing before   64
our eyes, and another, often of less architectural beauty, put up   78
in its place.   (S.I. 1.32)   80

UNIT 21   **138**

Unit 12

Skill building

Type each exercise (A, B, C, and D) *once* for practice, *once* for speed, and finally *once* for accuracy.

A. Review alphabet keys

1.   Through an involuntary error on your part, the question of the Zenith Club Dinner must be adjourned until next week.

B. Improve control of figure keys

2. tour 5974 tore 5943 your 6974 wore 2943 tier 5834 were 2343.

3. Add together 123, 234, 345, 456, 567, 678, 789, 890, and 91.

4. Sales: £20,846,000; Profit: £1,735,889; Assets: £12,451,469.

5. Dividends: 1959 — £293,617; 1960 — £485,732; 1961 — £86,247.

C. Build accuracy on shift key drill

6. Miss J. Levy, Mr. K. Yates, Mrs. D. Tate, Messrs. Rowe Bros.

7. Dear Sir, The Misses C. & E. A. Levy, Messrs. H. F. Gittins, I. Norton, P. St. John Clark, and O. Watson-Viney will visit the Mass X-ray Unit at Zephyr Street on Monday, 3rd October.

D. Improve concentration

8. Schon lange ist es mein Wunsch, in Deutschland eine dauernde Stellung zu erhalten, um den dortigen Handel kennenzulernen.

Accuracy/Speed Practice
Two-minute timing   *Not more than 2 errors*

	words
AS.15 There is a tendency for our lives to become fuller as time goes on,	13
and the problem is how to find time for all the things we want to do.	27
The best way is to decide what is the most important, and to use up as	41
far as possible the periods which have hitherto been idle. Those of us	55
who travel by train or bus can use this time if the train or bus is not	69
too crowded. Then again, there is always the week-end, part of which	81
should be set aside for the reading that we may not have had time to do	98
during the week. For though it is vital that the student should not	111
miss her daily study, we must not make cast-iron rules for any one thing	126
without bearing in mind all the other claims we may have on our time.	139
Our plans must always be flexible, and we must see that we have	152
time for relaxation as well as for study. (S.I. 1.24)	160

Job 67 Production Target—*10 minutes*

Type the following memo. Two carbon copies please—one for filing and one for Mr. T. Weston.

To – Sales Manager From – Chief Engineer
Our Ref: CE/TAM Today's Date
Subject – TYRE PRESSURES.
Further to our tel. conversation of yesterday, I give below / tyre pressures y. asked abt.

Model	Tyres	PRESSURE Normal Front kg/cm²	Rear kg/cm²	Fully Laden Front kg/cm²	Rear kg/cm²
1100 cc	5.50 x 12 Cross Ply	1.7	1.7	1.7	2.1
1300 cc	155 x 12 Radial Ply	1.7	2.0	1.7	2.0
G.T.	155 x 12 Radial Ply	1.7	2.0	1.7	2.0

Job 68 Production Target—*8 minutes*

Display the following notice of meeting and agenda on A5 paper.

BAXTER SPORTS & SOCIAL CLUB
ARIEL WORKS
29 Frederick Road, Birmingham B29 2XN

The A.G.M. of B.S. & S.C. will be held in / staff canteen on Thursday 11th March, 1971, @ 1700 hrs.

AGENDA

(1) Apologies. (2) Minutes of / last meeting (4) (3) Chairman's Annual Report (4)3 Matters arising (5) Treasurer's Annual Report & Bal. Sheet. (6) Election of (a) Officers (b) Committee (c) Hon. Auditor. (7) A.O.B.

R. Grace
Hon. Sec.

(Typist please display numbered items)

Technique development

The semi-blocked style differs from the fully blocked as follows:
(1) Paragraphs are indented (at least five spaces) from left margin.
(2) Subject-heading is centred on typing line, one clear line-space being left above and below the heading.
(3) Displayed matter is arranged in such a way that the longest line is centred on the typing line. To do this, find the centre point of the body of the letter by adding together the points at which the left and right margins are set, and divide by 2. Bring writing point to this scale-point and back-space once for every two letters and spaces in the longest line. Leave one clear line-space above and below the displayed matter.
(4) The complimentary close starts at approximately the centre of the typing line (or slightly to the right) and the name of the company is typed on the next line. There should be a minimum of 4 clear line-spaces between the name of the company and the signatory. If there is any designation, this should be typed on the next single-line space.

9. Practise typing semi-blocked letter. Type the following letter on A4 paper (210 × 297 mm) with margins 20/80 (elite), 12/72 (pica). Keep your typed copy for future reference in Folder No. 2.

JS/AKL   1st September, 1971

The National Bank Ltd.,
Davies Street,
LONDON.   W1Y 2AA

For the attention of Mr. H. Harper, Manager

Dear Sirs,

Appointment of Bankers

    We have to advise you that it was resolved at the Board Meeting held today that you should be appointed bankers to the Company.

    The following documents are therefore enclosed:

                1. Copy of the Directors' Resolution.

                2. Copy of the Company's Memorandum and
                    Articles of Association.

                3. Specimen signatures of those who are
                    to operate on the account.

                4. Certificate of Incorporation.

    Will you please return the last document at your earliest convenience.

                        Yours faithfully,
                        W. J. BUSH & CO. LTD.

                        John Scrivens
                        Secretary.

Encs.

Consolidation

Type the following letter on A4 paper. In addition to a carbon copy for filing, take bcc. copies for the Managing Director and Miss J. Smith.

Mrs. N. Bailey, 5. Gibson Rd. Stockport, Cheshire SK6 6LA

Continental Tours   We have much pleasure in enclosing set/ our current Programme of Motor Tours to the most uc beautiful parts of the continent. Each of these Tours is planned to give more passengers an absolutely carefree holiday amidst places of interest in Europe. First class hotel accommodation is throughout the Tours, & seats are reserved in a Luxury Motor coach. From the beginning to the end of the Tour our 1st consideration is our passengers' comfort. An experienced guide accompanies each party.

the finest scenery*

I Three weeks' Grand Tour of Italy. II Austria uc/ and the black forest. III Spain. Each of these wl appeal to the Tourist, since ea. has its own charm and interest. We hope to hv the pleasure of making a reservation for you to join one of our parties this year.
Yrs. faithfully, GRAFTON TOURS LTD.
Advert. Manager.

In response to repeated requests we hv included a new Tours as follows:

Typist
Numbered items should be in arabic figures and inset.

TYPIST
Please paragraph letter

Display the following Dinner Menu on A5 paper as effectively as possible.

Wednesday, 31st July.   MENU.
Melon Cocktail - Fillet of Sole Princesse - Roast Turkey with Sausages & Stuffing, French Beans, Vichy Carrots, Roast new Potatoes - Iced Savarin with Raspberries & cream. - Coffee

Postscripts

Sometimes a postscript has to be typed at the foot of a letter, either because the writer has omitted something he wished to say in the body of the letter, or because he wishes to draw special attention to a certain point. The postscript should be started two single-line spaces below the last line of signatory, and should be in single-line spacing.

10. Practise typing letter with postscript. Read the above explanation, and then type the following letter on A4 (210 × 297 mm) paper, with margins 20/80 (elite), 12/70 (pica). Keep your typed copy for future reference in Folder No. 2.

```
GAS/MBB                                (Insert today's date)

Stewart & Goodall Ltd.,
Norton Road,
IPSWICH.      IP4 1LU

For the attention of the Purchasing Officer

Dear Sirs,

                         Enquiry

     We thank you for your enquiry for details and prices of
our Shaped Covers for all makes of cars, and we enclose our
catalogue of these covers which, we may say, are a remarkably
quick-selling line.

     As you are in the trade, we are quoting below our whole-
sale prices, but would point out that these apply only to
minimum orders of ten covers in sizes of any assortment.

          Length 366 cm for small cars ... £3.45 each
            "    396 cm  "  medium  "   ... £3.75  "
            "    427 cm  "  large   "   ... £4.15  "

We look forward to receiving a trial order from you.

                    Yours faithfully,
                  for J. APPLETON & CO. LTD.


                  G. A. Sanders
                  Sales Department

PS.  Prices for smaller quantities will be quoted on request.

Enc.
```

Secretarial aid No. 4

One of the essential things that each of us must keep in mind when we work in an office is that we are responsible not only for the final product, but also for the work of all persons who share a job with us. Thus a typist may feel that all she has to do is to copy an invoice, quotation, pay-roll, etc., and that it is not her fault if the totals, which someone else has added, are wrong. But this is not the case. It is just as much the responsibility of the typist to see that the totals are right as it is the duty of the person who first added the figures and wrote in a wrong total. Check all totals by adding up the columns before you type the total.

If you do find a mistake, needless to say you do not shout about it and wait to be patted on the back; instead, you go quietly to the person who may have made the mistake and ask whether *you* are wrong in wondering about something that seems out of order.

Composing at machine

Type the following in double spacing, filling in the correct preposition in the blank space.

I am grateful *to* you *for* your help. I am not prepared to part *with* the box. We were annoyed *at* them because they acted contrary *to* our instructions. The girl was indebted *to* her teachers *for* the success she had. He is responsible *for* the cashier *for* the most unsatisfactory state of the books. He was quite oblivious *to* what was going on around him. This student is always amenable *to* discipline. This desk is different in size *to* all the others. Do you agree *with* me, and are you ready to agree *to* my proposal? The director is well versed *in* mathematics.

Review Quiz No. 4

Type the following on A4 paper in single-line spacing, with double spacing between each item, filling in the correct word or words in the blank spaces. Do not write on your textbook.

1. When typing on ruled lines, type very slightly *above* the line.
2. Headings typed in lower case characters must be *underlined*
3. Final punctuation marks should never be *underlined*
4. Thick carbon packs can be inserted into the machine by using the *paper release*.
5. A key which can be depressed without causing the carriage to move forward is known as a *dead* key.
6. An ornamental arrangement at the end of a section or chapter is known as a . . . . .
7. A document stating the work to be done by a contractor is called a . . . . .
8. When typing accounts with two sides, the space allowed for both sides must be . . . . .
9. The *left* side of an account should always be typed first.
10. Totals of an account or balance sheet must be . . . . . each other.
11. A Balance Sheet is a statement of . . . . . and . . . . . of a firm.
12. In a Bill of Quantities the separate items are typed in . . . . . spacing with . . . . . spacing between items.
13. The pages of a Specification and a Bill of Quantities are numbered at . . . . .
14. The last word of a paragraph or of a page must never be . . . . .

Turn to page 199 and check your answers. Score one point for each correct entry. Total Score: 16.

Type the following letter on A4 paper.

Yr. ref (Ref. from previous letter)
Our ref. JH/LP

J. Appleton & Co. Ltd.,
28 Broad St.,
NOTTINGHAM. N62 7 OP.

Typist: this letter is a reply to the one on page 74 Use suitable date

Thank y. for yr. ltr. dated   and f. yr. N.P. catalogue of car covers. [Attached please find our Order No. 218/40 for 10 of ea. size. / We shd. like dely. of these by Wednesday of next week *. Should this be impossible, please let us know immediately.

If this line sells well, we will certainly order in larger quantities and we wonder what additional discount y. wd. allow on an order such as

200 – 366 cm. @ £3.45 (Small cars) I.C.
150 – 424 cm. @ £4.15 (Large cars) I.C.

"1" "4" We note that all orders are /carriage fwd/; However, in / case of a large order /as above/ wd. y. be prepared to pay the carriage? [The next occasion yr. rep. is in this area, please ask him to call.

Yrs. ffy. Stewart & Goodall Ltd
J. Haddleton M.P.O.A.
Pur. Officer

150 – 396 cm. @ £3.75 (medium cars)

* Typist – please insert date

Please mark letter for the att. of G.A. Sanders & mark /alculation

Set out the following Minutes on A4 paper.

12½

MINUTES of a comm. meeting of the Guild of Students held in Room 4 @ 1 College of Commerce, Bristol, on first March --- @ 1700 hrs.

Present: G. G. Perrins (Chairman)

[circled list:]
S. T. Liggins
Miss K. G. Hamilton
K. Ryland, J Ryder, Mrs. A. Naylor
E Colley.

List in alph. order.

1. APOLOGIES — Apologies were recd from Miss J. Keeley, Mr. H. Rye, + Mr. R. Tippett.

2. MINUTES OF LAST MEETING — The Sec. read / mins. of the meetg held on Jan 3 --- These were signed as being a correct record. [circled: By / Chairman]

3. MATTERS ARISING
   Participation in Activities — The chairman sd th only 2.7% of / members took any part in / activities of / Union. After a lengthy discussion it was unanimously agreed th / a circular to all members outlining / activities taking place up to / end of June. [circled: the Sec. send]

4 RECORD PLAYER
   of Miss Hamilton — In reply to a question from Miss Hamilton, the chairman explained th / Record Player was not available because it had bn smashed by person or persons unknown + no action had bn taken abt

NP/lc/ a replacement [The Treasurer sd th there were insufficient funds available w. wh.

lc. To purchase anr record Player

5 A.O.B — (Date of AGM) — 1st Oct. of
   It was agreed th the AGM wd be held on 1st Oct.

6. DATE of next meetg — 30th June @ 1700 hrs

Type the following on A4 paper.

Typist — I would like this in draft form. Mark it
"Draft": use treble spacing and wide margins — say
left margin of 38 mm.

BACKFEEDING

consisting It sometimes happens that an addition or
alteration has to be made to a p. of a document/of
sev. sheets stapled together (wh. hv. bn.). This can be
done by what is known as back backward feed
i.e., inserting the paper into the m/c from front
N.P. of platen instead of in normal manner. [To do this
the following steps shd be taken:—

1. Erase neatly any letter(s) th. hv. to be
altered.

single 2. Insert a sheet of paper in the m/c in
usual way.

4 3. Turn the platen backwards so th. two
sheets are fed together sufficiently far
f. the loose sheet to be removed. The
typewritten sheet on which alteration is
to be made is held by feed mechanism firmly
+ by means of the paper release lever it
can be adjusted to the correct position
for addition or alteration & necessary
correction then made.

(without having
to unfasten
Trs. sheets)

Typist — please use
hanging paragraphs
for numbered
paras.

Typist 3. Between sheet of paper
inserted and platen, insert
bottom of page and note
alteration to be made to be
altered.

5 If letters next to alterations are light
when rubbing out may b also
rubbed over adjacent letters type
over these so that all letters are
same shade.

Production typing

Job 62
Production Target—*20 minutes*

Type the following Monthly Sales Analysis on A4 paper in double spacing, leaving 3 spaces between columns. Centre vertically and horizontally.

Monthly Sales Figures (all caps + underscored)

Typist - please put commas in figures

(in £'s)

Month	Credit	Cash	Hire Purchase
Jan.	2510	100466	25627
February	1445	129865	20446
March	1565	146400	23263
Apl.	3626	70121	10414
May	4324	85320	9648
June	6210	65812	8040
July	6384	74697	8762
Sept.	7123	73297	9142
Oct.	8354	78015	10092
Nov.	9364	102454	9555
Dec.	10450	94136	12465
August	4234	64110	7322

(trs. marks indicated)

Job 63
Production Target—*20 minutes*

Display the following on A4 paper.

EASTFIELD POLYTECHNIC (spaced caps)

Staff Vacancies (closed caps)

Dept.	Subject + Grade	Salary £
③ Mathematics + Statistics	Mathematics	
	Senior Lecturer	2,700
	Lecturer II	2,400
② Industrial Engineering	Management	
	Senior Lecturer	2,700
	Manufacturing Technology	
	Sen. Lecturer	2,700
	Metallurgy	
	Lecturer II	2,400
① Computer	Computers	
	Principal Lecturer	3,000
	Sen. Lecturer	2,700

(Please put in numbered order - do not type nos.)

UNIT 20

Unit 13

Skill building

Type each line or sentence (A, B, and C) *three* times, and, if time permits, complete your practice by typing each group once as it appears.

A. Review alphabet keys

1.   The take-over bid made was entirely unexpected, but was judged to be inadequate in view of the size of the business.

B. Build speed on common phrases

2. to go, to me, to do, to be, to say, to ask, to pay, to come.
3. It seems to me that you should be able to go home this year.
4. We hope to be in a position to ask you to come and visit us.
5. We do not know whether to pay or to return the damaged toys.

C. Build speed on common prefixes

6. complete, commerce, compare, combine, comply, commit, common
7. Compare the completed contract with the one now recommended.
8. She will be compelled to comply with the complete programme.
9. To avoid complicating the issue, he will not commit himself.

Accuracy/Speed Practice
Three-minute timing   Not more than 3 errors

		words
AS.16	The interview is a two-way process. The interviewer must find out	13
	if you have the desired qualifications and suitable personality. You	27
	must try to size up the job to see if it is what you are looking for.	41

Before the interview, the interviewer will have studied your **53** Application Form and Job Sheet to find out what the job is about — what **67** has to be done, how it has to be done, and where it has to be done. He **81** will then be ready to ask you a number of questions designed to confirm **95** statements made on your Application Form and to find out other facts **109** about you. **111**

When the most suitable person has been chosen, her references are **124** checked. This may be done by mail or by telephone. If they are in **137** order, the chosen person will be offered the job. **147**

When you receive a letter offering you a post, see that you write **160** back straight away, thanking the writer for the offer and giving your **174** decision. **176**

In a new job there are many things to learn. No matter how well **188** you have been trained, your new employer is sure to ask you to do one **202** or two tasks in a different way. When he does so, carry out all instruc- **217** tions he gives. If, later on, you feel your way is better, there is **231** usually no harm in saying that you think it is.   (S.I. 1.33) **240**

5. Practise typing columnar work with heading. Type the following table on A5 paper (210 × 148 mm), centring vertically and horizontally. Leave three spaces between columns.

PURCHASE TAX REDUCTIONS

Gift No.	Description	Old Vouchers	New Vouchers
215	Transistor Radio	5,800	5,500
218	Record Player	4,900	4,300
902	"Convertible" Compact	460	400
903	"Convertible" Compact	530	470
1005	Dressing Case	1,350	1,350

6. Type the following financial statement on A5 paper (210 × 148 mm), centring vertically and horizontally. Leave three spaces between columns.

NORTHERN CONSTRUCTION CO. LTD   *c — Centre + u/score*

Financial Statement.

Trading Results

	1969	1970
	£	£
Trading Profit before taxation	1,917,204	1,649,482
Profit/taxation ~~taxation~~	864 361	733 143
Less dividend to shareholder	6/440/686	493 797
Less profit retained in business	259,675	239 346
Group turnover (approx.)	9 250,000	8,250000

(marginal notes: "after before sp/", "trs.", "uc")

Numbers

Many offices do not insert a comma to separate millions from thousands, and thousands from hundreds. In this case the figures are typed as follows:

(a) Numbers comprising *five* figures or less are blocked together, e.g., 1723, 26785.

(b) Numbers comprising *six* or more figures are grouped in threes (starting from the unit figure) with one space between the groups instead of commas, e.g., 9 687 253.

NOTE: If commas are used to separate millions from thousands, and thousands from hundreds, leave no space before or after comma, e.g. 9,687,253.

10. Display the following on A4 paper. The rectangle should measure 203 mm × 70 mm. Keep your typed copy for future reference in folder No. 2.

<u>Sizes of Envelopes</u>

Post Office Preferred Sizes

Minimum size: 140 mm length x 89 mm width

Maximum size: 235 mm length x 121 mm width

Note: Envelopes coming within these sizes are:—

Also   229 x 102 mm
        89 x 152 mm

C6 114 x 62 mm
DL 110 x 220 mm

<u>Post Office Regulations</u>

1. Post Office regulations require address to be parallel to the length and not to the breadth of the envelope.

2. Postal town should preferably be typed in capitals.

3. The <u>postcode</u> should be typed as follows:

   a) It is always the last item in the address and should have a line to itself.

   b) If it is impossible, because of lack of space, to put the code on a separate line, type it <u>six</u> spaces to the right of the last line.

   c) Always type code in block capitals.

   d) Do not use full stops or any punctuation marks between or after the characters in the code.

   e) Leave <u>one</u> clear space between the two halves of the code.

   f) NEVER underline the code.

   Examples:

   Block style — standard
          punctuation

   Messrs. W. H. Ramsay & Co.,
   Mortimer Street,
   LONDON.
   W1N 8BA

   Indented style — open
          punctuation

   Messrs W H Ramsay & Co
          Mortimer Street
              LONDON
                  W1N 8BA

3. Practise typing column work. Display the following table in double-line spacing on A5 paper (210 × 148 mm), leaving 5 spaces between columns.

LIST OF SCHOOL OFFICERS' BADGES AVAILABLE

Captain	Monitor	Physical Education
Vice-Captain	Monitress	Birthday
House Captain	Leader	Merit
Form Captain	Sports	Good Conduct
Head Boy	Swimming	Department
Head Girl	Netball	Punctuality
Prefect	Football	Courtesy

4. Type a copy of the following on A4 paper in double-line spacing. Keep your typed copy for future reference in Folder No. 2.

COLUMN HEADINGS

In addition to /main headings, ea. column usually has its own headings which must be taken into a/c when deciding on /longest line in a column. ← then/longest item in the column,

1. If /heading is shorter, it must be centred over the longest item

u.c. 2. to do this, find the centre point of /column by tapping /space
l.c. bar once for every 2 letters & spaces in the longest item. Begin from for the scale point set for /start of the column.

3. From the centre point thus reached / backspace once H for every 2 ltrs & spaces. Start to type /heading from this point. (in the heading)

4. If /heading is /longest line in /column, /column items must be centred under it as follows:

H (a) Type the heading @ /scale/point set for /start of the column. (spaces in /heading)

(b) Find /centre point of /column by tapping /space bar once for every two letters, beginning from / 1st ltr of the heading.

(c) Fr. /centre point thus reached, back-space once for every 2 letters & spaces in /longest column item under /heading.

H (d) Reset tab stop (or margin stop if in first column) at this scale point for /start of /column items.

Before typing /column headings therefore, take the following steps:

(upper - block paras; please for numbered items)

11. Type a copy of the following on A4 paper in single-line spacing with double spacing between the items. Keep your typed copy for future reference in Folder No. 2.

(circled note: Please use hanging paras)

ADDRESSING ENVELOPES, POSTCARDS, ETC.

(a) Always be sure to use an envelope sufficiently large to take/letter/bearing in mind | P.O. preferred size/.

(b) Many firms hv their name/printed in / top left corner. This ensures/safe & speedy return of / ltr *(+ address)* if/for any reason/ it cannot be delvd.

(c) Always type / envelope of ea. ltr immediately after typing the ltr.

(d) Single/line spacing +block style are preferable on a small envelope. With larger envelopes/ address may be better displayed + more easily read by being typed in double-line spacing.

(e) On most envelopes the address shd be started/ *about* 50 mm fr the l edge +/ 1st line shd be approx ½ way down.

(d) Remember to type the envelopes of any extra carbon copies) to or offices or persons of their informⁿ.

(f) *(circled: wh may be sent)* Special instructions/ shd be typed/ in caps. + underscores, 2 spaces above /name of the addressee. (such as personal/confidential/ private,)

(h) Some firms prefer open punctuation, i.e., no punctuation whatever is inserted in name + address.

12. Cut slips of paper size 229 × 102 mm and type the following addresses in block style.

```
Richard Daniel Ltd., 11 Canal Street, Manchester.  M4 6HD
Miss A. Blackie, 15 Hall Lane, Upminster, Essex.  RM14 1AP Private
Wilson & Mansfield Ltd., Market Street, Leicester.  LEI 6DF
International Co. Ltd., 101 Hempstead Road, Watford, Herts.  WD1 3EY
Mrs. A. M. Little, 10 Sealand Road, Bristol.  BS1 3BQ
Mr. M. Jones, 4 Clitton Road, Northampton.  NN1 5BQ
Dunn Bros. Ltd., 320 High Street, Huddersfield.  HD1 2NE
F. Ferguson Ltd., St. Giles Street, Edinburgh.  EH1 1YW
Everitt Ltd., 20 Thomas Street, Liverpool.  L1 6BJ (Confidential)
B. France & Co. Ltd., 439 Oxford Street, London.  W1A 1BH
```

2. Type a copy of the following on A4 paper in single-line spacing with double between paragraphs. Keep your typed copy for future reference in Folder No. 2.

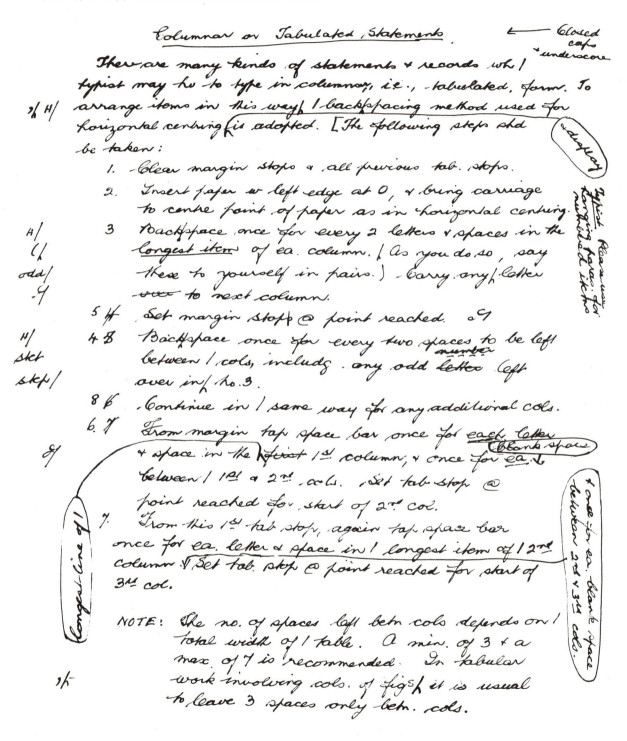

<u>Columnar or Tabulated Statements</u>. ← Closed caps + underscore

There are many kinds of statements & records wh 1 typist may hv to type in columnar, i.e., tabulated, form. To arrange items in this way 1 backspacing method used for horizontal centring is adopted. [The following steps shd be taken:

1. Clear margin stops & all previous tab. stops.

2. Insert paper w left edge at 0, & bring carriage to centre point of paper as in horizontal centring.

3. Backspace once for every 2 letters & spaces in the <u>longest item</u> of ea. column. (As you do so, say these to yourself in pairs.) Carry any 1 letter over to next column.

5. Set margin stop @ point reached.

4. Backspace once for every two spaces to be left between 1 cols, includg any odd letter left over in 1 no. 3.

8. Continue in 1 same way for any additional cols.

6. From margin tap space bar once for each letter & space in the 1st column, & once for ea. 1 between 1 1st & 2nd cols. Set tab stop @ point reached for start of 2nd col.

7. From this 1st tab stop, again tap space bar once for ea. letter & space in 1 longest item of 1 2nd column & Set tab stop @ point reached for start of 3rd col.

NOTE: The no. of spaces left betn cols depends on 1 total width of 1 table. A min. of 3 & a max. of 7 is recommended. In tabular work involving cols. of figs it is usual to leave 3 spaces only betn. cols.

13. Type a copy of the following on A4 paper in single-line spacing with double spacing between the numbered items. Keep your typed copy for future reference in Folder No. 2.

FORMS OF ADDRESS

1. Courtesy titles must always be used when writing to individuals.
2. Use Mr. OR Esq. (NEVER both) if writing to a male person.
3. Address a married lady and a single lady as follows:

   Mrs. L. Brown and Miss J. Clark (if names are different).

   Mrs. L. and Miss C. Brown (if names are same).
4. If the word 'Sen.' (Senior) or 'Jun.' (Junior) is used, this comes immediately after the name & before Esq., and is preceded & followed by a comma. Always leave one clear space after the comma.
5. Letters after a person's name must be arranged in order of importance, as follows: (a) military decorations, (b) Civil Decorations; e.g., O.B.E. (c) University Degrees; e.g., M.A. (d) M.P., (e) J.P.
6. Rev. or Dr. or Sir replaces Esq., (Mr. or)
7. Use the Misses . . . when writing to more than one single lady w. same name.
8. Use Messrs. when addressing more than one male person.
9. Letters after a person's name do not require a space between them, but a space must be left between ea. group of letters.
10. Use no courtesy title for limited companies, even if the name includes a personal name.
11. Address 2 married ladies of the same name as Mesdames
12. Use no courtesy title with impersonal names or those beginning w. 'The'.

14. Cut slips of paper size 229 × 102 mm and type the following addresses in block style. Use standard punctuation and insert any courtesy titles that have been omitted.

Holt & Marsdon, 1 Southsea Rd., Portsmouth, Hants. PO5 3JD

Rev. P. H. Rose, The Vicarage, St. Anthony's Rd., Exmouth. EX8 3AF

Valerie Ryan-Miller, The Bridge, Bury, Lancs. BL9 0SW (Private)

The New Dry-Cleaning Co., 40 Thames Street, Bath, BA2 3LA

Jas. L. Marlow, Jnr., OBE, The Gables, Alfreton, Derby. DE5 7JA

Joan & Betty Hayward, Halifax St., Brighouse, Yorks. HD6 1AY

Arthur & John Paton, 57 Kings Rd., Norwich. NOR 01A

Monkhouse & Sons Ltd., 171 Newbury Rd., Romford, Essex. For the attention of Mr. M. V. Monkhouse

Unit 20

Skill building

Type the alphabetic review *once* for practice, *once* for speed, and *once* for accuracy.

A. Review alphabet keys

1.   Amongst the junk she bought from the auction sale was a
unique glazed pottery case which was in excellent condition.

Accuracy/Speed Practice
Five-minute timing   *Not more than 3 errors*

words

AS.24 A remarkable young Roman slave earned his own freedom by invent-	13
ing a system of shorthand in the last century before the Christian era.	27
His name was Tiro, and he was born south of Rome in the year 103 B.C.	40

In 96 B.C. this bright young slave was sent to Rome to study with | 54
his master's two sons, who were called Marcus and Quintus. They were | 68
about the same age as Tiro, and treated him like a friend rather than a | 82
slave. As the boys advanced in their studies their friendship grew | 95
stronger, and when the master died, Marcus became Tiro's legal owner. | 109
He made Tiro his secretary. | 114

It is not quite clear just when Tiro invented his system, and some | 127
people go as far as to say that he stole a system already in use in | 140
Greece. Others say that he merely perfected abbreviating devices used | 154
by the Greeks. However, most agree that Tiro's "notes" were the first | 168
organized system that enabled a writer to take down the spoken words as | 182
fast as they were said. In those days the notes were written on clay | 196
tablets. According to some sources, Marcus himself picked up a short- | 210
hand system during one of his trips to Greece and taught it to Tiro, who | 225
adapted it to Latin. Whether this is true or not we do not know, but it | 239
was Tiro who wrote the shorthand treatise that was soon distributed | 252
throughout the Roman Empire under his name. | 261

The system was taught in schools to children of all classes, and | 274
the Romans were quick to realize the value of it. | 284

Tiro was a great help to Marcus, and, as a result, he was made a | 297
free man. He showed his gratefulness by remaining Marcus's friend as | 310
well as his devoted secretary. | 316

Tiro wrote several books on the Latin language, but his greatest | 329
contribution to the advancement of civilization lies in the widespread | 343
use made of the Tironian shorthand. Not only was the system taught in | 357
the Roman Empire, but with the advent of Christianity, it was adopted | 371
by the early Christian churchmen as a practical means of spreading the | 385
new religious doctrine and recording the deeds of the saints and martyrs. | 400

(S.I. 1.38)

Job 36

Type the following on A4 paper in single-line spacing with double between numbered items.

(NOTICE TO ALL OFFICE STAFF) → ← *Closed caps & underscore*

DECIMAL CURRENCY ← *Spaced caps & underscored*

To ensure consistency in all office documents, please ~~following~~ follow very carefully the instructions given below:

1. Cheques. When handwritten

Figures	Words
£140-05 *	One hundred and forty pounds 05
£70--00	Seventy pounds
£0-45 †	Seventy-five pence
£60-23	Sixty pounds 23

* note use of hyphen instead of decimal point

→ When typed

Figures	Words
£80.00	Eighty pounds
£73.42	Seventy-three pounds 42

(† Always have at least one figure (a nought if necessary) between the pound sign & / hyphen (or decimal point))

2. P is / abbrev. for new pence. It is placed after the amt & there is no full stop unless it ends a sentence.

3. Any amt over 99½ new pence must be expressed as pound(s), e.g., 80p + ~~30p~~ 50p = £1.~~70~~30 (one pound thirty), & NOT as 130 pence.

4. Amounts in whole pounds *(std be written :)* £5, £324,000, OR £5.00, £324,000.00 *(Typist: in this case raise these 2 points)*

5. When typing column work :
   (a) w. pounds & pence the £ sign always goes over the unit figure of the pounds column.
   (b) w. pounds only - centre the £ sign over / longest line in the column.

A.C. BANKS
OFFICE MANAGER

Typist. I want to put an advert in the Brighton Handbook in which the pp. measure 178mm x 203mm. Please Type the following on the handbook size of paper & let me see how it looks.

A.A. * * * * R.A.C.

THE COURT HOTEL
St Mary's Road, Brighton BN7 1NP
Tel: 0243 567229. Telegrams: Panoramic

* Faces south. Adjoins Town centre} all caps.
& all entertainments.

* Ballroom   * Table Tennis   → Put in
* Lounge   * Crazy Golf.   two
* Cocktail Bar   * Lift to all floors columns
* Lock-up Garage * Billiards   in alpha.
                  * Night Porter   order.

* NEW HEATED SWIMMING POOL

ACCLAIMED AS ONE OF THE MOST
FAMOUS HOTELS IN EUROPE

FULL BOARD TARIFFS

Off Season — £25 - £35
Season⁺ — £27 - £37

Daily rates available on application

⁺ Applies: May/September

← 31mm →

Typist please draw to size and leave blank.

153mm.

Display the following on A5 paper. Make full use of closed capitals, spaced capitals, underscore, etc.

ST. JOHN/S MUSICAL SOCIETY

Presents

The Pearl Fishers (spaced caps)

by

BIZET

in

ST. JOHN'S CONCERT HALL

KINGSHURST ROAD

WARWICK

Wednesday 13th May 1970

to

Saturday 16th May 1970

Commencing @ 7.15 pm.

PRICES OF ADMISSION

Wednesday to Friday		Saturday	
Stalls	35P	Stalls	45P
Balcony	40P	Balcony	50P

ALL SEATS ARE NUMBERED T RESERVED.

Applications for tickets should be sent to:

Hon. Sec.

St. John's Mus. Soc.

" " Road

Warwick.

Typist : Please draft this on a sheet of A4 paper. Tomorrow it must be put on an offset-litho stencil.

McGRAW-HILL PUBLISHING COMPANY LIMITED

1971 METHODS CONFERENCE

FOR BUSINESS TEACHERS.

UNIVERSITY OF SUSSEX, BRIGHTON

28th - 31st JULY, INCLUSIVE   ← lc.

PROGRAMME

The lecture programme wl incorporate a wide range of topics of practical value & significance to all teachers of business subjects. Practical workshop sessions wl alternate w./ more formal lectures. There wl be an exhibition of teaching aids.

(of business machines)

FEES

The conference charge is   for residents and for non-residents. The conference charge for delegates incorporates board + lodging, the cost of the special dinner on 30th July, tea + coffee, transport during the conference and entertainment. (Insert 'A'   .) non-residents are asked to indicate below whether they wish to join / party attending / Chichester Festival Theatre for an extra charge.

APPLICATION FORM

Please complete + return to: Miss B.M. Abbott,
Conference Secretary, McGraw-Hill Publishing Co. Ltd.

Surname _____   Initials _____ . for mrs. Date ____
                                                     mrs
Address _____   mrs

School or College _____

Please submit your application form NOT LATER THAN 29 MAY, + enclose a deposit of £1.50.

non-Residents: I wish / do not wish to join the theatre party.

non.   'A' The conference charge for residents includes tea, coffee + luncheon.

┌─────────────────────────┐
│ I wish to attend   │
│ as a   │
│ RESIDENT / NON-   │
│ RESIDENT   │
└─────────────────────────┘

Unit 14

Skill building

Type each exercise (A, B, and C) *once* for practice, *once* for speed, and finally *once* for accuracy.

A. Review alphabet keys

1.   Jack was quite delighted when they visited the tropical
zone and was impressed by the exotic colours of the flowers.

B. Build accuracy on shift lock drill

2. WHAT'S-HIS-NAME, GO-AS-YOU-PLEASE, EIGHTY-TWO, MOTHER-IN-LAW
3. WHAT'S-HIS-NAME should call and see his MOTHER-IN-LAW today.
4. I do not like your GO-AS-YOU-PLEASE attitude one little bit.

C. Build accuracy on concentration drill

5. As a teacher of pharmaceutics, pharmacognosy, pharmaceutical
chemistry and forensic pharmacy, I use an old PHARMACOPOEIA.

Accuracy/Speed Practice
Four-minute timing   Not more than 3 errors

	words
AS.17 What a grand place Majorca is for a holiday. In fact, it seems to me	14
that nature designed it as a holiday playground. The climate is pleasant	28
at any season, with cool sea breezes on the hottest day. Along the coast	43
line there are fine sandy beaches and you can swim all the year round.	57
Palma, the capital, is a fine city with its port and old town all in	71
one. To the east of Palma is Pastilla where there is a perfect stretch of	85
golden sand running along the bay to Arenal. Also there are two or three	100
smaller beaches where the soft sand and shallow waters make bathing safe	114
for children, and there is plenty to do — water ski-ing, horse riding,	128
bathing, boating, etc., and, by night, a variety of bars and night clubs	143
where you can enjoy music and dancing.	151
Arenal has the finest beach on the island. Here you will find a three-	165
mile sweep of golden sand, gay night life in clubs and cafes, many shops,	179
and yet only twenty minutes from Palma. A short distance beyond Arenal,	194
among the rocks, there are ideal conditions for snorkel and skin-diving.	208
Palma Nova has superb sandy beaches with safe bathing for all ages,	221
and rocky coves for the more daring. There are excellent shops, bars and	236
cafes and plenty of evening entertainment. Palma Nova is set in some of	250
Majorca's most delightful countryside with warm-scented pine woods and	264
hills, yet with the delights of Palma only eight miles away.	276
If you prefer a quieter holiday, you will like the fishing village of	290
Porto Cristo, which is forty miles east of Palma. Here there are fascin-	305
ating hill walks which reward you with wonderful views of the island's	319
coast.	320

(S.I. 1.37)

Type the following extract of Bill of Quantities in correct form on A4 paper. Rule necessary columns.

Page 1 Bill of Quantities for the Erection of a 2-storey house at The Oaks, Wood Lane, Streetly, Staffs, for Mr J L Wilkins. Walter Archer, A.R.I.B.A., Chartered Architect & Quantity Surveyor, High St, Sutton Coldfield. — May 19--

PRELIMINARIES

Item Closed caps →

Contract Conditions

Item		Qty	Unit
A	The prices in this Bill of Quantities will be deemed to cover the cost of complying with the Clauses contained herein ~~with the Clauses~~ as set forth below:		
B	Clause 1. Interpretation.		
C	Clause 2 Specification & Dimensions		
D	Clause 3. Additional or Extra Works.		
	Carried to collection	£	

Page 2 Substructure ← Closed caps

Excavating AS GP 103 ← Closed caps

Item		Qty	Unit
A	Starting from natural ground level		
↓	Surface to reduce levels	860	cu. m
B	Starting from reduced level		
↓	Surface average 100 mm deep to reduce levels	10	sq. m
C	Rubble-filled cellar not exceeding 1.50m deep.	15	cu m
D	Trench not exceeding 1.50 m deep for foundation	90	cu. m
E	Pit not exceeding one cubic metre for ditto (In no. 2)	1	cu m
	Starting from about 600 mm below natural ground level		
F	Rubble-filled cellar not exceeding 1.50 m deep	75	cu m
G	Trench not exceeding 1.50 m deep for foundation	100	cu m
H.	Pit not exceeding 1.50 m deep for ditto	10	cu m
J	Trench over 1.50 m but not exceeding 3.00 m deep for ditto	1	cu. m
K	Pit not exceeds one cubic metre for ditto (In no 1)	1	cu. m
	Starting from abt 1.70 m ~~deep for~~ below ~~foundation~~ natural level		
L	Trench not exceeds 1.50 m deep for foundation	1	cu m
	Carried to collection	£	

Technique development

Carbon copies

It is necessary to keep, for filing purposes, at least one carbon copy of each letter or document typed. To take a carbon copy, take the following steps:

1. Place face downwards on a flat surface the sheet on which the typing is to be done.

2. On top of this place a sheet of carbon paper with the coated surface upwards.

3. On top of these place the sheet of paper on which the carbon copy is to be made. Pick up all sheets together and insert in machine with coated surface of carbon paper facing the platen.

Headings

Main headings, paragraph headings, and shoulder headings are used in letters in the same way as in manuscript work, see instructions on page 4.

6. Practise typing letter with headings. Type the following letter, taking a carbon copy for filing. Use paragraph headings for sub-headings.

John Gosnell & Co. Upper Duke St, Liverpool. (Insert Date)
We have pleasure in enclosing our new illustrated Price List wh gives
full details of the attractive range of gifts we have available for
Christmas. Selection of Gifts. You wl notice th on the back page we
hv illustrated in full colour a representative selection of the gifts
we can supply. Display of Xmas gifts. The full range of Xmas
gift packs is permanently on view in our Ln Showrooms + also
in the main provincial cities. Order Form. We hv also included
an order form for the convenience of those wishing to place their
orders direct. May we ask you to keep this letter for ref. purposes? NP
Yrs ffy, E. H. BUTLER & Sons, Sales Mgr.

Additional carbon copies

In addition to the carbon copy required for filing, many business letters are typed with extra carbon copies, which are sent to any persons who may be concerned. If a copy of a letter is sent to someone other than the addressee, the letters cc. (= carbon copy) are typed at the left margin (usually at foot) followed by the name of the recipient. Where a copy is being sent to more than one person, the names are typed after cc. one underneath the other, and the name of the person for whom the copy is intended is either ticked at the side or underlined, e.g.,

(First copy)	(Second copy)	(Third copy)
cc. Mr. Jones ✓	cc. Mr. Jones	cc. Mr. Jones
Mrs. Stone	Mrs. Stone ✓	Mrs. Stone
Mr. French	Mr. French	Mr. French ✓

Job 58 Production Target—*20 minutes*

Type an original and one copy of the following portion of Specification in correct form on A4 paper, using a continuation sheet if necessary. Fold the Specification and endorse in the correct position. All items underscored to be in closed capitals unless otherwise instructed.

SPECIFICATION of works to be done & materials to be provided in the erection of a house in Hardwick Rd., Streetly, for Mr. Walter Carroll.

William Dixon, ARIBA,
Architect & Surveyor,
128 Parade,
Sutton Coldfield. Warwicks

MAY 1971

PRELIMINARIES

SITE — The site is situated adjoining No. 45 Hardwick Rd., Streetly, and may be inspected at any time.

SCOPE OF CONTRACT — The work included in the contract comprises the erection and completion of a house and garage complete w. all drainage.

CONTRACTOR — The contractor must provide all necessary plant, scaffolding, ladders, etc., required for the proper execution of the work for the use of workmen and sub-contractor, & f. maintaining same during the progress of the works, & f. removing when no longer required.

NOTICES & FEES — The contractor is to allow for giving all requisite notices to the local authority, obtaining permission & paying all fees legally if required.

WATER — The contractor shall provide water for the use of the works.

ATTEND — Each trade is to attend upon all others and perform all jobbing work throughout.

End of preliminaries

EXCAVATOR & CONCRETOR — centre → to raft, walls, piers & for drains as shown on plans.

EXCAVATE — Excavate for all foundations & trenches & well ~~run as the work proceeds~~

SAND — The sand to be clean, sharp, pit or fresh water river sand & to be of quality & type approved by architect.

FILLING — Fill in to foundations & trenches & well ram as the work proceeds.

CEMENT — The cement to be 'Super' Cement.

AGGREGATE — The aggregate is to be composed of approved clean hard stone, all broken to the gauges described.

FOUNDATIONS — The cement concrete raft foundations to comprise . . . .

7. Practise letter with cc. Type the following letter with a carbon copy for filing and extra copies for Office Manager and Supplies Dept. Insert date. Use A5 paper.

John Wilkes (Printers) Ltd., Halifax St., Brighouse, Yorks. HD6 1AY

Dear Sirs, Will you kindly quote yr price for typing 1000 copies of the enclosed letter, stating also the approximate time reqd. to carry out this work. Each letter should be typed separately, not ~~printed~~ duplicated. [N.P.] [Yr price shd include the cost of addressing envelopes from a typewritten mailing list, & typing the name & address on each letter. Envelopes & letter-headings wd be supplied by us. [N.P.] [The letters & envelopes wod be returned to us for enclosing & despatch. We sh appreciate yr. early reply. Yrs. ffy., R.A. Cripps & Son Ltd., Manager.

Blind carbon copies

It sometimes happens that the writer does not want the addressee to know that copies have been distributed, in which case the typist types a bcc. (blind carbon copy) note. When the letter is finished and the carbon paper removed, the carbon copies are reinserted into the machine. At the foot of these copies the typist then types the bcc. note at the left margin, as follows:

> bcc. Mr. Jones
> Mrs. Stone
> Mr. French

marking the name of the recipient as before. The bottom copy on which all the bcc. notes appear is the one kept for filing.

8. Practise typing letter with blind carbon copies. Take one file carbon and one bcc. copy for Mr. J. Overton. Keep your typed copy for future reference in Folder No. 2. Use A5 paper.

Ref FWG/GFD   Today's date

JAMESON

Walter Jameson Ltd., 24 Milton St., Bury, Lancs. BI9 OSW
For the attention of ~~the~~ Mr. J. G. Brown, Chief Buyer.

Dear Sirs, <u>Office Supplies</u> Although we [hv] serviced yr typewriters for several yrs, you may not hv. realised th we are specialists is of office machinery & stationery. In any case, we shd appreciate the opportunity of submitting our quotations for any of yr office requirements the next time you are in need of supplies. [N.P.] [In particular, we [hv] an exceptionally attractive line in "Everclear" Carbon Paper, of wh we enclose a specimen sheet, & we sh be pleased to quote for either standard or special sizes in this carbon. [N.P.] [We look forward to hearing fr you whenever you are interested in renewing yr equipment. Yrs ffy, Office Requisites Ltd., Sales Manager

Item		CONCRETE WORK (cont'd)				£

CONCRETE WORK (cont'd)

27 _Mild steel bar as in appendix_
    B; cutting, bending & securing w.
    tying-wire, distance-blocks [SPACERS]
    & ordinary spacers."

A	12 mm diameter bar in lintels.	24	kg		
B	10 mm Ditto in ditto.	250	kg		
C	10 mm diameter links, stirrup, binder or special spacer.	350	kg		
D	8 mm diameter Ditto.	29 7	kg		

[BENDING]
28 _Standard grade steel deformed_
    bar as Appendix B; cutting,
    bending & securing w. tying-wire,
    distance-blocks & ordinary spacers.

E	25 mm diameter bar in lintel.	32	kg		
F	20 mm Ditto in ditto.	82	kg		
G	16 mm Ditto in ditto.	305	kg		
H	12 mm Ditto in suspended floor.	42	kg		
J	12 mm Ditto in lintel on staircase.	4 44	kg		
K	10 mm Ditto in ditto.	2 89	kg		

29 _Welded steel wire fabric as_
    Appendix B; cutting, bending
    & securing w. tying-wire &
    distance-blocks.

L	100 mm × 100 mm mesh fabric weighing 0.76 kg per sq. metre w. 200 mm side & end laps; wrapping around horizontal steel beams.	10	sq. m		
M	Horizontal soffit of suspended floor or landing.	19	sq m		
N	Sloping soffit of staircase	15	sq m		
P	Side or soffit of horizontal beam-casing or lintel.	256	sq m		
Q	caps → carried to summary				£

31

Continuation sheets for letters

A long letter may require a second sheet. This is called a Continuation Sheet, and sometimes the name or initials of the sender are printed in the top left-hand corner. Otherwise, always use a plain sheet the same size and colour as the previous page.

The only details which you should type are the following: Name of addressee, page number, and date, starting on 4th single space from top.
In fully-blocked letters, all these details are typed at the left margin in double spacing, in the following order: Page number, Date, Name of addressee.
In semi-blocked letters the name of the addressee is typed at the left margin, the page number is centred in typing line and typed as follows: - 2 - and the date ends at the right margin. The letter is continued on the third single-line space below the continuation sheet details.

When a continuation sheet is needed, the letter must be so arranged that at least three or four lines are carried to the second page. On no account must the continuation sheet contain only the complimentary close and name of writer. Also at least two lines of a paragraph must be left at the bottom of the first page.

NOTE: The word 'Continued' or 'P.T.O.' should not be used in letters. A catchword, i.e., the typing of the first word appearing on a continuation sheet at the foot of the preceding page, is sometimes used.

Open punctuation

When open punctuation is used in business letters, no punctuation is used up to and including the salutation, after initials in the body, or in the complimentary close and below.

9. Practise letter with continuation sheet. Type the following letter on A4 (210 × 297 mm) paper, with a continuation sheet. Use margins of 12/72 (pica) and 20/80 (elite), and single-line spacing.

Our ref FLK/MKJ   (Insert date)

Miss L M Johnson
29 New Road
Birkenhead   L41 6NH

Dear Madam

    Thank you for your letter dated   about a book suitable for Secretarial Students taking the shorthand-typist's and audio-typist's examination. SECRETARIAL TYPING by D M Sharp and H M Crozier is an integrated course of dictation, typewriting, English usage, and secretarial duties for shorthand-typists, audio-typists, and personal or private secretaries. The correlation of general office and duties is an essential part of the text. The inclusion of comprehension, written and spoken communication and basic English usage provides continuing and ample training in accurate & speedy transcription.

    The following are the outstanding features of the book —

Planned Text
27h Each of the units deals with some aspect of applied office or secretarial typing. With few exceptions, the units may be taken in any order, thus enabling the work of the typing room to be linked with that being done in Office Practice and Clerical or secretarial duties. u.c.
(Insert A) ~ currently
Correlation of Shorthand and Typing

    The accompanying Gregg Secretarial Dictation text contains, unit for unit, ample informative and office-style dictation practice. This Dictation practice requires the application of typing skills to real- l.c. istic office problems.

10. Practise typing Bill of Quantities. Type a copy of the following extract of a Bill of Quantities on A4 paper, following the layout and the rules given on Page M2, Reference Manual. Please use hanging paragraphs as in copy.

Item	CONCRETE WORK (centre in spaced caps.)			£
	IN-SITU PLAIN CONCRETE WORK			
A	l.c. 1:2:4 Medium Gravel-concrete) 50 mm × 55 mm kerb; tamping) surface to form key for) trowelled bed.)	~~147~~ 147	~~m~~ m	
B	Wrought formwork; 50 mm) side of kerb.)	147	m	
	IN-SITU CONSULTANT-DESIGNED REINFORCED CONCRETE WORK			
l.c.	1:2:4 Medium Gravel-concrete			
C	Casing over 0.10 m sectional area) to horizontal steel beam;) packing around steel fabric) wrapping.	1	cu m	
D	Horizontal lintel over 0.05 m) but not exceeding 0.10 m sectional) area.)	3	cu m	
E	Ditto not exceeding 0.05 m) sectional area.)	13	cu m	
F	Step and staircase.	3	cu m	
G	100 mm Bed; trowelling surface;) laying on cork insulation of) suspended floor. (Insulation) and suspended floor measured) separately.)	5	sq. m	
H	130 mm horizontal suspended) landing; tamping surface to) form key for screeded bed.)	20	sq. m	
J ;h	150 mm horizontal suspended) floor & trowelling surface.)	10	sq. m	
K	150 mm horizontal suspended) landing; tamping surface to) form key for screeded bed.)	2	sq. m	
L	210 mm Ditto; ditto.	3	sq. m	
M	Carried to collection			£

30

Secretarial Duties

The ~~acquiring~~ *acquisition* of secretarial skills and knowledge, in addition to the ability to apply typing skill, is treated as essential. Much of the text and many of the exercises cover the office practice and secretarial duties examination requirements. As the teacher of type-writing often teaches office practice or secretarial duties, the text brings flexibility to the planning of courses and classroom teaching.

Typist: Please turn these 2 paras.

Audio Typing

The additional practice of the Secretarial Dictation Text meets *l.c.* the requirements for examinations for audio-typists.

English Usage

N.P. Teachers recognize the importance of correct English usage in transcription, but many find it difficult to ensure that their students use in transcription and in the typing room the skills learned in the English lessons. The text contains ample exercises for punctu-ation, spelling, meaning and use of words, and correct sentence con-struction.

Exercises

An outstanding *immediately* feature is the wide range of practical exercises. These are included after the teaching and learning situation to which they relate. All the exercises can be typed, thus encouraging the use of the typewriter as a machine for communication. If this is not practicable, many exercises can be handwritten either in class or as *H* out *H* of class preparation. In addition to a wide range of office typing jobs, English usage exercises comprising spelling and correct use of words, punctuation and styling, clear and concise expression, provide excellent transcription training for the shorthand-typist and audio-typist. The composition of letters, reports and memos, and summaries, ensures that original work is not overlooked. *& correction of errors*

Knowledge of secretarial duties and aptitude for secretarial skills are ensured by the inclusion of a *wide* range of exercises, many of which have been taken or adapted from past examination papers.

Closed caps for words underscored

Gregg Secretarial Typing is a follow-on text for full-time, part-time and evening students who have completed the basic keyboard training and are preparing for office jobs, and shorthand-typist's or audio-typist's examinations.

I am sure you would find this book ideal for the students you have in mind.

(A) In addition to applied l.c. typing practice, each Unit contains simple practice exercises to develop secretarial skills, correct English usage & comprehension.

Yours faithfully
McGRAW-HILL PUBLISHING CO LTD

M J Thorrowgood
SALES MANAGER

9. Type a copy of the following layout of a Bill of Quantities on A4 paper. Keep your typed copy for future reference in Folder No. 2.

(1) B I L L   O F   Q U A N T I T I E S

for

ALTERATIONS AT 'THE HAVEN'

QUEEN'S ROAD, DUDLEY

for

Mr. H. W. JOHNSON

(2) J. W. WALTERS, A.R.I.B.A.,
Architect,
4 Stoke Road,
DUDLEY.

(3) MARCH 19..

(5) P R E L I M I N A R I E S

(6) (7) (8) (9)

(4) Item £

1 The works covered comprise: extending)
   ground floor of house a distance of)
   1.210 metres at rear and then   )
   building on new Sun Room 9.500 m x)
   3.060 m with glass roof and sides.)

2 The Contractor is referred to the   )
   Conditions of the Contract issued   )
   by the Royal Institute of British   )
   Architects and must allow for com-   )
   plying with them and for any cost   )
   incurred therewith.   )

3 The Contractor can enter the site and)
   commence work immediately after the)
   Contract is signed which date   )
   should be a few days after the   )
   acceptance of the Tender.   )

Carried to collection £

Columns: (1) Heading. (2) Name and address of architect. (3) Date. (4) Item No. (5) Name of trade centred. (6) Measurements. (7) Nature of measurements. (8) Unit price. (9) Total.

Typist: This will be a two-page circular letter which I will be sending to about 50 selected firms. Put in tomorrow's date and leave room for name and address *(and address of)* which you will type in later. When I have seen yr. typed copy, I shall want an offset litho master cut. Better leave out the salutation for the time being.

DRAFT

¶ It is not enough to have a good product; people ¶ buy the branded ~~goods~~ foods in wh. sincere & successful advertising has 1st given confidence to (them). Foodstuffs are sold by *the creative* ~~original~~ ideas wh. fix their excellence in /

N.P. public mind. [Yet ideas alone are not enough] the ⊙ v.c.

selling/theme] must be directed by those who understand modern commerce/ men with long successful experience of / food market.⌐

Run on] ¶ Advertising/ when rightly handled/ is no longer a matter of chance/ it is/ scientific application of creative experience to a tested market.

⌐A market ~~survey~~ *survey* is not a / *hasty* glance @ / latest Digest of statistics & a few tentative questions to friends of the family; it is as highly-skilled a part of modern advertising as/ etching of colour plates. ⌐Indeed, the market must be tested & / campaign controlled @ every step by a team wh. specializes in measuring public reaction. ⌐Typist: Start new para at "Indeed" & then run on.

¶ That is a picture of the food manfr's ideal advertg. agency. Such an agency can help to inspire yr. whole sales effort. *(insert ⅓ here)*

v.c. Quality advertg. is such an agency. We hv. specialized in food advertg. for a ¼ of a century — a long time/ rich in experience. 6n many a lesson well learned we hv. perfected a service wh. can sell confidently.

¶ These are our credentials—here is what we offer:

H 1. 25 yrs' advertising & marketing co-operation w. leading manfrs. in / food industry. (Typist—please do not put in a full stop after the nos., 1, 2, 3, etc., leave 4 clear spaces after each no. & use block paras.)

2. An integrated team of artists & writers, *men* ~~men~~ *who specialize in food publicity* ¶ men not content with smart ideas unless they also sell the product.

contd.

Specification (Contd.)

EXCAVATOR AND CONCRETOR

EXCAVATION   Excavate under all walls to a solid foundation.

N.P. [British Portland Cement to be obtained from approved
manufacturers and to comply in all respects with the
latest British Engineering Standard specification
97 for Portland cement*, + to stand the tests named herein.*

The concrete raft to be cement concrete 153 mm
thick and composed of four parts clean gravel, two
97 parts sand, and one part of cement, reinforced with
97 B.R.C. Steel Mesh *no. 65.*

SAND   Sand to be supplied from an approved Sand Pit.

A + for providing storage tanks + tools; + for removing at completion.

End of Excavator and Concretor

B CLEANING ON COMPLETION Remove all rubbish + surplus material on completion, + leave site clean + orderly.

ENDORSEMENT

Typed on right-hand
side of middle fold as
specimen opposite, or,
in the case of a bound
Specification, on the
front cover.

April, 19..

SPECIFICATION OF WORK

to be executed

at

Coppice Lane,

CHURCH STRETTON

for

Mr. William Simpson

J. Wilkinson & Co. Ltd.,
Architects & Surveyors,
80 High Street,
Church Stretton.

Bills of quantities

A Bill of Quantities is a document showing details and prices of materials to be used in building, etc., its purpose being to obtain tenders for the work to be done and materials required. It enables the architect to make an accurate estimate of the work to be carried out, and it is usually prepared by a surveyor, the Contractor completing it with the prices quoted by him for each item. Ruled sheets are normally used, although the document is sometimes typed on plain paper and ruled afterwards. A specimen is given below, but there may be slight variations in the layout and ruling. For full instructions concerning the typing of Bills of Quantities, study page M2, Reference Manual.

3   A research dept. wh. includes a housewives' panel,
field workers & a modern kitchen, supported
by a completely mechanized statistical dept. for
obtaining reactions to food products & their
sales & advertising methods.

6 X   Complete photographic & film unit.

4 X H   A display unit for designing & mfg. point/of/sale
displays.

     A good chess player never forgets th. he is in/game
for/ thing: he wants to checkmate his opponent's king.
He may be able to do it in 2 moves, or he may take a
hundred moves. But th. is/ thing wh. he is after. ← He
may be moving/ pawn of general publicity, he
may be making any one of a 1,000 advertg. moves, but
ultimately he expects his advertising by its effect on
sales to make his business bigger, or steadier, or all
these together.

v.c.   Quality advertising is at the service of
all go-ahead organizations for home &
export publicity.

     We shd. like to meet yr. executives
to discuss informally how we can
help to put yr. products on the
housewives' shopping list.

      Yrs. ffy,
      QUALITY ADVERTISING. LTD

      J.L. LEE
      DIRECTOR.

Please insert at 'A'
     It can, in time, make the name of yr. product
an automatic reaction in every housewife's mind
when she enters a food store.

5.   A series of 6 shop windows for constructing
     experimental display work.

(margin notes, right side):
He may be/protecting
a castle of/field
force,

And so/ good advertise
never loses sight of the
fact that it is aiming
finally @ sales.

or more permanent,
more profitable,

Technique development

Specifications

A Specification is a document detailing the work which a contractor proposes to do on any particular job, and shows the quality and measurements of materials to be used. The description of the work to be done and the materials to be used are divided into the different trades, which follow the order in which the work would normally be carried out. The specimen below shows the general layout of a Specification.

8. Practise typing Specification. Type a copy of the following extract of a Specification on A4 paper, following the layout and scale-points given and the rules on pp. M6—7, Reference Manual. Complete with endorsement.

35(30)

S P E C I F I C A T I O N of works required

40(35) to be executed in the erection of a house

at Coppice Lane, Church Stretton, for

Mr. William Simpson.

J. Wilkinson & Co. Ltd.,
Architects & Surveyors,
80 High Street,
Church Stretton.

30(25)
APRIL 19..

44(39)

P R E L I M I N A R I E S

12(10)
DRAWINGS   *l.c.*   This Specification must be read in conjunction with the general design of house as shown on drawings and */site*/ layout already deposited.

NOTICES AND
FEES   The contractor must comply with any regulation and Bye-Laws of local and other authorities, give any notices, and pay any fees if required.

MATERIALS AND
WORKMANSHIP   The materials and workmanship throughout are to be of the best quality of the respective kinds. The work is to be carried out to the satisfaction
    N.P.   of Mr. William Simpson or his Surveyor.

WATER   *u.c.*
    l.c.   The contractor is to allow for giving notice and paying fees for tapping the Water Main and providing all temporary services for the supply of
    /   water to all parts of the works/ *(Insert A)*

INSURANCE   The Contractor must insure all workmen under the Workmen's Compensation Acts, Health and Unemployment Acts, etc.

    Insert B

FROST   Work executed at a time when frost is likely to occur is to be adequately covered up and well protected at night.

ATTEND   Each trade is to attend upon all others and perform all jobbing work throughout.

End of Preliminaries

Unit 15

Skill building

Type the alphabetic review *once* for practice, *once* for speed, and finally, *once* for accuracy.

Review alphabet keys

1.   The magic of the peace and quietness was broken when an
extra noisy jet plane flashed overhead across the azure sky.

Accuracy/Speed Practice
Five-minute timing   *Not more than 3 errors*

words

AS.18   Why do so many visitors to Britain include in their tour a visit | 13
to 'leafy Warwickshire'?   This is a well-wooded area, nearly in the | 26
centre of England, and has a maze of narrow, winding lanes of great | 40
beauty.   In the summer it is leafy in all truth, as one would expect | 53
when one recalls that it is all that is left of the once great Forest | 67
of Arden.   This forest was once of great size, and the woods were so | 81
thick that they became the home of hosts of robbers, who made the | 94
journeys of merchants full of danger.   Even now many ancient trees are | 108
to be found, trees which have lived for many times the span of a man's | 122
life. | 123

        The Romans, who had landed on the south shores of the country, | 135
slowly forced their way into the centre of the land, and many signs | 148
of their occupation can still be found in the country.   Four great | 161
Roman roads enter the district at different points — Watling Street, | 175
Icknield Street, the Ridgeway, and the Fosseway — all of which can | 188
still be traced.   It is easy to follow, at least for parts of these | 201
roads, the course along which Roman soldiers marched forth into the | 215
unknown. | 216

        There are two great feudal castles within its borders — that at | 229
Warwick, from the outside scarcely changed since the Middle Ages, and | 243
that at Kenilworth, once a great regal building, but now just a heap of | 257
ivy-clad ruins. | 260

        These things, however, are not the reason for so many people from | 273
so many lands making this journey.   They come to honour the memory of | 287
William Shakespeare, called the world's greatest poet, who was born and | 301
lived for most of his life at Stratford-upon-Avon.   His works are known | 315
and admired all over the world, and it is no wonder that people from | 329
afar should want to see where he lived and worked, and to take the walks | 343
he quite likely took in his lifetime. | 350

        A lot of villages around Stratford are mentioned in his works, | 363
and students of the poet, as well as many others, get much pleasure from | 378
finding these places and building mental pictures of the days of long | 392
ago.   This, truly, is Shakespeare's country.   (S.I. 1.30) | 400

Unit 19

Skill building

Type each line or sentence (A, B, and C) *three* times. If time permits, complete your practice by typing each group once as it appears.

A. Review alphabet keys

1. An exceedingly smart native boy operated the punka with zeal, by jerking a quite frail rope attached to his big toe.

B. Build speed on common letter combinations

2. anything anxious change answer annual thank than can and an.
3. Thank them. Anything they can do will be more than welcome.
4. We are anxious to have your answer about the annual meeting.

C. Build speed on fluency drill

5. That boy said the baby was very ill when the lady went away.
6. The four men went off down the road when that shop was shut.
7. They said that the tour was good but that the food was poor.

Accuracy/Speed Practice
Four-minute timing   Not more than 4 errors

words

AS.23   You may not find shopping much fun if you can only buy absolute   12
necessities on a shoe-string, but at any rate you can spend a most   26
interesting morning looking around some of the curious shops to be   39
found in London. The Old Curiosity Shop, which dates back to the   52
sixteenth century, is well worth a visit. Or, if you like books, you   66
could pass a whole morning browsing in certain bookshops in Charing   79
Cross Road. The large stores, too, will be found of interest. Some,   93
we are told, sell everything from an elephant to a pin. Youngsters   106
will be thrilled with the animals and birds which are on sale in the   120
pet store, whilst you can wander around at your leisure in the fashion   134
department.   136

Visitors to London should not fail to see Kew Gardens — a favour-   149
ite spot, particularly in lilac time. These gardens were originally   163
the grounds of Kew Palace, which goes back to the Hanoverian period;   176
these are now botanical gardens, which contain some thousands of rare   190
plants, and there is never a time when they are quite bare.   202

Another place of interest is Kenwood House, standing in its own   215
grounds in the middle of Hampstead Heath. There you could think you   228
were in open country. The park, designed in the eighteenth century,   242
has a lovely view from the house; and in the spring there are daffodils   256
in profusion, followed by a wonderful display of azaleas and other   269
flowers. A fine collection of old furniture and pictures in the house   283
also makes Kenwood House a place which is well worth a visit, and one   297
which could not fail to please. Next time you are in London, why not   311
make a special point of visiting these places?   (S.I. 1.37)   320

Technique development

Personal letters

(a) *Personal Business Letters:* Used when writing to an unknown person or firm about a personal business matter. The layout is similar to that of a business letter. If your home address is not printed on your stationery, type it about 25 mm from the top and centre on page, or in such a way that the last line ends flush with the right-hand margin. Date in usual place. Name and address of addressee may be typed in usual place or at bottom left-hand margin, two spaces below your name.

(b) *Formal Personal Letters:* Used when writing to someone older than yourself or to whom you owe respect. Layout as for Personal Business Letter. Salutation is formal, e.g., Dear Miss Brown, Dear Mrs. Taylor, Dear Dr. Emery.

(c) *Personal Letters:* Used when writing to a personal friend. Your address and date as in a Personal Business Letter. No name and address of addressee. Salutation is informal, e.g., Dear Mary, Dear Arthur, Dear Uncle George.

2. Practise typing Personal Letters. Type the following personal business letter on A5 (148 × 210 mm) paper, using suitable margins.

> 12 Warwick Road,
> Kenilworth,
> Warwickshire,
> 14th May, 19-

H.M. Inspector of Taxes,
Coventry 3rd District,
94 Gosford St.,
Coventry.   CVI 5RS

Dear Sir,

Your Ref. 70/75 O/D 2116

I hv today recd Form P2 (notice of Coding) & find that th an error has bn made in allowances. [For the past two yrs I hv bn given an allowance of £75 for my widowed mother w whom I live & whose annual income for last yr was £150. [Please be kind enough to include this allowance & amend my code no. accordingly.

Yrs ffly,   Doris McLean

3. Type the following Formal Personal Letter on A5 paper, using suitable margins.

> 25 Warwick Road,
> Hampton-on-the-Hill,
> Warwick,
> 14th June, 19--

Dear Mrs. Ingram,

Thank you for yr letter abt the Club's visit to Chatsworth House on Sat, 2nd July & my mother & I wl look fwd to this trip & I enclose a Postal Order for £5.

Yrs sincerely.

Mrs. J. Ingram,
The BUTTS, Warwick.

Enc.

UNIT 15

91

Production typing

Type in correct form on A5 (210 × 148 mm) paper a three-column invoice for the following items sold to Morris Blythe & Co., Ferry Road, Kingston-upon-Hull. HU1 2AA, by Carnival Supplies Ltd., 12/18 Booth St., Manchester. M60 2JT.

> 150 pkts crepe Throw Streamers (asstd in 3 colours) @ £2.50 per 100 = £3.75) Purchase Tax 19p; 300 Frolic Hats (@ 60p 100 (in bags of 10) = £1.80 P.T. 9p; 600 Domino Eye (@ 25p 100, £1.50 P.T. 8p; 10 sets Indian Chief Characters @ 37½p per set, £3.75 PT 17½p; 150 boxes Confetti @ £1.04 100, PT 8p; 100 75mm Taffeta Plain Rosettes @ £2.50 100, £2.50 PT 20p; 100 113 mm ditto @ £4 per 100, £4. PT 26p; 700 Zoo Hats @ 65p 100, £4.55, PT 25p; 150 Pirate Captain Character Sets @ £3 100, £4.50, PT 22½p. Cash discount 2½% 14 day.
>
> *(masks) £1·56*
>
> *Typist - Please insert total*

The Midland Iron & Steel Co. of Bridge Street, Derby. DE1 3LD, sent a statement at the end of February to their customers W. & J. Richards, of High Street, Coventry. CV1 5RS, for the items appearing in their Sales Ledger (Folio 101). Make out the statement as per Specimen No. 1 covering these items as follows:

> Balance b/f from Dec. £10.53. A/c rendered for Jany £20.80 Goods sold during mth. Feb 1. £15.63; Feb 10. £20.44; Feb. 15 £8.60; Feb 24 £14.50. On Feb 3 W. J Richards returned goods valued £2.50 for which they received credit note for £2.50 on Feb 10. On Feb. 12th they sent cheque for £10.53
>
> *Typist Please show balance owing*

The Ledger Account for James Wood & Son, of High Street, Bradford shows the following items outstanding in your firm's Sales Ledger. Type out a statement from your firm for the above customer, showing balance owing. Your firm use statement forms as per Specimen No. 2.

> Balance outstanding at end of Feb. £4.35. Goods supplied during March: March 6 £13.63 March 12 £15.80. March 15 Credit Note sent for £2.33 for gds returned. March 25. They sent you a cheque to cover amount of Feb. a/c. £14·63

Formal notes

It is customary to use formal wording when sending out invitations to weddings, twenty-first birthday parties, etc. The invitations are written in the third person with a blank space left for the insertion of names of the guests in ink. The invitation begins with the name(s) of the writer(s) whose address is placed at the bottom left-hand margin. The date and R.S.V.P. are at the lower right-hand margin. Invitations are not signed.

4. Practise typing formal invitations. On postcards, or postcard-size paper, type the following invitation from Mr. and Mrs. Hubbard and the reply from the Facchino family. Use double spacing and centre each line.

(a) **Formal invitation**

Mr. and Mrs. Eric Hubbard request the

pleasure of the company of

[ENRICO] Mr. & Mrs. Enrico Facchino & Jane (write this line)

at their daughter's twenty-first birthday

party on Saturday 20th September, at 8 pm.

The Braff
Newbould-on-Stour,
Warwickshire.

1st September, 19..

R. S. V. P.

(b) **Reply to formal invitation**

Mr. and Mrs. Enrico Facchino and Jane

hv. pleasure in accepting the invitation

of Mr. & Mrs. Eric Hubbard to their

daughter's 21st birthday party on

Sat., 20th Sept, @ 8 pm.

Fern End House,
Knowle,
Warwicks.

4th Sept, 19..

Variable line spacer

You will find the variable line spacer (sometimes called platen release) on the left cylinder knob. By pressing in (or pulling out on some machines) the variable line spacer, you release the spacing mechanism, and the platen roller can be moved to any desired position.

It is used for:
Filling in form letters;
Typing on ruled lines;
Finding the correct alignment when paper has been reinserted to make a correction.

11. Type a copy of the following statement on A5 (210 × 148 mm) paper, unless you have blank ruled forms. Place your paper over the statement below and lightly mark the position of the vertical lines.

Phone: 0274 19265

STATEMENT

HUGHES & PROCTER LTD.
158 Garnett Street
BRADFORD.

Messrs. King & Co.,
City Square,
Sheffield. S1 1RJ

31st January, 19..

Fo. 55

Terms: Nett monthly

Date	Ref. No.		Debit	Credit	Balance
			£	£	£
197 Dec.		A/c rendered			71.20
197 Jan. 2	415	Goods	10.08		81.28
5	564	"	25.72		107.00
10		Cheque		71.20	35.80
15	664	Goods	30.50		66.30
25	999	"	45.25		111.55
30	342	Credit		5.72	105.83
		E. & O.E.			

12. Type the following statement from W. & T. Jones Ltd., of City Square, Dundee. DD1 3EP to J. & W. Bolton Ltd., George St., Edinburgh, EH2 3DA. Use A5 (210 × 148 mm) paper.

Date	Ref No		Debit	Credit	Insert Date Balances
197- May		a/c rendered.			64.60
June 3	621	Goods.	10.50		
" 5	690	"	30.75		
6		Cheque		60.60	
10	725	Goods.	20.60		
12	109	Credit.		4.00	
15	784	Goods	35.00		
20	844	"	15.90		
25		Cheque		50.00	
		E. & O.E.			

(handwritten note: Typist – Please insert Balances)

(margin note: 6/)

5. Type the following on A4 paper in single spacing with double between lettered and numbered items and for the memo. heading. Keep your typed copy for future reference in Folder No. 2.

<u>INTER-OFFICE MEMORANDA</u>

The memorandum (usually referred to as 'memo.') is one of the most convenient ways of sending messages from one person to another in the same firm or from the head office to a branch office or agent. A memo. may be typed on any size of paper, and firms have the headings printed and the paper cut to the size required. The layout of headings varies, the following being one example:—

<pre>
                              (1)
                          <u>R. B. BENSON LTD</u>
(3)   (5)   (4)   (5)
To: ....   Date: ....
(2)   (2)
              (5)
From: ....
(6)
_____

              (5)
SUBJECT: ....
</pre>

(1) Name of firm — usually centred on page.
(2) Margins — 25 mm either side. Where the headings are printed, it is normal practice to set the left margin to coincide with the beginning of the headings.
(3) When typing in the headings, start left-hand side at 25 mm. Headings are ALWAYS typed in double spacing.
(4) Right-hand headings start at approximately 45 Pica and 55 Elite.
(5) Insertions start two spaces after end of heading. It is absolutely essential that these are consistent throughout.
(6) Line normally from edge of paper. Some firms do not have a line here.

<u>Other points to remember</u>

(a) No salutation or complimentary close. (b) Body. Single spacing with double between paragraphs. Block or indented paragraphs used. (c) Some firms have the writer's name or initials typed two single-line spaces after the last line of the body. Do not do this unless specially instructed to do so. If they are to go in, then they end level with the right-hand margin. (d) If there are dotted lines after the headings, then you must type slightly above these. If there are no dotted lines, align paper by means of variable line spacer, so that insertions are in alignment with headings.

6. On memo. paper prepare an original and one carbon copy of the headings set out above. On the original insert the following:
To: Managing Director. From: Sales Director. Subject: Sales — January—June 19.. Suitable date. The following are the sales figures for the 1st six months of this year. January £10,750, Feb. £9,830, March £11,620, April £14,560, May £14,000, June £19,740. (Typist: Set out these details in two columns.)
On the carbon copy insert: To: Chief Cashier. From: Man. Dir. Subject: Overdue A/cs. Suitable date. Please let me have a list of overdue a/cs as at 30th June.

At the end of each month, statements are sent out for each customer, showing any balance owing from previous months, details of goods supplied during the current month, and the total amount due. The statement not only reminds the customer that he owes the money, but it enables a comparison to be made of the buyer's and seller's books, so that any discrepancy can be discovered and rectified. The specimens given show the usual types of statements, though the forms vary from firm to firm.

10. Practise typing statements. Type a copy of the following statement. If you do not have blank ruled forms, use A5 (148 × 210 mm) paper: place this over the statement below and lightly mark the position of the vertical lines.

STATEMENT

Phone: SPENCER & CHAPMAN LTD.
061-764   Newhive Works
2267   Bury, Lancashire.   BI9 0SW

(1)

Messrs. Wilfrid Everitt & Co.,
High Street,
Edgware, Middx.

                                      (2)
                               30th April, 19..

(4)   (3)
Fo. 16   Terms: 2½% monthly

19..		(6)	£	£
(5) Mar.		A/c rendered		24.60
Apr.	2	Goods	30.60	
	15	"	20.75	
	18	"	25.50	
	24	"	13.25	
			90.10	
	25	Cheque	24.00	66.10
				£90.70
		(7) E. & O.E.		

(1) Customer's name and address. (2) Last day of month. (3) Terms of payment. (4) Customer's ledger folio in Sales Ledger. (5) Date of transactions. (6) Details. (7) Errors and omissions excepted.

Production typing

Job 39 Production Target—*10 minutes*

Type the following letter on A4 paper ready for signature by the Sales Manager (Mr. John A. Grey) of Taylor and
Law Ltd. Type an extra carbon copy for Accounts Department.

S.W. Mackellar & Co Ltd., Wage St., Lichfield, Staffs.
For the attention of W. Robinson Esq. We are pleased to open
an account with you, & to give you full credit facilities.

l.c. → We appreciate your choosing us to supply y. w. the goods
N.P. you require. The information we have rec'd. concerning
stet. you is completely satisfactory, and.
all/ We assure you of our full co-operation at L times,
and of our efforts to help you. The first order which N.P.
you have placed with us is receiving our immediate
attention. In securing increased profits through the sale
of our goods. We are packing with it our latest assortment
tr. of display window cards, w. detailed suggestions on
u.c. how to make the display attractive. At regular intervals
you will hear from our business promotion dept.,
of which is organized by us solely for our customers'
N.P. benefit. If you find that there is anything further
we can do for you, please h. no hesitation in writing
to us.

Job 40 Production Target—*8 minutes*

Type the following memo. on A5 paper. Insert paras.
From: R.P. Freeman To: Sales Manager
Subject: Canning & Co., 34 Frederick Rd., S. Shields
Thank y. for yr. memo. dated Aug. 21st. I called
yesterday to see Mr. P. Scott, Chief Buyer, Canning
& Co., & he informed me th. a cheque in full
settlement of their a/c was sent on 23rd Aug.
Please let me know whether or not the cheque
has been received. CC. District Manager.

UNIT 15   94

8. Practise typing three-column invoice. Type a copy of the following three-column invoice on a blank ruled form (if you have this) or, if not, use A5 (210 × 148 mm) paper and place this over the invoice below, and lightly mark the position of the vertical lines. Keep your typed copy for future reference in Folder No. 2.

Phone:
0532 22005

INVOICE No. 45556

HUGHES & PROCTER LTD.
Manufacturing Stationers
158 Garnett Street
LEEDS   LS1 3AE

C. W. Field Ltd.,
Mansfield Road,
DERBY.   DE7 2FL

15th August, 19..

Order No. 3486/210/VP

Terms: 2½% Monthly Account

		Unit Price each	Purchase Tax	Value of Goods	Amount payable
			£	£	£
20	Standard grade Black/Red Ribbons, medium inked	13p	0.85	2.60	
10	reams White Duplicating Paper, A4	50p	1.37	5.00	
5	reams White Bond, A4	41p	0.65	2.05	
3000	small Bendover Fasteners, boxes of 100 per 1000	75p	0.88	2.25	11.90
			3.75		
	Plus Purchase Tax				3.75
					£15.65
	E. & O. E.				

9. Type a copy of the following two-column invoice, using a blank ruled form or A5 paper (210 × 148 mm). Rule when completed.

Buyers - Wilfred Everitt & Co., High St., Edgware, Middlesex. Sellers - Educational Supplies Ltd., 131 Richmond Rd, Kingston-upon-Thames. Invoice No. 341/2. Use today's date. Terms: nett monthly acct. Order No. A1576/2. 1 only 'Mediaeval England' (M. Black) @ 25p, 10 'Modern Everyday Science,' Book 3 (D.H. Damsell) @ 32p, £5.00 £3.20 5 'From Sea to Sea' (John G. Field & Lloyd A. Dennis) @ 90p £4.50 Total £13.95 10 'Footprints in Time - Canada' (H. Murray Smith) @ 50p £5.00 Less 10% Trade Discount £1.29 nett total £12.56 £11.66 Postage 15p. Sent by post. Typist. Please insert final total.

Type the following in double-line spacing exactly as it appears. Remove from the machine and mark in ink any necessary corrections with the recognized correction signs. From your corrected copy type a fair copy.

We have today sent you a telegram as follows, "No definite information obtainable byt everything point to a general increase in material prices.

Their was allready some talk of this advance in prices before Mr. Thorne our purchasing agent left on 21st. September for a visit to London but he has evidentally obtained further information There to strengthen the belief that such an ad vance is like to place take. Present conditions are are such as to make an increase in the London prices almost inevitable.

Job 42   Production Target—*10 minutes*

Using postcard-size paper, type one original and three copies of a formal invitation asking friends to attend a dinner at your home next Friday evening. After typing the invitations, write your friends' names in ink.

Job 43   Production Target—*5 minutes*

Type the following on a postcard, or postcard-size paper, ready for mailing.

From H. H. Bray & Co. Kingsthorpe Road Northampton. To J. F. Bird & Co. Ltd., Ware, Herts. Thank you for your order No 125/67 dated 23rd February. The garden ornament that you require will be despatched on the 27th May.

7. Practise typing invoices. Type a copy of the following two-column invoice. If you do not have blank ruled forms, use A5 (210 × 148 mm) paper, place it over the invoice below and lightly mark the position of the vertical lines. Keep your typed copy for future reference in Folder No. 2.

INVOICE   No. 5656/3/A

Phone: SPENCER, CHAPMAN & CO. LTD.
061-764 2267   Newhive Works,
                  Bury, Lancashire.   BI9 OSW

SOLD TO:

Potter & Clarke Ltd.,
    City Square,
        DUNDEE.   DD1 3BP

ORDER NO. X6546   14th September, 19..

                  Terms: Nett monthly account

(1)	(2)	(3)	£ Per 1000	(4) £	(5) £
2,000	Screws, Round Heads, 6 mm		0.50	1.00	
2,000	" " " 16 mm		0.90	1.80	
1,000	" Cheese " 38 mm		2.85	2.85	
1,000	" Countersunk Heads, 38 mm		16.75	16.75	
1,000	" " " 45 mm		18.50	18.50	
1,000	" " " 57 mm		32,25	32.25	
				73.15	
	Less 10% Trade Discount			7.31	£65.84
	Per British Road Services				
E & O E					

1. Quantity (left margin set).
2. Description (Tab. stop set).
3. Unit price (Tab. stop set).
4. Total price (Tab. stop set for units of pounds).
5. Final total (Tab. stop set for units of pounds).

Addressing machines

Addressing machines, which operate on a similar principle to that of duplicators, are used for imprinting the names and/or addresses on statements, ledger cards, envelopes, wage packets, etc. The names and/or addresses are typed on metal plates or stencils which are placed in cardboard frames. The frames are passed through the addressing machine, which can print as many as two thousand an hour.

Secretarial aid No. 3

It is a well-known fact that a good personality is an asset to the office worker. She must be a person who is liked by her employer or supervisor, by her fellow-workers, by the salesmen who call at the office, and by the public who are the customers or clients of the business of which the office is a part. You should know yourself, not as you think you are, but as other people think you are. If you find that your personality is less pleasing to others in some respects than you had thought, you should remedy the defects.

It is not assumed that the following characteristics are the only ones that make for the best personality, but they are important:

Punctuality: You must always be on time, and begin work at once.

Cleanliness: Clean hair; clean, well-kept hands and finger-nails; clean, well-brushed clothes suitable for an office; clean teeth.

Courtesy: Say 'please' when asking a favour; 'Thank you' when one has been granted. Do not interrupt the work or conversation of others.

Co-operativeness: Maintain team-work with your supervisor and other members of staff; assume responsibility for everything you do.

Cheerfulness: Respond to questions and requests with a smile, and cultivate a bright and happy disposition.

Composing at machine

Type the following in double spacing, correcting any errors.

We have no demand from our customers for these kind of materials.
In unity consists the welfare and security of society in general.
If I were him, I would not let anything come between you and I.
These two girls do good work, but the eldest is the most careful.
Neither the boy nor his brother were able to find their way home.

Review Quiz No. 3

Type the following on A4 paper in single-line spacing, with double spacing between each item, filling in the correct word or words in the blank spaces. Do not write on your textbook.

1. In an indented paragraph the first line is indented . . . . . spaces.
2. In a hanging paragraph the first line is typed . . . . . spaces to . . . . . of the rest.
3. In a fully-blocked letter all lines start at . . . . . margin.
4. The complimentary close is typed . . . . . single-line spaces below last line of body.
5. An enclosure in business letters is indicated either by typing . . . . . at . . . . . margin below . . . . . or by affixing a . . . . . at foot of letter.
6. When typing sums of money the . . . . . sign and . . . . . sign must . . . . . be used together.
7. Inset matter in a letter is usually . . . . . on writing line with a space . . . . . and . . . . . it.
8. A continuation sheet for a business letter contains . . . . . name, ... number, and . . . . . , all usually typed on . . . . . line in a semi-blocked letter.
9. In addressing envelopes the postal town must appear on a . . . . . line.
10. In addressing envelopes the postcode should be typed on the . . . . . line without . . . . . and with . . . . . space between the two halves.
11. If initials are to be typed on a memo, instead of the signature, these should end at . . . . . margin.
12. 'For the attention of' is typed on the . . . . . single-line space after the last line of address at . . . . . margin.
13. Invitations to weddings, etc., are written in the . . . . . person.
14. When using Roman numerals for enumerations, ... should be typed under . . . . .

Turn to page 199 and check your answers. Score one point for each correct entry. Total score: 29.

Technique development

Invoicing

Commercial Invoices give details of the goods sold and the prices to be paid. They are usually typed on specially printed forms. These forms contain certain particulars and rulings which vary from firm to firm, but the most usual are as follows:

1. *Contents*. Printed: (a) Invoice number; (b) Name, address and phone number of seller; (c) Terms of payment; (d) Ruled columns. Typed: (a) Quantity of goods supplied; (b) Description; (c) Unit prices; (d) Total prices; (e) Carriage or postage (if any); (f) Trade discount; (g) Method of despatch.

2. *Carbon copies*. Small firms usually have one carbon copy of the invoice for their own records. Larger firms have extra copies, the top copy being sent to customer, and the carbon copies for any department of the firm, or other particular purpose to suit the method adopted by the firm, e.g., Advice Note, Despatch Note, Delivery Note.

3. *Ruling*. The most common and simple form of invoice for small firms has one or two money columns. Other more elaborate invoices may have additional cash columns. Vertical lines may or may not separate the £ and p columns.

4. *Margin and tab. stops*. The left-hand margin stop is used for the start of the first column for the quantity, and tab. stops are set for the start of each of the other columns, as required.

5. *Spacing*. Single-line spacing is used when items are long or numerous. Double spacing for shorter items.

6. *Horizontal rulings for totals*. The first horizontal line is ruled underneath the last item without turning up the paper. The total is typed on the second single-line space below the horizontal line. The bottom underscore is ruled after turning up one single-line space under the total. If a double horizontal underscore is used underneath the total, the interliner is used, the paper being turned up very slightly for the second underscore.

Export Invoices. Firms sending goods abroad use an export invoice which contains, in addition to the particulars given in an ordinary commercial invoice, the name of the vessel on which the goods are shipped, any shipping marks, and also shipping charges.

Consular Invoices. When goods shipped abroad are subject to import duties in the country of destination, a consular invoice is made out. This contains a declaration made before the Consul of the country to which the goods are being exported to the effect that the details and prices given are true and correct, and that the goods are of British manufacture or origin. Such a consular invoice bears a consular stamp. On pages 114 and 115 are examples of two of the many types of invoices in use. Study these carefully.

Inserting thick carbon packs

If you find difficulty in inserting into the machine thick sets of invoices or other documents, you will find it helpful to disengage the paper release lever which opens up the paper grips under the platen, and the pack of paper can then slide into position.

Continuous stationery

When typing invoices, the typist has often to take a number of copies (one for Accounts Dept., one for Despatch Note, etc.), and to speed up the operation she may use continuous stationery. This type of stationery is fed into a continuous stationery machine (a typewriter fitted with a special attachment), and, as each set of documents is completed, the carbon, by the push of a lever, is automatically fed into the next set; the typed set is then torn off, and the next set is in position ready for typing.

Job 44   Production Target—*20 minutes*

Type the following on A4 paper, using shoulder headings and block paragraphs. Use double spacing except for paragraphs lettered (a) and (b) or unless otherwise instructed.

LETTER WRITING *

Simple consise English is best for writing letters. In this unit you will learn / techniques required for , which , modern letters / while rigorous in style / maintain a good tone + are courteous in their wording.

[margin note: Typist— most this para + use block style.]

PLAN THE LETTER * Make a note of / points ; Then arrange them in the most effective style / order ✗ Lack of planning leads to afterthoughts......... + indicates careless thinking.

[margin notes: you wish to include] *[Deal w. ea. point once only.]*

USE ACTIVE CONSTRUCTIONS Active constructions are more forceful than / passive / + save words.

(b) Passive: The goods wh. were ordered by us a considerable time ago hv. not yet bn. received. (16 words)
( ).

Active: We hv. not yet reed. / gds ordered on 3rd. March. (11 words)

USE SINGLE WORDS INSTEAD OF PHRASES & CLAUSES.

(a) In / event of yr absence continuing for more than three days, you shd. submit a med. cert. (18 WORDS) / After three days' absence fwd a med. cert. (8 words)

(b) He made a decision wh. it was impossible to justify. (10 words) / He made an unjustifiable decision. (5 words) /

OMIT NEEDLESS WORDS

Please see text book.

AVOID BUSINESS JARGON   *Insert 'A' here*

AVOID READY / MADE PHRASES

These hackneyed or long / winded expressions only hide yr. meaning. Omit them or replace them by suitable

[right margin vertical note: (a) Passive: I understand tt he is at present employed by you as a sales manager. (14 words) Active: I understand tt. y. employ him as a S. Man. (10 words)]

[left margin notes: which, / gr / gr let / ⁊h / Insert (a) + (b) please / H H H]

Unit 18

Skill building

Type each exercise (A, B, and C) *once* for practice, *once* for speed, and finally *once* for accuracy.

A. Review alphabet keys

1.   The physical fitness of the walkers was really amazing, and at the request of the judge extra big prizes were given.

B. Build accuracy on shift lock drill

2. SEVENTY-FIVE, NO-MAN'S-LAND, NINETY-SIX, DO-OR-DIE, Cardiff.

3. SEVENTY-FIVE men were lost in NO-MAN'S-LAND and they all had to make a DO-OR-DIE effort to escape their WOULD-BE captors.

4. NINETY-SIX members of the party would like to stop at Largs.

C. Build accuracy on common prefix drill

5. per, permit, person, perfect, perhaps, permanent, personnel.

6. Perhaps you would see that all permanent staff report to the Personnel Officer. It would be perfect if you could give us permission to question all persons who perused the document.

Accuracy/Speed Practice
Three-minute timing
Not more than 3 errors

	words
AS.22 Not only does the Private Secretary or the Personal Assistant have to	14
attend meetings and take down Minutes, but she also has to see that the	28
agenda is sent out and that the conference room is ready for the meeting	42
at the proper time.	46
The first thing to do, as in any job, is to avoid last-minute snags.	60
It could happen that you have had to deal with a most important telephone	74
call, and when you do at last reach the meeting you find all the chairs	88
round the table taken, and there just isn't room for you to squeeze in.	103
The result of this is that you will find yourself in a corner of the room,	118
unable to hear either the main speaker or any of the others. On another	132
occasion you may find that you are seated next to a member who really needs	147
a table to himself, because he always tends to spread his papers over the	161
place just where you want your shorthand book to rest.	172
To avoid these snags, see that the room and the table are adequate and	186
that there is plenty of seating — have a chair or two more in case extra	201
people arrive. Keep for yourself a seat near the chairman.	213
One secret of a successful meeting is to start your plans early. See	227
that all those who are entitled to attend have a copy of the agenda.	240

(S.I. 1.32)

short phrases or simple words. Many ready-made phrases are still current. Lavish use of them robs a letter of meaning or personality & makes it needlessly long.

Typist —
Insert & display
in single
spacing

Instead of	Use
In the near future	soon. uc
Wholly at a loss to comprehend	cannot understand v.c.
Institute enquiries	u.R.c. ask, enquire
In a large percentage of cases	Usually, as a rule
Use our best endeavours	Try.

COURTESY & CORRECT TONE Courtesy is more than the use of a

⊙ polite word or phrase & the reader's response shd be sket constantly borne in mind & tactful phrasing ~~used~~ sought. The purpose of good letter writing is to convey information & or ask for ,however 'A good letter & is more than / communication of facts. The sh lay-out shd be correct & pleasing & the presentation of / facts gives scope for style. Business ltrs. help to create good public

⊙ relations & they indicate an efficient organisation.

Insert at 'A'   It will not impress yr. reader.
Business jargon is an artificial vocabulary........ now
⊙ becoming obsolete & Some of / worst examples occur in / introductory & concluding paras. of letters.

* Extract from SECRETARIAL TYPING.
  By kind permission of the authors
      D. M. Sharp
          and
      H. M. Crozier
  Book published by :
      McGraw-Hill Publishing Company Ltd.,
      Shoppenhangers Road, Maidenhead, Berks.

Type the following Programme on A4 paper as a folded leaflet, displaying it as effectively as possible.

Front page - Birmchester Civic Hall - London Philharmonic Symphony Orchestra - Concert - 8th May, 19-- 7 p.m. Programme 10p.

Centre these lines across P 2 + 3

Page 2   The London Philharmonic Symphony Orchestra
Leader: Leonard White   Conductor: Hans Wassermann

Programme

Overture 'Russian Easter Festival'   Rimsky-Korsakov
'Pavane pour une infante défunte'.   Ravel
Piano Concerto No. 3 in C minor   Beethoven
Soloist: ALEXEI PUSHKOV

Interval   (Refreshments on Sale)

Page 3

Prelude and Liebestod
(Tristan und Isolde)   Wagner
Fantasia on a Theme of Thomas Tallis   Vaughan Williams
Symphony No.1 in F minor   Shostakovitch

LIEBESTOD

Centre these lines as a blocked paragraph

As this concert is being broadcast, the audience are requested to be in their seats five mins. prior to the commencement of the Programme.

Please send the following note to Miss A.M. Brown of 28 Crescent Road, Brighton, Sussex. BN2 3RP. Use plain A5 paper and date for today. My address is 4 St James's Road, Croydon. CH3 6YU

Dear Miss Brown, As you were unable to come to the concert last week, I thought you might like to hv a copy of the programme, wh I am sending you herewith. I wl advise you well in advance when the next concert wl be held. Sincerely yours,

Type the following letter on A4 paper ready for despatch today. Sub-headings to be in the form of paragraph headings. Take one carbon copy, and address an envelope.

J.W. Kingsley + Keith Ltd., Gnome Corner, Caerphilly Rd. Cardiff

Dear Sirs, Your letter No. 210. Order: We have pleasure in enclsg an order from one of our customers which we shall be glad if you will execute as soon as possible. Payment: We have now received a cheque in Escudos in settlement of our invoice no. 1446/EX from our customer Oliveira + Cia, which amount is to be placed to the credit of our Commission Account. Commission: We shall be glad if you will remit the amount in question through our bankers as usual. Yrs. faithfully, F. CABRERA + COMPANHIA —COMPANHIA

NB We thank you for your statement of a/c showing the amount of commission due to us for the qtr ended 31 May, and

Type the following letter on A4 paper, taking two carbon copies: one for file and one for Despatch Manager. Use shoulder headings for sub-headings.

Paines + Byron Ltd, North Bridge Road, Berkhamsted, Herts.

Dear Sirs, Order No. A430. We thank you for your order received with your letter this morning and, as requested, we will arrange for the goods to be ready by the end of the month. Despatch: We sh. await the instructions of your forwarding agents w. whom we will communicate as soon as the goods are ready for despatch Payment: At thirty days from date of despatch less 2½% discount or in cash at time of despatch with 3% discount. Packing: the goods will be packed in 4 cases. Please let us know which method of payment you decide to accept, so that we may make our invoice out accordingly. We look forward to hearing from you.

Yrs faithfully, W. LAMBERT + CO. LTD. Sales Dept. || Typist: please insert the section about PACKING before the para. headed PAYMENT.

Production typing

Job 50
Production Target—*5 minutes*

On A5 paper type an original and two carbon copies of the following form letter from Newbury's Limited, 79 Victoria Street, London, WC2 8ND.

Dear Sir(s), We thank you for yr. Order No.
dated   for
These goods will be despatched as requested.
yrs. ffy,

Job 51
Production Target—*10 minutes*

(a) Address the top copy of form letter (Job 50) to E.G. HALL & Co.
Ltd., King Charles Street, Surbiton, Surrey. Insert Ref. F13/OP.
today's date; Order No. 1516/70; dated (insert suitable date).
For: 12 doz. 'Lion' Brand Stockings, 15 Denier, F.F, Size 9.

(b) Address first carbon copy to H. TIBBETT & SONS, 7 GLOVER'S
COURT, Preston, Lancs. PR1 2RL. Insert Ref. SC/B7. Today's date;
Order No. 6154; dated ... (insert suitable date). For: 4 only
HI-FI Equipment Cabinets (Leak).

(c) Address second carbon copy to F. L. BRIDGES & CO. LTD.,
45 Sackville St., Manchester. M60 3BB. Insert Ref. DBL/40;
Today's date; Order No. PUR/15/70; dated .. (insert suitable date).
For: one Tubular Trolley with Formica Trays — No. V.306,
size 915 × 458 mm.

Job 52
Production Target—*5 minutes*

Type an original and one copy of the following form on A5 paper. Use double-line spacing. On the carbon copy insert suitable details.

Hon. Sec., Birmingham Indian Assoc.,
156 Orphanage Rd., B'ham. B24 6EU

Please reserve   seats for members, and   seats
for guests for the Dinner to be held on 26 Jan, 19...
The names of those attending are:
_____
_____
_____

Cheque for   enclosed. 1
Signed _____
Address _____

Unit 16

Skill building

Type each exercise (A, B, and C) *once* for practice, *once* for speed, and finally *once* for accuracy.

A. Review alphabet keys

1.   Even in her wildest dreams she had not expected such an
amazing stroke of luck by the sale of her queer lot of junk.

B. Improve control of figure keys

2. w2 e3 r4 t5 y6 u7 i8 o9 s2 d3 f4 g5 h6 j7 k8 19 12 34 56 788

3. Tariff (1970): 7 days £20.50; 14 days £27.80; 21 days £38.70

4. Dividend increased by 1½% to 15%. Profits £96,250 higher at
£10,304,000. Shares rose by 7p to £1.40 — 2p up on 1969/70.

C. Build accuracy on common letter combinations

5. in ink into find line kind thing think going indeed interest

6. Indeed, if they follow the thing through, we think they will
find that line of thought interesting. The ink dripped from
the pen into his pocket — in minutes his pocket was stained.

Accuracy/Speed Practice

You should now aim at increasing your speed by 5 words a minute.

One-minute timings   *Not more than 1 error*

words

AS.19   We often have a warm spell in March, sometimes earlier, sometimes   13
later, but when it arrives it means for many of us that spring is not   27
far away. This is a comforting thought, for we know that the weary   40
winter, with its snow and ice and biting winds, is at last drawing to a   54
close, and a feeling of hope is awakened in our hearts. No wonder that   68
spring is the season of hope and all things look brighter.   (S.I. 1.26)   80

AS.20   A flower delivery service is a useful method of sending flowers to a   14
sick friend or as a present, but it does mean that you do not see the   27
flowers sent, so that, unless your friend tells you what she received, and   42
in what state these reached her, you will never know whether the flowers   56
sent were worth the money paid for them. You can only depend on the   70
honesty of the florist to whom you gave the order.   (S.I. 1.29)   80

15. Practise typing on ruled lines. Read the explanation given on page 108 and type the following form letter on A5 paper (210 × 148 mm) in double spacing, taking a carbon copy. Take it out of the machine, reinsert the carbon copy, and fill in the details given below. Use a 60-space typing line.

Ref. _____   Date _____

_____

_____

_____

Dear

          Re _____

On the _____ we quoted you £_____ for carrying out the necessary repairs to the above appliance. Please let us know whether you accept our quotation, so that we may proceed with the repairs, which will take about _____ days.

                    Yours faithfully,
                    NORTHERN ELECTRICAL SERVICE LTD.

Details: Ref. RT/0/46. Today's date. Addressee: Mr. H. Wadsworth, 40 Chapel Street, Liverpool. LI 6BJ. Salutation. Re: Electric Iron. Date of quotation: 5th of last month. Amount £2.25. Time: 3 days.

16. Type the following Order Form on A5 (210 × 148 mm) paper. Then take it out of the machine. Reinsert it in your typewriter and fill in the details given below.

Order Form ← Spaced caps
James H. Wilkins Ltd   Order no. _____
Great Winchester St., London. WIN 8BA

Mr _____   Date _____

Dear Sir
    Please supply us w. the under-mentioned gds. ─ goods)
         Typist — leave 6 single line spaces here for ~~detail~~)
Delivery _____   Carriage _____
Terms of payment ─

              Yrs ffy, James H. Wilkins Ltd.,
                         Chief Buyer

Details: Order no. 546/4. Today's date. Addressee: Office Equipment Co., 10 Leake St., Bristol. BS1 5TN. Goods: 1 14-tray Kardex Visible Index Cabinet for 204 × 127 mm cards @ £37.50. Delivery: 7 days. Carriage pd. Terms of payment: As usual.

Technique development

Civil Service letters

DATE
(a) Unless otherwise indicated by the letterhead, the date is typed on the right-hand side at a standard tab. stop—if possible the same one as is used for typing the writer's telephone extension number —opposite the last line of the address.
(b) To be simplified to 19 October 1971, instead of 19*th* October 1971. Dates in the text should be similarly simplified.

REFERENCES
Unless the placing of 'Our Reference', and 'Your Reference', is indicated by the printed letterhead, they should be placed at the left-hand margin.

NAME AND ADDRESS OF ADDRESSEE
(a) To be positioned at the top left-hand side of the letter, and blocked; i.e., all lines starting at the left-hand margin.
(b) Full stops (after initials, etc.) and commas to be omitted entirely.
(c) Officially recognised abbreviations for departmental and establishment, etc., titles (like HMSO, UKAEA, LOB, etc.) should normally be used in addresses, instead of the full names.
(d) Postcodes to be typed as the final line of an address, with a single space between the two parts of the code.

SALUTATION
At left margin. No final comma.

SUBJECT HEADING
(a) Start at left-hand margin.
(b) Typed in capitals rather than underlined lower case letters.

BODY
(a) Blocked paragraphs.
(b) No full stops after, or unnecessary spaces between the separate letters of contractions and familiar abbreviations; e.g. Appx, Sgd, SEO, NATO, DTI, etc, eg, ie, para.
(c) Sub and sub-sub-paragraphs to be indented from the left-hand margin only and typed in blocked style.
(d) Spacing after punctuation—after a comma, a semi-colon or colon: one space; after a full stop, question or exclamation mark: two spaces.

(e) In the absence of clear directions to the contrary, paragraphs should be numbered '1.', '2.', etc. (figures followed by full stop) rather than '(1)', '(2)', etc. (figures in brackets). In sub-paragraphs 'a.', 'b.', rather than '(a)', '(b)'. Paragraph numbers should start at the left-hand margin and the full stop should be followed by 3 clear spaces.
(f) Catchwords should not be used.
(g) Pages should be numbered at foot of the page and centred where there is more than one sheet.
(h) The second page is typed on the back of the first and the margins are reversed.

COMPLIMENTARY CLOSE
(a) Typed at left margin; or
(b) at the same right-hand tabulation stop as the date.
(c) No comma at end.

NAME OF WRITER
(a) Typed under the signature space and without brackets.
(b) Either at the left-hand margin; or
(c) at the same right-hand tabulation stop as the complimentary close.
(d) Omit full stops after initials of name.

TITLE OR BRANCH/DIVISION, ETC., OF WRITER
Typed immediately under the typed name of writer. (The Branch, etc., may of course already be included in the printed letterhead, or it may not be needed at all.)

ENCLOSURES
To be indicated by typing ENC or ENCS (no full stop) followed by a figure denoting the number, at the bottom left-hand side of the letter, rather than by typing dashes or dots in the margin opposite the mention.

AMPERSAND
To be used instead of 'and' in such branch, etc., titles as 'O & M', 'Messrs. Jones & Smith'.

SECURITY CLASSIFICATION
Typed (in capital letters and not underlined) at the centre of the top and bottom of each page, if neither pre-printed paper nor stamps are available.

Technique development

Form letters

Form letters are printed or duplicated forms or skeleton letters, the object of which is to save the typist time when dealing with routine correspondence. As a general rule, all that the typist has to do is to fill in the date, name and address of addressee, and insert a few details in the body of the letter.

When preparing form letters for duplicating, care must be taken to see that the type on the machine to be used for inserting the particulars is the same size and kind as that used in the duplicated portion, and that the ribbon matches in colour and depth the duplicated part of the letter. (A different colour, e.g., red, is better than a bad match.)

The following steps should be taken when you fill in a form letter:

1. Insert the form letter into the machine so that the first line of the body of the letter is just above the alignment scale.

2. By means of the paper release, adjust the paper so that the base of the entire line is in alignment with the top of the alignment scale (this position may vary with certain makes of machines) and so that an 'i' or 'l' aligns up exactly with one of the white guide lines on the alignment scale.

3. Set margin stops and paper guide. The margin stops should be set to correspond to the margins already used in the duplicated letter.

4. Turn the cylinder back two single-line spaces, and, if not already typed, insert salutation at the left-hand margin.

5. Turn the cylinder back a sufficient number of line spaces to provide the correct space for the reference and name and address of the addressee, and the spaces between, to reach the line for the reference and date.

6. Type the reference at left-hand margin.

7. Move carriage to right-hand margin, back-space, and type date.

8. Return carriage to left-hand margin and type name and address.

9. Insert any details required in body of letter.

10. Check carefully.

14. Practise filling in form letters. Read the above explanation and then type the following form letter on A5 (210 × 148 mm) paper in double spacing, leaving 6 single-line spaces at top to represent heading. Take your typed copy out of the machine, reinsert it, and fill in the details given below. Margins of 25 mm on each side.

```
Dear

     We acknowledge receipt of your cheque for                in

payment of our account to the end of

                    Yours faithfully,
                      F. W. JACKSON & SON LTD.
```

Details to be filled in: Today's date. Salutation: Madam. Addressee: Mrs. J. Jones, 56 New Road, Solihull. Amount £20.30. End of . . . (Insert month prior to present date).

Typing on ruled lines

In some form letters and forms you may have to type on ruled lines. In this case it is better to type slightly above the line, and it is recommended that the base of the characters should be about 1 mm above the ruled line.

7. Practise typing Official Letter. Study the instructions on page 101, and then type a copy of the following on A4 paper.

No. 56497/1964

A W Tennant Esq
20 Miller Street
Manchester
M4 8AA   5 October 1970

Sir

With reference to your application of the 30 September,
I am directed by the Commissioners of Customs and Excise to
inform you that the authority granted to you by their letter
of the 9 July, 1955, No. 45500/1955, has been extended to
cover the use of the Industrial Methylated Spirits at your
premises at 20 Miller Street, Manchester, in making a Liniment
in accordance with the following formula:—

Oil of Eucalyptus   142 ml

Oil of Turpentine   142 "

Compound Liniment of Soap
(made with Industrial
Methylated Spirits)
sufficient to produce   2841 "

This extension of your authority is granted subject to com-
pliance with the appropriate provisions of the Methylated
Spirits Regulations, extracts from which are reproduced in
the enclosed Notice. It is not to be taken as implying that
the above formula, or any of its constituent parts, complies
with the provisions of any non-Revenue Act or Regulations.

I am, Sir
Your obedient Servant

H J Ward
Secretary

Enc

Unit 17

Skill building

Type each line or sentence (A, B, C and D) *three* times. If time permits, complete your practice by typing each group once as it appears.

A. Review alphabet keys

1.   The block pavement is extremely uneven, and many of the children, jumping quickly, fell down and grazed their knees.

B. Build speed on common suffixes

2. being, going, making, showing, getting, shipping, regarding.
3. Are they going to return the damaged crate during next week?
4. They are making enquiries about hiring a hall for the dance.
5. Are you showing anything of your own making at the carnival?

C. Build speed on common phrases

6. you can, you may, you are, you will, you should, you are not
7. If you are not too busy, you may call when you are in Devon.
8. You must not delay; otherwise, you will miss the next train.
9. You should ask if you will be required after eleven o'clock.

D. Build speed on fluency drill

10. John says they went down this lane past that path each time.
11. That poor girl will soon need some help with such hard work.
12. They will only wait till next week when that tour then ends.
13. When they come back home from that long trip they must rest.

Accuracy/Speed Practice
Two-minute timing

Not more than 2 errors

words

AS.21   Years ago, when education was reserved for the rich, and life moved | 13
more slowly, a 'good hand' was an accomplishment. For the daughters of | 27
gentlemen, it was rated as high on the social scale as music and paint- | 42
ing, and examples of some fine handwriting may be seen in most art | 55
galleries. In these days, life is much more hectic, and typewriters are | 69
in common use, so that there is less need to write well, and writing by | 84
hand is not of such great importance. The typewriter is the main cause | 98
of handwriting's fall from status, but the fountain pen and, worse still, | 112
the ball-point, have added to this decline. As a result, handwriting is | 127
now quite illegible in some cases. Yet, although it is not so necessary | 141
as it was in the past, it is still required. So you must try to write in | 156
a neat and clear style.   (S.I. 1.30) | 160

Proof-reading

In Secretarial Aid No. 1, page 26, we drew your attention to the importance of always proof-reading your work. We cannot stress too strongly the necessity of reading through your typescript and making any alterations before a document is removed from the typewriter. Look particularly for the following types of errors:

1. Mis-spellings, including misuse of the hyphen in compound words.

2. Incorrect division of words at line-ends.

3. Wrong choice of words when there are two or more words of similar sound, such as plain, plane; already, all ready; advice, advise.

4. Incorrect punctuation.

5. Incorrect use of capitals.

6. Failure to correct obvious errors in grammar.

7. Wrong use of abbreviations.

8. Inconsistencies of all kinds.

9. Typing errors, such as: (a) mis-strikes; (b) overtyping; (c) transposition of letters; (d) faulty erasures; (e) errors in spacing; (f) faulty shift-key operation for capitals, resulting in bad alignment; (g) irregular paragraph indentations.

10. Names, addresses, and figures need special attention.

8. Practise proof-reading. Read the above, and then carry out the instructions given.

The following letter contains a number of errors.

(a) On A4 paper write down the numbers 1 to 20, and opposite each number make a note of the error(s) to be found in that line in the letter. Check your list with the one given on page 199.

(b) Type a fair copy of the letter.

```
1   Barrett & Patterson
2   Newport.

3   Dear sir.

4       It has bn. kindly sugested to us by the Oldham Manufacturing
5   Co. of Oldam, Lancs. that we invite your advise on the following
6   prolbem. —

7       We are re-modeling out 2 storey factory in Cardif and wishto
8   instal the most up to date automatic sprinlker equipment procure-
9   able. We should appreciate your answer to the folowing questi-
10  ons:— 1.  What would be the approx. cost of instaling a satis-
11  factory sprinkler systerm on both flors.  (2) How soon after you
12  recieve your order could instalation be completed? 3. Judge-
13  ing by our experiance what is the average %-age of saying in
14  insurance costs resulting from such instalations.

15      we are encl. the floor plans of the Factory.  If you re-
16  quire further information in order to anser the forgoing
17  please le us know.

18      You early reply will be apreciated.

19                          Yrs. Faithfully,
20                          J. Haywood — Sec.   J. M. Steel & Co.
```

order : (b) Investment income for the current yr. (a) Supplies income accumulated from 1 previous financial year. Chapter XI Suggestions for appointment (Typist: Indent-(a) & (b) above and use single spacing) of an Assistant

stet Administrator. Rule eight. The officers form the

shall uc. board for the management of 1 affairs of 1 Assoc. should be an Administrator, an Assistant Administrator, a secretary & a representative assistant from ea. deanery. Rule 9 (Take in 'A') The Assistant Administrator sh. be chosen by the Board from among their own members. Rule 10. The Administrator, if present, sh. take 1 chair at all meetings; in his absence the Board will elect a chairman from the meeting

(who shall act as chairman)

" " 'A' The words [Assistant Administrator] could be inserted
" " after [Administrator] in the first line or 1 rule modified to read as follows:

Type a copy of the following letter on A5 paper, using suitable margins.

Wm. F. Jackson, 26 Grove Crescent, Solihull, Warwicks. Dear Sir, Having heard that you have just

stet / bought purchased a new house in the neighbourhood [we are enclsg

" " our brochure entitled [Garden Planning]

/-/ We are old established garden craftsmen and would like to h. the opportunity of quoting you for laying out your garden.

stet Run on The services of our Estimating Dept. Department are

N.P. entirely free & without obligation. [May we hope to hear from you? Yrs. faithfully, W. BROWN & SONS LTD. [Typist: 2 extra copies please - one for Mr Jones & 1 for Mr McNicol].

Type the following official letter in correct form on A4 paper. Insert date and paragraphs. Address to R. W. Herdman, 214 Bath Street, Birmingham B31 2JB.

Ref. No. 4065/5 A. Sir, with ref. to yr enquiry of the (insert date), I am directed to give you the following information concerning the changes in arrangement for recruitment in connection w. the Student Apprenticeship Scheme in Research & Development Establishments. The two main streams of entry to Student Apprenticeships will be at G.C.E. 'A' level and G.C.E. 'O' level, but there are two important changes: (i) The age limit for the 'A' level entry is now $19\frac{1}{2}$ years instead of 19 years. (ii) The entry requirement for the 'O' level stream is now four 'O' level subjects instead of five, & a pass in English Language is not a requirement. The examination requirements referred to are normally applicable to England & Wales. Equivalent qualifications for Scotland & N. Ireland are acceptable. Details of these equivalents are given in the regulations for the competitions, which are now available. 'A' Level Entry – Mechanical, Electrical, Chemical & Metallurgical Engineering. The entry qualifications for this competition are a minimum of 5 subjects in the G.C.E. Exam, of which 2, Maths & Physics, must have been passed at 'A' level. English Language must be one of the other subjects. The age limits for the 'A' level entry are over 16 and under $19\frac{1}{2}$ yrs. of age on 1st Sept. Industrial scholarships are granted to student apprentices as part of their apprenticeship to enable them to study for a Degree in Engng or Metallurgy at a University or a Diploma in Technology (equivalent to a Degree) at a College of Advanced

Technology. 'O' Level Entry — Mechanical & Electrical Engineering. The entry qualifications for this competition are for 4 subjects in the G.C.E Exam at 'O' level. These must include Maths, & either Physics or Mechanics or Physics w. Chemistry or Engineering Science or Science (Building & Engineering) wh. wl. enable the candidate to enter the O1 year of the new Ordinary National Certificate Course. The age limits for this competition are over 16 & under 17½ years of age on the 1st Sept. Details & entry forms for the competitions are now available. The Official Regulations are enclosed, and Entry Forms are obtainable from the Industrial & Technical Education Officer, Room 503, 55 High Holborn, London, W.C.1. I am, Sir, Yr obedient Servant, A. W. Walker, Secretary.

Job 48 Production Target—*12 minutes*

Type the following on A4 paper in double spacing, making any necessary corrections. Centre chapter headings and use shoulder headings for sub-headings.

Chapter VIII Grants. Proposed Modifications in Rules. Rule 30. The funds of the society sh. be applicable for the relief of infirm, sick & aged members of the Society. [Relief may be voted & paid by the Committee in such manner and to such amount, as the Committee may and for such periods from time to time direct, having regard to the circumstances of each case, the funds available, and the calls or probable calls thereon. All reliefs so voted sh. be reported to the next General Meeting. Rule 31a: The funds available for grants in any financial year sh be limited after deductions of all Rule 31: to be omitted management and salaries expenses, to the following sources which sh. be applied in